RECREATING YOUR SELF

RECREATING YOUR SELF

*Help for Adult Children
of Dysfunctional Families*

—

NANCY J. NAPIER

W · W · NORTON & COMPANY

NEW YORK LONDON

For information on prerecorded audiotapes of
the exercises in this book, write to:

Nancy J. Napier
Post Office Box 153
New York, New York 10024

Copyright © 1990 by Nancy J. Napier
Printed in the United States of America.
The text of this book is composed in 11/13 Avanta,
with display type set in ITC Fenice Bold.
Composition and manufacturing by the Haddon Craftsmen, Inc.
Book and ornament design by Margaret M. Wagner

First published as a Norton paperback 1991

Library of Congress Cataloging-in-Publication Data
Napier, Nancy J.
Recreating your self: help for adult children of dysfunctional
families/by Nancy J. Napier.
p. cm.
Includes bibliographical references.
1. Adult children of dysfunctional families—Rehabilitation.
2. Autogenic training. 3. Self. 4. Psychotherapy. I. Title.
RC455.4.F3N36 1990
616.89'162—dc20 89–28106

ISBN 0-393-30804-9

W. W. Norton & Company, Inc.
500 Fifth Avenue, New York, N.Y. 10110
W. W. Norton & Company Ltd.
10 Coptic Street, London WC1A 1PU
6 7 8 9 0

To Nell, without whose legacy I would never have known the heights of inspiration or the depths of vulnerability that have fueled my journey of reclaiming the wounded child and recreating myself.

And to Michael, without whose guidance and reassurance I would not have reached beyond myself into the future that has become the present.

CONTENTS

7

ACKNOWLEDGMENTS

So many people have contributed to the journey that has resulted in the approach reflected in this book that it would be impossible to name them all. In recent years, Garrett Oppenheim, Ph.D., has been a willing "navigator" during expeditions into the far reaches of my unconscious. His willingness to enter into new territory and his helpful questions along the way provided an essential focus to our work together. Rafaela Valdez Echeverria, C.S.W., a good friend and colleague, has been generous in sharing her ideas and creative work with sexual abuse survivors. Our long lunches and talks on the telephone have provided a trustworthy and helpful sounding board as my ideas developed. Emily Marlin, C.S.W., has also been a wonderful resource and I will always be grateful to her for prompting me to take the plunge and write this book. Karen Peoples, Ph.D., has been an ever-present inspiration and friend for many years. Our talks about self psychology, hypnosis, and things spiritual have nurtured the soil in which important ideas have taken root. Now that we live on different coasts, our talks are fewer and farther between, but they still serve to inspire.

The opportunity to work with Kitty LaPerriere, Ph.D., has contributed immeasurably to my understanding of families and the intricacies of communication. The healing process I have experienced personally as a result of her wisdom and skill has also enhanced my ability to listen to the child within of my clients and workshop participants with a more studied ear. I hear more deeply now.

To Patricia Jobling, especially, go thanks beyond words for the transformational journey she's been willing to share as collaborator, friend and teacher. With her background as a business consultant and Ericksonian hypnotist, she has always added grounding and perspective to my work. As our collaborations have developed, her consistent demand for excellence and clarity has proven invaluable. Our many conversations—and energetic debates—have sparked the fires of creativity in productive and useful ways. In particular, I remember a day in 1982 when we sat at a restaurant in Stockbridge, Massachusetts, and "discovered" the title of this book. As I look back now, I can see that the seeds of ideas contained in the pages that follow were already germinating then. It's taken time for them to evolve and, at this writing, they are probably in their adolescence. I can picture a conversation yet to come that will focus on the offspring of seeds planted now, as we discuss future projects.

Bob Markel, my agent, provided encouragement and essential feedback as the manuscript developed. His willingness to critique the material in the book provided many important insights. Susan Barrows, my editor at Norton, gave needed guidance in turning the manuscript into a useful, coherent manual for moving through the self-hypnotic process described in the book. Her support has been a source of real encouragement.

Without my family, of course, there wouldn't be any child to talk about, and within the richness of family life were laid the foundations of what follows here—the wounds, the tragedies and traumas, as well as the warm, magical moments I remember with such gratitude. Included in so many memories is Ellen Weisman Morehead, with whose family I had many wonderful adventures.

To Jeri Love, also, go special thanks for being my first teacher about the pain of childhood abuse. Having known Jeri has allowed me to trust the stories told by the children within my clients with an equanimity and belief that even the worst of experiences can be faced and healed.

And to my clients and workshop participants, I offer my thanks and gratitude for all they've been willing to share, for all they've taught me over the years. Without them, there would be no book, no understanding of what it means to reclaim the wounded child and recreate the self.

PREFACE

I have a love affair going on with the unconscious. I admit it. I also have an underlying faith in the unconscious as a creative resource, a friend who is *always* looking out for me, even if at times it uses old or outmoded strategies to keep me safe.

The approach encompassed in this book has emerged and evolved from my own process, both as a client and as a psychotherapist. As a client, I have made a long journey from experiencing life as a wounded, unevolved "child in an adult's body" to being a healthier, more empowered person in my own right. As a clinician, I have made an equally long journey of discovery, theoretically and practically, to find ways to help others heal their own wounded selves.

Most influential in my journey as a psychotherapist have been training and work with Ericksonian hypnosis and an interest in the concepts encompassed by the maturing field of self psychology. As an individual, what has been most important in my development is a long-held fascination with, and exploration of, human consciousness, particularly the realms of intuition and nonrational ways of knowing. I see the most promising and intriguing "new frontier" as the inner space of human consciousness rather than the outer reaches of the astronomical universe.

In this book, I will share with you some of the exciting, inspiring things I have encountered as I have explored the tremendous potential of the unconscious—a potential that resides in all of us. It encompasses an inherent talent to express ourselves in creative and surprising ways. I will also share with you some of my own healing journey and that taken by my clients, workshop participants, and members of my self-hypnosis groups.

Examples drawn from my own life will be presented as they actually were experienced. The client stories I share here, though, are composites: none is exactly as it happened in sessions. In fact, any resemblance to actual people is purely coincidental. The cases presented represent common issues and descriptions derived from many hours of hypnotic work with individuals and groups, rather than specific instances from specific client work. And yet, it is only through the rich variety of the experiences of real people dealing with real issues—and through their generosity—that any of this is possible.

Underlying the ideas and cases shared in this book is an assumption that the unconscious has the capacity to draw on a deep well of inner resources. These resources operate to promote a healing, integrative journey of reclaiming the wounded child within from the past and recreating the self in the present. Taking this journey evokes the potential for an internal, ongoing experience of "selfhood," which is both empowering and satisfying. Every one of us has a right to achieve this, and yet, we often find ourselves thrown off track by wounds that were inflicted early in life.

The process of reclaiming the child within and recreating the self is undertaken with the firm belief that we humans are surprisingly resilient: the seeds of our potential to be whole, creative, and comfortable are ever-present. What these seeds need is a supportive internal environment in which they can germinate.

The promise of change can be found, also, in a challenge that awaits us everyday, if we choose to meet it. Life experiences constantly invite us to let in new information and create new concepts about ourselves and the world, and to try out new responses and risk new behaviors. We are also given an opportunity to let go of once cherished beliefs, after they have served their purpose.

As this book has evolved, the same challenge has emerged for me. As a clinician, I have moved through phases of theoretical understanding, beginning with training in psychoanalytic approaches and evolving through cognitive and systems therapies. Included has been a long-standing interest in transpersonal psychology. As I look back over the past 15 years, I can see how some of my dearly held convictions have changed as new information has become available. At times, it was hard to shift my perspective on how people heal and what to emphasize in the therapy process. At other times, letting go was easy, as new information was more compelling and immediately useful.

And so, the ideas presented in this book have continued to evolve for me, even as I wrote them. In psychology, as in other disciplines, new challenges constantly arise and new solutions inevitably emerge. It is for this reason that some of what is offered here will look different to you, and to me, after the passage of time and experience. That's fine. It's the way things are, the way the mind inevitably moves on to new understandings when life presents new experience. It is my hope that, as you read what is contained here, you will also allow your ideas to develop along lines you may not have expected. It's all part of the ongoing process of recreating yourself in better and more meaningful ways.

RECREATING YOUR SELF

Chapter 1

CAN THE SELF
BE RECREATED?

Someone once said that it is amazing we survive growing up in families. Although this may seem like a strange statement on the face of it, if you think about the current revelations about child abuse, there does appear to be reason for concern about how we make it from here to there—from childhood to adulthood—in a reasonably healthy and functional way. Often, as I am walking to and from my office, I look at the many windows in the tall apartment buildings along the way and I wonder. I wonder what is happening inside those apartments, behind those outer walls. I wonder who is being terrorized. I wonder who is being berated verbally. I also wonder who is having a wonderful birthday party or getting ready for a delicious trip somewhere special. It is impossible to say what is really going on behind those walls. As I listen to clients in my office, I hear life stories that seem so very benign on the outside but, behind the walls of another time and another place, they are stories of terror and abuse.

In my work as a clinician, I have had the privilege and the heart-wrenching honor to share with many people the stories of their struggles in the journey from childhood to adulthood. I have also had the opportunity to participate in the discovery of healthy, creative, expressive selves, waiting deep inside for the proper environment of safety and respect to begin to emerge.

Much of this book will, by necessity, focus on healing the wounded child each of us carries inside. It will also look at family patterns of intimacy, family myths, family values and expectations that comprise the fabric of understanding that each child creates while growing up. These family "heirlooms" are powerful unconscious elements and play a significant part in shaping our view of the world and our place in it.

Even with an emphasis on healing the wounded child, there will be ample space given to the considerable *resources* we each bring to the process. No one is *only* a wounded person. The unconscious of each of us contains, at the very least, an inherent urge to be healthy and well. This urge is transformed into active participation when a context is created in which we are willing to listen to ourselves in a new way and discover parts of ourselves that we may not have guessed are available to us now.

Some of these parts may be familiar to you from approaches such as psychosynthesis and gestalt therapy. They comprise the parts of the self that function as guide, wise person, protector— and many more. We will spend some time exploring the important concept of "ego states," those parts that developed when you were young to keep you safe and alive psychologically and physically. Also, we will focus on aspects of the self that may be new to you—particularly the future self. These are parts of you from beyond your current timeframe, from a time yet to come. These are the parts of you that have achieved already the things you seek, and they become important resources in the process of healing the wounded child and empowering you in your current life.

To make sense of these and other concepts I'll be presenting, let me first share with you my current view of the unconscious. I say "current view" because when you explore a new frontier things are always changing as unexpected discoveries are made. I expect my perspective on the unconscious to keep evolving and changing as this fascinating terrain reveals more of itself.

If necessary, feel free to suspend any disbelief you may experience as we make this journey together. Ultimately, what is useful will make sense to you. The rest can just become something curious you thought about one time and then tucked away in that place of forgetting that seems to have all the room it needs to store seemingly non-essential pieces of learning that might be useful someday.

What Is the Unconscious?

First, I want to define for you what I mean by "unconscious." For me, the unconscious is the sum total of human consciousness that operates outside the linear, concrete day-to-day awareness we use to write a check or add up a series of numbers. I find it difficult to draw a distinction between conscious and unconscious, because I'm not really sure where one begins and the other ends.

In hypnosis, we talk of going into a trance state and entering a realm of experience that is generally outside conscious awareness. Unconscious awareness seems a contradiction in terms; however, it is a valid and viable kind of knowing that often finds its way into conscious awareness through sudden insights, dreams, flashes of recognition. Ultimately, we need the "conscious" mind—the rational, linear part—to translate the unconscious and make useful sense of it.

It's rather like the right brain/left brain concept. We now know there is not such a definitive distinction as a left brain that is logical and a right brain that is illogical.[1] In the whole brain, right and left share many similarities, with a bias towards verbal functioning in the left hemisphere and nonverbal functions in the right. Where one leaves off and the other begins is not clearly defined; that is true of conscious/unconscious functioning as well.

For me, the unconscious includes all we have ever learned and then forgotten, all that is stored away for future use. It encompasses unresolved conflicts and unrealized wishes. It reaches into realms of awareness called *transpersonal* and *paranormal*. It is the source of those creative breakthroughs and inspirations that become peak experiences and the seeds of new awareness. It is the repository of things positive and negative. Most of all, the unconscious is our ally and protector—always seeking the best for us, even if sometimes misperceiving how to go about doing that.

In terms of how the unconscious becomes conscious, think of a prism. When no light is shining through the prism, what you see is glass, with no color at all. When light is shown through one of the facets of a prism, the colors are suddenly visible. They have been there all along but not in a way you could perceive them.

Or, think of a radio. Even though you are tuned to a particular station, that doesn't mean the others aren't still there, playing on frequencies that are all around you, passing through your body. You are just not tuned in to them. You can change the station or turn the radio off and all those frequencies *still* exist. It's the same with your conscious awareness. It is tuned to one station at a time, in a linear fashion, but the unconscious is there, operating fully, even though it is outside conscious awareness. Dreams are like a sleep-snooze alarm. You have turned off the radio— your conscious mind—and the unconscious wakes you up with a dream, turning on that awareness again.

So, when I say "unconscious" I mean a sum total of all the levels of your consciousness—whether you are aware of them or not. And I mean the positive and seemingly negative, constructive and seemingly destructive elements of that consciousness. I say "seemingly" before negative and destructive because it has been my experience that unconscious impulses are often misdirected, intending to be of help but not knowing how.

My approach to accessing the unconscious draws heavily on the hypnotic techniques of Milton Erickson.[2] This method of hypnosis has gained tremendous popularity in therapy circles in the past 10 years. One of the main things that originally attracted me to Ericksonian hypnosis was that, using this hypnotic approach, there is no right way to have a trance experience. There are as many ways as there are people. Accepting each individual's unique trance abilities can convey a powerfully affirming message. In this approach, the conscious mind becomes a translator of the underlying activity of healing that the unconscious sets in motion in response to trance work—healing that may only become apparent, consciously, long after the unconscious has received suggestions for change.

I value the conscious mind as the means by which unconscious resources can be brought into awareness. Such awareness is not always essential, however. You didn't learn to walk because you understood, consciously, about walking. You learned to walk because you followed your body's unconscious impulses.

This kind of learning reminds me of the story of the frog and the centipede.[3] One day, a frog was sitting on a lily pad in the middle of his favorite pond. Along the shore came a centipede, walking rapidly on all his hundred legs. Curious, the frog said, "Hey! How do you get all those legs to work all at once without tripping? It seems like a complicated business to me." The centipede stopped in his tracks and said, "I don't really know, now that you mention it. Let me think about it." As he was thinking, the centipede began to walk again. Much to his astonishment, he fell flat on his face!

And so, your unconscious takes care of some things a lot better than your conscious mind can. When you learned to read, you used the conscious mind to feed information into the unconscious. It was in your unconscious, though, that those three lines that looked like a teepee suddenly came together as the letter A. It was your unconscious that understood, all of a sudden, that the two bumps and a line were the letter B, and the half circle was the letter C.

You can trust your ability to learn unconsciously and discover those times when it's just as well to leave the unconscious to its own devices and keep your conscious mind out of the way. You might wonder about this kind of learning. It's really second nature and you know much more about it than you realize. And, maybe that's a nice thing to discover as you begin this journey into your own unconscious.

THE TIMELESS NATURE OF
THE UNCONSCIOUS

One of the most important characteristics of the unconscious is its timeless nature. Everything in the unconscious is taking place in the "now." There is no "then" or "when." In our usual, everyday, linear awareness, we tend to think in terms of "yesterday," "today," "tomorrow," "this page," "the last page," "the next one." We make rational sense of our world this way, organizing the natural progression of days into weeks, weeks into months.

In the unconscious, however, things are quite different. For instance, think of something that happened to you several weeks ago, or a long time ago, that was really upsetting. Maybe you were angry or hurt. If you think about that upsetting event and just let yourself drift into a reverie about the memory, chances are good that you will find yourself back there, feeling as though you *were* there again, right now. The anger or hurt or humiliation may even feel as strong as it did then. Whenever you drift into a reverie about something, you are entering the timeless unconscious and the "memory" becomes a current, immediate experience.

If you were to begin to daydream about an upcoming event, *really* to be there imagining yourself doing something you are truly excited about, or something you dread doing, chances are you would begin to feel as though you were actually there right now. Memories are not the only way to enter the timeless unconscious. Anticipations about the future can take you there, too.

It is the timeless nature of the unconscious that makes the approach presented in the following pages possible. Entering the "eternal now" provides a framework for moving through time in any direction and interacting with parts of the self that exist in the past, the present and the future.

The timeless nature of the unconscious is central to our consideration of the wounded child. Because the unconscious is timeless, the child you *were* actually exists in the present, psychologically. Think, for a moment, of times when you have had an interaction with your boss, or a colleague, and you suddenly felt intimidated, or frightened, or enraged, and you just couldn't get hold of yourself. Chances are good you were experiencing yourself as the child, that you engaged the current situation as if you *were* a child rather than an adult. You might remember a time when you were in an interaction with a loved one and suddenly felt powerless or overwhelmed by some emotion that you couldn't seem to control. Again, the child within was probably responding to some old pattern you learned in the family, as if no time had passed and as if the adult's present *were* the child's present.

In any of these cases, the timeless unconscious is playing out early learnings and responses as though it were still *then* instead of *now*. While this may cause problems at times, because the old patterns get in the way of current relationships, there are also patterns and parts of you in the unconscious that express in empowered and positive ways.

For example, think of a skill you have developed that you feel really comfortable using. How about a time when you were experiencing something in a way that everything felt just right? These are examples of resource states, developed within the unconscious and available to you at a moment's notice.

The timeless unconscious is a treasure trove of resources and learnings that can be accessed consciously. One way to do this is by entering into a self-hypnotic trance, which you will be exploring extensively in the exercises in this book.

WHAT IS TRANCE?

Whenever you shift your attention from the outer world to your own inner awareness, you enter a state of trance. In fact, one definition of trance in Ericksonian hypnosis circles is "focused attention."

You have a lot more experience with trance than you realize, even if you've never done hypnosis. We all experience what are called "naturalistic trance states" throughout the day.[4] Whenever you are daydreaming, staring off into space, you're in a natural trance state. Whenever you're swept up in a strong emotion or listening raptly to beautiful music and have forgotten all about where you are, you're in a natural trance state.

I'll talk more about trance in the chapter on self-hypnosis. For now, the thing that may be helpful to know is that you're already familiar with the state of mind you'll be entering in the exercises in the book. As is true with many people, you may find trance so familiar that you won't sense any difference between self-hypnosis and meditation or visualization experiences you may already have had many times.

PARTS OF THE SELF

In my work with clients, I emphasize a process of engaging the many parts that make up an individual's psychological life. In later chapters, I'll go into some detail about these parts and how to work with them. For now, let me simply say that your best resources are the many parts that come together to make up the intricate and complex creature you are, psychologically. Learning to communicate and cooperate with these parts opens up areas of potential that may have been unavailable to you for much of your life.

I have a favorite story about the desert in the Antelope Valley in California. When you visit this area during most times of the year, there is a vast landscape of dirt and scrub. It doesn't look like the kind of place where things can grow easily. For as far as the eye can see, the predominant colors are brown, beige and dun. You may see some of the gray- or brown-greens that characterize much of the flora of California, but all in all it appears to be a rather inhospitable environment.

During the spring of most years, the rains come to the California desert. When the rains come in the desert, they arrive in a torrent, bringing a great abundance of water. Within that new, moisture-rich environment, something miraculous happens. Almost overnight, that arid, dusty desert landscape is transformed into fields and fields of colorful wildflowers.

To me, the message conveyed by the California desert wildflowers is a message of hope. It says to me that no matter how hostile an environment may appear, the seeds of our potential lie under the surface just waiting for the right time and conditions that will allow them to emerge and come into full bloom. For the wounded child in each of us, this message becomes a promise: all is never lost and there is always hope that you *can* become the best of what you have always had the potential to be.

Throughout the book, I'll be emphasizing the fact that we are resilient creatures by nature. You have survived whatever your childhood brought your way. Having survived, you can now develop in ways that were not possible in that old context. If you are still carrying around that old context inside—as many of us are—you can develop a new internal environment that promotes and supports what is best in you.

A FEW WORDS ABOUT "FUNCTIONAL" AND "DYSFUNCTIONAL"

In recent years, as the family therapy movement has grown, a great deal of research has been done on styles of coping and communication in families. Alcoholic families have been a main source for these studies.[5] The burgeoning Adult Children of Alcoholics (ACOA) movement has emerged as another force in defining and describing family patterns and their effects on family members.

The terms "functional" and "dysfunctional" refer to the *kinds* of coping strategies and communication patterns a family uses. Functional strategies and patterns are those that allow the family to negotiate challenges and traumas effectively. Those that are dysfunctional get in the way of the family's ability to deal as effectively with stressful events.

Here are some examples of these different coping strategies:

• In a functional family, children are encouraged to have friends, outside activities, independence. In a dysfunctional family, children are kept close to home. Strangers and outsiders are not welcomed. The family has secrets—alcoholism or incest, for example—that it cannot share.

• In a functional family, children have reasonable privacy. In a dysfunctional family, a child's diary might be fair game for anyone who finds it and wants to read it.

• In a functional family, individual differences are applauded and respected. In a dysfunctional family, differences are experienced as threatening—as a sign of disloyalty.

• In a functional family, conflict is accepted and resolved. In a dysfunctional family, conflict is denied. Among ACOAs, there's the story of the elephant living in the house that no one talks about. If you grew up in a home where there was substance abuse or sexual abuse, you are probably particularly familiar with this kind of denial.

Functional and dysfunctional are not the same as good and bad. They do convey, though, the premise that dysfunctional responses tend to be maladaptive and not the best choices for coping with life's challenges and stresses. Children raised in dysfunctional families are likely to have less resilient coping styles as adults. By identifying dysfunctional patterns from your own family, you give yourself an opportunity to review your coping skills and change them to more functional patterns.

ABOUT PARENTS AND PARENTING

If you are a parent now, there are a few things I'd like to say to you before you begin to work with the material in the book. As you engage the process of recreating your self, you begin to realize the effects your family's patterns of communication and style of intimacy had on you. So often, I've heard clients and workshop participants express feelings of devastation or guilt when they realize how they have passed these dysfunctional patterns along to their own children. If you run into any feelings like these, please remind yourself that it is absolutely normal— and nearly inevitable—for you to do to your children what was done to you. The thing to keep in mind is that you've done the best you could all along and that now you're learning something new. And, do remember how resilient children are. Yours are no different. They, too, have the resources to heal the wounded children in them.

What may surprise you is how quickly you begin to experience your children in new ways, as you come to know the child in yourself. The approach presented in this book offers ways to break patterns of abuse and craziness that, most often, have been passed down through *many* generations. And so, you may discover things you wish you hadn't done. Please allow yourself to treat these discoveries as important pieces of information that are helpful to know about. You're on a journey of learning something new. Celebrate that journey, even as you find family patterns you want to eliminate from your own parenting style.

Even with all the awareness in the world, it is virtually impossible for parents to be consistently supportive to their children or to do the "right" thing every time. Parent training—the most important training I can think of—isn't commonly available to most people. From the beginning, parents are "thrown in the deep end" and are expected to have perfected their swimming strokes before having had any training or practice. Be gentle with yourself—as gentle as I hope you'll be with the child in you.

ABOUT THE STORIES IN THIS BOOK

Throughout the book, I use the male and female gender inter-changeably to represent the generic person. My choice of when to use each is purely arbitrary.

As mentioned in the Preface, the stories of individuals woven throughout the book are composites created by me and do not reflect any one person's experience. I chose to use composites for two reasons. First, I wanted to protect the identity and confidentiality of the people who have trusted their stories to me. Secondly, over the years, I have observed that there are primary themes that run through the experiences of adult survivors of dysfunctional families. Because these themes are so common—and so many of us recognize ourselves in them—I wanted to be able to present a broader picture of how these themes operate than is possible with just one person's experience. Using the composite form allowed me to illustrate more elements of each theme.

Also, the stories I've chosen to share with you cover a wide range of experiences. They are not the most horrifying of the stories that have been shared with me. I chose less dramatic themes because of the tendency of those of us from dysfunctional families to discount our experiences. If we hear something that sounds worse than what we went through, it's too easy to say our experience didn't really matter. I wanted to leave room for the whole range of childhood woundings—from the most dramatic to the most seemingly insignificant. I honor them all as important to the child who had them. I'd like to ask you to do the same as you proceed through the book. Pain and injury are relative—they feel bad to the person having them and that's all that really matters.

A TECHNICAL NOTE: EXERCISE FORMAT

The exercises in this book provide one way for you to develop a supportive internal environment. Most of the following chapters contain self-hypnotic exercises that guide you in developing new and healthier relationships with parts of yourself.

Each exercise is presented in two forms. First, you'll find a full self-hypnotic induction that guides you into trance and on to an exploration of some part of you. I recommend that you tape record the entire induction and then play the tape back to yourself as you do the exercise. Hearing your own voice on tape is a powerful way to connect with your inner process. In case you don't have a tape recorder available, you'll find a short version of every exercise at the end of the book. If you choose to use the second, shorter version of the exercise, I recommend that you read the entire induction first to get a feel for what you're doing. Then, you can glance occasionally at the short form as you go along. You'll find that the taped version of the exercise will probably allow you to go more deeply into your experience than the shorter form.

MY OWN STORY

As a final note to this first chapter, I briefly want to mention my own process of healing the wounded child in me. A keynote to my childhood—and to the child within who has accompanied me into adulthood—has been a fear of humiliation. As strong has been a lifelong conviction of not deserving—not deserving to get my needs met, not deserving reliable, trustworthy love, not deserving acclaim.

The seeds of these internal fears and expectations were sown early in my life—as they are for most of us. I began as a cross-eyed kid, terribly self-conscious and embarrassed whenever I had to speak or perform in public. The ridicule of some of my school-mates early on left an indelible imprint—I was the "cross-eyed monkey born in a zoo" and I did not know how to see beyond that humiliation. That, accompanied by early sexual abuse by my father, and then the loss of him to divorce when I was six years old, left me with my fair share of dysfunctional patterns in life and relationships.

I began to work with the child within in the ways described in this book a number of years ago. Much of what has evolved in the work I do with my clients has emerged from my own process. Fundamental to the shifts I've felt in my own relationship with parts of myself has been the development of an underlying sense of *self-acceptance*. With the increasing self-acceptance I've experienced over the past few years, I have also discovered how to give myself permission to have a better life than I ever imagined possible.

Through the process of working with the child within and accessing resource parts I had not imagined were available, I have discovered a person inside whom I truly love. I am now comfortable speaking to large groups and conducting large workshops. In fact, I now enjoy sharing my ideas and myself with others without the grinding fear of being exposed to incapacitating humiliation.

My wish for you is that what is contained in this book will provide a foundation for your own process of reclaiming and recreating yourself. It is possible to develop a relationship with *all* the parts of you, a relationship that is an empowering, enabling one. You can become a friend to yourself in a healthy and comfortable way, giving yourself permission to have the best life possible. Your relationship with the parts of you can become one of cooperation, validation and self-affirmation in ways that give you an opportunity to be more comfortable within yourself and more available to others in positive and meaningful ways.

And so, I ask you to explore the pages that follow with the thought in mind that your unconscious understands so much more than your conscious mind does of what is contained here. Allow yourself to give permission to your unconscious to do the important learning for you and for your conscious mind to discover, in its own ways, the things you need to know to recreate yourself in the most powerful and positive ways possible.

Chapter 2

ᴍᴍ

EARLY LEARNINGS:
LAYING THE FOUNDATION

In most of my workshops, I use an exercise in which I ask people to imagine a beautiful, mature adult tree. They begin in a natural setting where there is a large tree—their favorite kind. I ask them to notice the trunk of the tree—its color, its texture, to become aware of branches, foliage, and the roots that show just above the surface of the ground. I ask them to notice how the branches reach up and reach out, taking in the sunlight, swaying in the breeze. I wonder if I might ask you, right now, if you can imagine the root system, hidden under the surface, that reaches down and out to provide balanced support for that tree. You might explore, for a moment, how it feels to be such a strong, healthy adult—as strong and healthy as that tree. You might become particularly aware of the fact that the seed from which that healthy adult developed had within it, from the very beginning, *all* it would ever need to grow up and mature.

Sometimes, the beginning is difficult. The sprout that emerges from that seed must find its way up to the surface. There may be barriers, obstacles to get around. The sprout seems so fragile and yet it keeps on developing and finally breaks through into the light of day. Then, it may be pelted with rain-drops or pushed around by strong winds. Or, it may be growing in the shadow of the adults around it, barely getting enough sun to sustain itself. You may wonder how so much adversity is over-come. And yet, it is. Every mature tree you see proves that sprouts *do* make it to adulthood.

Then, as a seedling and a sapling, the young tree must adapt to its environment to survive. Trees have rings in their trunks which are graphic evidence of good times and bad times. A fat ring tells of a time of abundance and support. A thin ring reveals a time of difficulty, a time when the environment may have been particularly brutal or withholding. Most trees have both kinds of rings and carry a visible record of what their early years were like.

The child within is like the seed of that tree. Each of us begins life filled with the potential to develop into a healthy, mature adult. The difference with us is that evidence of what our early years were like usually is hidden from view, invisible except in the way we feel about ourselves and the quality of the adult life we create.

If it's true that the child within is like the seed of a tree, filled from the very beginning with the potential to be a fully mature, healthy adult, what is it that locks us into self-destructive behav-iors or keeps us in abusive adult relationships? What happens to the potential inherent in the seed of our being?

Even as you think about these questions, you might want to keep in mind the wondrous fact that you have made it anyway. Something in you pulled you through all the early learnings, experiences and traumas. Throughout the coming chapters, re-mind yourself again and again that, in spite of whatever healing you may seek now, you are *here.* That, in itself, is a testament to the potential inherent in you.

DEVELOPING A SENSE OF SELF

Let's look at how that potential becomes blocked or thrown off track. In order to become healthy, mature adults, we, unlike trees, must deal with more than physiological development. We must engage a complex inner world that gives us the potential to create a positive, coherent *sense of self.* [1]

As I define it, a coherent sense of self is an internal feeling of solidity—an experience of yourself as a person who has a place in the world, the right to express yourself, and the power to affect and participate in what happens to you.

However, for those of us from dysfunctional families, our sense of self is often characterized by feelings that are anything but empowered. Instead, we may feel ashamed, enraged, terrified, guilty or helpless. These internal experiences can lead to a feeling of being unglued, fragmented, unable to cope, powerless to change things. How do we come to feel this way?

The development of a strong sense of self requires an environment in which good psychological food is available. Positive psychological nourishment most often comes from experiencing *empathic* responses from the people around us. [2]

Empathy means many things to many people. Being empathic, to me, means you have the space inside to listen and respond to another person without getting caught up, or stuck, in your own point of view. Do you know the saying that goes something like, "Walk a mile in my shoes before you judge me"? That's empathy—putting yourself in the other person's shoes.

When I speak of *non-empathic* responses, I mean those times when you are so caught up in yourself that there's just no room for another person's point of view or need. Most of us become non-empathic when we're scared, even when we don't know we're scared and think we're angry, instead.

We learn about empathy first from our families. For young children—right from birth and throughout development—both empathic and non-empathic responses have a definite impact on the developing sense of self. These responses need not be conveyed in words to affect a child. In fact, for infants and young children, words don't yet carry the meaning they will later. What carries meaning are the more subtle expressions—body language, a caretaker's emotional state, tone of voice, facial expression.

Let's look at what can happen to a child who is treated nonempathically early in life. An example that comes to mind is a hypnotic session with a client, Andrea. Andrea's family style was characterized by blaming. Whenever conflict or tension arose in her family, someone would be blamed. The blame wasn't always expressed directly. It often took the form of impatience or indifference.

In the particular session I'm thinking of, Andrea went back to an early memory of being quite young. She was lying on a table near the kitchen and her mother was changing her diapers. Andrea's first impression was that her mother was impatient with her. Her mother seemed to be handling her roughly. She felt displeasure from her mother, but she didn't know why. As soon as the new diaper was on, Andrea soiled it, much to her mother's mounting consternation. What surprised Andrea was how bad that little child felt—as though she had done something terribly wrong. The hardest part was that she felt her mother didn't like her. Andrea was stunned to experience how much her mother's annoyance conveyed dislike and rejection to that young child.

Andrea realized experientially something she already knew in her head—that children inevitably think they are the cause of other people's responses. A young child doesn't yet have the ability to experience things from another person's point of view. For Andrea, there was no other available response to her mother's annoyance than that she must have done something wrong, that she was bad, and that her mother didn't like her.

As she reexperienced this memory in hypnosis, Andrea also observed it with her adult mind. She had a feeling that her mother was getting ready to give a party that night. From her adult point of view, Andrea could well imagine how frazzled her mother must have been. Having to change diapers twice would certainly have intensified her fears that she wouldn't be ready in time. As an adult, Andrea could understand. As a child, she felt rejected and bad.

A sense of yourself as bad or worthy of rejection can leave you feeling ashamed and sensitive to criticism, or afraid of engaging in confrontations with others. This was true for Andrea. Later, we'll be looking at what to do to ease this kind of vulnerability.

For now, let's look at another example of how your sense of self develops. One of the primary ways of enriching a developing sense of self is to have your perceptions validated. When someone agrees that something is sad when you also feel it is sad, you are likely to experience a feeling of being all right. Things are okay in your world. However, when someone tells you that a sad thing is really a happy thing, you might suddenly feel off balance, or that something is wrong with you.

For example, imagine Joey, a perky five-year-old, who sees his Aunt Mary crying. He runs up to his mother and says, "Why is Aunt Mary crying, Mom?" An empathic response might be something like, "Oh, she just heard that a friend was hurt and so she's sad. She'll be all right after she's cried for a while."

In a non-empathic environment, Joey might get yelled at for bothering his mother with nonsense. She might say, "Aunt Mary has something in her eye. Stop being so nosy." This kind of response might confuse Joey, or make him angry. It's so different from what he thought was going on that he might question his own perceptions. When these kinds of responses happen consistently, over time, you learn to deny, rather than listen to, your own sense of what's going on in your world.

Another important kind of empathic response in creating a healthy sense of self is respect for the child's uniqueness as an individual. When your uniqueness is respected, you learn to tolerate differences between yourself and others. You learn that it's *interesting* to discover differences and to deal with them constructively.

Dealing with differences can be particularly challenging in families where it is assumed that children are being disobedient when they disagree with parents' wishes. For instance, did you ever sit at the dinner table long after everyone else had left, staring at a plate of cold vegetables? I did. I particularly remember the plate of *very* cold peas. I sat with those peas throughout the entire evening, even missing television, until bedtime. I can't remember now if I ever actually ate them, but I do recall how it felt to dislike something that much and have to eat it anyway.

I recall hearing stories of children who were served the same bowl of cereal the next day if they didn't finish it the first time around. There are children who have been force-fed foods they really didn't like or that didn't agree with them. I remember one person's story of how he was punished because his mother thought he was deliberately disobeying when he threw up some liver she had made him eat.

In many dysfunctional families, it seems hard to acknowledge that it's normal for people in the same family to have different preferences. There seems to be, instead, an assumption that differences represent a power struggle, with the child trying to "win" or to control caretakers. And so, perhaps my parents felt that I didn't eat my peas because I was being difficult, not because I couldn't stand the taste or consistency of them.

In a similar vein, there may be great value placed on loyalty to the family, so that, "in our family, we love sports." Translated, this means any child who prefers reading to sports is letting down the family. Regardless of the specifics, to be punished or blamed for being different from other members of the family means, to the child, "I am bad."

When our individual preferences are respected, we tend to feel, "I am all right. The world out there says so, so it must be true." These basic assumptions, conveyed to a growing child, promote a sense of self characterized by feeling worthwhile and loved.

Your developing sense of self is also enhanced when people let you know there's a difference between who you are and what you do. For example, do you remember a time, growing up, when someone said you were "selfish," "lazy," or "stupid"? Most people have had this kind of experience—either at home, or at school, or maybe somewhere else, like church.

In a home that is primarily empathic and functional, there tends to be a distinction drawn between the child, "We love you and are delighted you're so creative," and the behavior, "but when you draw on the walls with your crayons, it makes us angry." Hearing this distinction enables you to know that you are a good person, worth loving, but that certain *behavior* brings disapproval and isn't okay.

And so, there are many ways to enhance or diminish a child's developing sense of self. For most of us, growing up had its fair share of messages from others that made us feel shaky inside. For many of us, there were also those messages that bolstered our sense of self and, at times, allowed us to feel good about ourselves.

Your sense of self, however, is only one part of development. There is also your ability to adapt to changing or unexpected circumstances: your psychological resilience or rigidity.

PSYCHOLOGICAL RESILIENCE AND RIGIDITY

Let's look more closely at how you developed psychological resilience or rigidity when you were a child. When I say *resilience,* I mean the ability to "bounce back" like a schmoo doll.[3] In case you haven't seen one, a schmoo doll is a large, plastic, egg-shaped doll that rests on a sand ballast. No matter how hard you try to push it down, the doll always bounces back to an upright position. It always regains its balance quickly.

Psychological *rigidity,* as I use the term here, describes a person who withdraws, becomes defensive or angry, or in some other ways acts threatened when confronted with something unexpected or new. This psychological stance reminds me of Humpty Dumpty. There is such a fear of being shattered that the person must protect herself at all costs. This kind of rigidity expresses a need to push away, rather than to invite, challenging or novel experiences.

Your basic style of coping was created from the very beginning of your life, as a means of dealing with situations in which you found yourself. It began as a response to nonverbal, experiential interactions you had with your caretakers and your environment. The particular style you developed way back then, whether you would now describe it as resilient or rigid, was the best option you had at the time.

Let's look at how an infant develops either resilient or rigid coping strategies. To do this, I'd like to ask you to imagine an infant in a crib. Remember, this infant is the seed of a healthy adult, newly emerged into her environment. In her earlier experience in the womb, she was held within a certain kind of connection, all the time. Now, she is alone in her room, crying. She is hungry and has no understanding of time. There is only now, and now lasts forever, and forever is too long to wait to be fed. She has no way of knowing that her mother will come with food in a few minutes. To the infant, there is an immediate need for food and the threat of starvation if that food doesn't arrive.

Imagine that this infant's mother, who is calm and reassured, responds quickly, picks up the baby and soothes her with both the right kind of food and a gentle tone of voice. Mom's internal state of comfort and ease with her baby constitute an empathic response. The infant feels reassured and safe. The infant learns, nonverbally and in a deeply unconscious way, that she *can* get what she needs, when she needs it, and that all will be well. Her first step towards psychological resilience has been taken.

The unconscious, internal experience that everything will be taken care of, that she is responded to adequately when she has needs, translates into an ability to *self-soothe*. Self-soothing promotes a psychological resilience that will enable her to respond to anxiety and stress with a deep-seated tendency to bounce back. If she feels knocked off balance by some experience, she'll get back on track quickly. As an adult, she will probably be able to cope well in ambiguous and uncertain situations.

Imagine, now, another infant who is also hungry and crying. He has a nervous, insecure mother. He's her first child and she's unsure of how to handle him. His helplessness and the immediacy of his needs tap into his mother's own fragile sense of self. Instead of responding calmly and with a sense of confidence, she comes to her son with mounting anxiety. The nonverbal message to the infant is that things are *not* safe. Rather than experiencing the welcome relief of a soothing response and receiving the food he needs to avoid starvation, the infant feels escalating distress. As his distress escalates, he develops an internal experience of being out of control. And, of course, the more distressed he gets, the more distressed his mother becomes. Even the food cannot soothe him now. He's too overwhelmed by the quality of the psychological environment in which he finds himself. The nature of the psychological food he received has taken precedence over the physical nourishment he sought.

This infant could well grow into an adult who is unable to soothe himself effectively, who lacks the resilience to roll with the punches. He may feel off balance and distressed when circumstances are challenging or ambiguous. He is developing expectations, already, that things will *not* be okay, that he *cannot* get what he needs and that the world is *not* a safe place.

It's important to note here that there are also individual differences in children, right from the beginning. Some infants are inherently more resilient and are not as vulnerable to the inevitable lapses in empathy that occur in nearly every family. Also, some children are inherently sensitive and are much more vulnerable to non-empathic responses. Even as infants, we are not simply mirror reflections of our home life. We are all magnificent combinations of personal and interpersonal factors.

At this point, you may be feeling that if you didn't learn to self-soothe as an infant, all is lost. Nothing could be further from the truth. Remember, you have inside a seed of potential to be a healthy, mature adult. That potential *can* still be developed.

For some children, the world can seem unsafe for reasons other than having anxious caretakers. There are infants who are left alone for long periods of time, whose caretakers are distracted by too many demands. There are infants who hear parents arguing loudly, and the noise and intensity are frightening. There are infants who receive unpredictable and changing responses from a parent who is loving one time and punishing the next. All of these are reasons an infant might experience escalating distress rather than soothing. Or, the child may live in an environment that is itself hostile or non-nurturing. There may be too little food or heat or fun. There may be too much quiet or too much noise. As you work with the exercises in the book, remember how diverse and complex we humans are: for any given individual, *any* situation may be experienced as non-empathic and wounding to a developing sense of self.

Unconscious Beliefs and Expectations

Early interactions with caretakers and the environment in general become the foundation for beliefs and expectations about the self and the world.[4] These beliefs and expectations are usually unconscious, and bring about instantaneous responses to events that may be characterized by comfort, anxiety, ease or despair. Often, you may not have a clue about why you're reacting so strongly to a given situation. The unconscious responds on auto-pilot, acting on these deeply held beliefs and expectations without consulting your conscious mind.

To think about this in terms of yourself, recall a time when something happened that threw you off balance and you just could not get yourself together. I can remember a time in the fourth grade when I was asked to sing a song for the class. There were several weeks for preparation. I remember obsessing over that song everyday, scared out of my wits at the prospect of singing in front of my classmates. I just couldn't get myself calmed down enough to imagine singing alone. I finally soothed myself from the outside in: I got a friend to sing with me.

As an adult, I remember the first time I was scheduled to present at a conference. About 150 people were expected. The entire night before that presentation I was awake with waves of intense panic flowing through me. That time, I was forced to soothe myself—I didn't have the option of asking a friend to perform with me! I used up so much energy that night worrying about standing in front of so many people that I wore myself out.

I had almost no energy left the next morning to be afraid. I gave the talk and survived—an important new learning.

In later years, I learned how to soothe the child within myself. This discovery created a much greater sense of internal equilibrium and taught me something else that is important. Self-soothing can be learned long after the time when it is usually developed.

What times come to mind for you, now, from your childhood or your life as an adult, when you were unable to soothe yourself or shift out of a distressing feeling? How about those times you have succeeded in doing so? How effectively have you learned to calm and reassure yourself, or validate and encourage yourself, or help yourself take risks? Take a moment to think about it. Remember, part of what you're doing is exploring what you need to learn in order to soothe yourself. You are discovering the kind of nourishing psychological food you need. This discovery itself tells you something about how you went through the early phases of development as a child, something about the expectations and beliefs you created back then.

At this point, I want to say something about asking yourself questions like these. This kind of exploration sometimes brings distressing or frightening memories. Or, you may be surprised by unexpected memories of times you felt strong, competent, together in a way you had forgotten. I encourage you to approach the journey with the curiosity of an explorer. *Everything* you discover provides information you need—information about places in you that seek healing and places of strength you didn't know you had.

"RAPPROCHEMENT"

The stages of development from about two to four years of age build on the infant's early, basic learnings. They involve the child's increasing discovery that he is a separate, autonomous self.[5] It is a time characterized by excitement, challenge, frustration and tremendous developmental achievement. It is the time in a child's life when a period of "rapprochement" with reality is engaged—when the child discovers that the world is not always his oyster and that there are certain limits he must accept.[6]

This "rapprochement" is often a surprise and bitter disappointment for the child. Suddenly, he can't just scream and Mom or Dad will come running immediately, every time. He's getting old enough to begin to learn that he's part of a larger context. Being part of a larger context means learning new rules. "No, you can't bite your brother." "Don't touch that." "I'll feed you in a little while."

Rapprochement is a period of learning another important internal state—*frustration tolerance.* It's important to be able to handle life's inconvenient or unplanned moments without feeling powerless or overwhelmed. If you haven't developed a degree of frustration tolerance, it's easy to feel knocked off balance. As with everything having to do with developing a solid sense of self, interactions with caretakers form the basis of the child's early learning.

For example, if your Dad is too busy to help you wind up a favorite toy, it may be that a small delay, say, two to three minutes, would be tolerable. Some frustration is there, but it is soon relieved when Dad responds. If the delay is longer, or Dad never does make time to help you, your frustration might continue to escalate. It's at this point that you might have a tantrum, or just give up, pushing away your anger. If this happens all the time, you don't have the opportunity to learn that things have a way of working out, eventually.

Developing an ability to tolerate frustration is important. I have met people who are so consumed with anger because of disappointments and frustrations that they feel off balance nearly all the time. The anger and feelings of being victimized are so strong that these people have little room left over for feeling satisfied or calm or at ease. Also, they sometimes feel so powerless that they are unable to go after what they want if any obstacles come their way. I always think of the child within—how frightened, alone and helpless that child must feel, and how out of control everything must seem.

And so, we're learning monumentally important things during this early phase of development. During this time, it is also essential that the child have experiences that validate her ability to be separate without being abandoned. As a child, you are learning that you have two levels of need. On one level, you still must have physical caretaking, and you also have an emotional need to feel loved by people who are important to you.[7] On another level, you have a mounting need to find your *own* place in the world and to have your natural urges towards independence acknowledged and supported.

Sometimes, caretakers—parents, teachers, babysitters—have a hard time allowing both dependence and independence. For instance, a child might prefer to color alone rather than to sit with the family and watch television. If disapproval is aimed at the child for his preference, the developing sense of self may be injured. Again, the child may be left feeling he is bad.

Other kinds of interactions may undermine a child's sense of competence. For example, when a child is learning to walk, a parent who feels competent herself might respond with appropriate support, applauding each small success. If the parent is anxious or insecure, though, she might respond by ignoring or withdrawing from the child as he stumbles through his first steps. Instead of encouraging steps forward, this parent might feel comfortable only when the child is dependent and needy. Responses of this sort may leave the child feeling confused and inadequate.

These kinds of wounds create an internalized experience of the self as unworthy, bad, shameful, or monstrous. The sense of self becomes increasingly negative as non-empathic responses accumulate. Later, in adult life, our negative sense of self affects the quality of relationships we are able to have with mates, friends and authority figures. It's not at all uncommon to discover that you have been, unconsciously, expecting and experiencing the same struggles with closeness and distance in your adult relationships that you had in childhood. This is something we'll look at in later chapters.

I'd like to say a word here about only children. Only children may feel swallowed up by their parents, or they may experience an overwhelming responsibility for their parents' happiness. Parental expectations, dreams and wishes may be put onto the only child, and there are no siblings to share the load. Also, the only child may become the primary companion to a parent. Moves towards independence on the part of the child may threaten the parent and create guilt in the child. Actually, in dysfunctional families, it's not at all uncommon for parents to turn to their children to get unfulfilled needs met. When this happens to an only child, there may be nowhere to turn for help or for validation of the child's feelings of being overwhelmed by parental demands.

For example, if you were an only child and you preferred to play with other children rather than stay home with your mother, you might have sensed your mother's distress as you got ready to go out. Because young children don't have names for feelings, the guilt or fear you may have felt becomes an uneasiness you can't express or understand. In time, this uneasiness becomes part of your self-image. You may decide, unconsciously, that you hurt people. You're not sure why. There must be something terrible about you or about doing what you want. It must be that you're only good when you're doing what others ask of you.

Of course, you don't have to be an only child to have experienced this kind of role reversal. Even when there are brothers and sisters to share the load, the demand to respond to a parent's need places a burden on a child.

What a different scenario it is for the child whose parents are secure in their own sense of self and who rejoice in their child's moves towards independence, even as they teach her how to deal with necessary limits in the real world. What a difference for the child who learns that reality has limits that can be managed even as she experiences an anticipation of future, new adventures. What a difference to go through each day with an inherent sense of safety.

For all children, this early phase of development is characterized by a need for give and take, freedom and limits, acceptance and frustration on the part of both children and caretakers. The child needs caretakers who give permission to explore and, yet, set appropriate limits to ensure the safety and acceptable socialization of their energetic and curious offspring.

MIRRORS—REFLECTIONS OF THE SELF

During the rapprochement phase of development, the child constantly references back and forth, from self to the caretaker, to validate that it is all right to move out on his own. This process validates and affirms the child's budding sense that he has the right to be an *active* participant in life. Throughout development, we check with the mirrors in our environment, just as we did as children.[8]

To explore this for yourself, think for a moment of a young child you've had an opportunity to observe. Can you recall how that child looked at you, or at other adults, to see if anyone was watching? Do you recall ever seeing the way a child's eyes light up when someone important to her responds with a smile? In essence, the child is looking into "reflections of the self." She's checking facial expression, body language, tone of voice—reflections of herself from people, mirrors, who are significant to her. Ongoing, daily interactions such as these communicate to a child what kind of person she is.

If these mirrors are smiling, a child feels wonderful; if they are frowning, she may feel frightened and become quiet and subdued. The mirrors in a child's life convey a wide variety of messages about the self. They may say a child is worthwhile, or lovable, or horrible, or a nuisance, or . . . what comes to mind for you?

These reflections create a powerful foundation for the child's internal sense of self. If parents are habitually irritated, hostile or remote, messages coming to the child will be what I call "self-diminishing." These kinds of messages may create in a child a certain lack of acceptance of himself because, as children, we *believe* what people reflect to us. As children, we have neither the cognitive nor the emotional sophistication to know that Mom had a hard day and would snap the head off *anyone* she had to deal with. Children don't know how to know that a father who gets drunk and yells or hits is caught in his *own* lack of control. We, as children, believe that *we* are the cause of these responses. We conclude that there is something wrong with us, or we are bad, or we do not deserve to be treated well, or that, if only we were good enough, it would all be fine. These beliefs become unconscious as we grow up and can be a source of great discomfort in adulthood. In fact, it's these kinds of beliefs that often propel people into therapy because it's just too uncomfortable to feel so bad about yourself all the time.

Think of a time when everything seemed to be going along just fine and you felt on top of the world and in charge of yourself. Then, without warning, a look or tone of voice from someone transformed you into feeling like an insecure, inadequate person, or you became so enraged you could hardly contain it.

I can think of the many times people have described feeling great, having a productive rewarding day, and then speaking to a family member on the phone and suddenly feeling terrible. It's as though they went into an old, familiar state of mind from childhood as they talked, and went back to another time, another place when they were very young. This is a common experience—and not just with family members.

These responses are so deeply unconscious, so thoroughly automatic, that we tend to accept them as inevitable. Rarely do we have a conscious appreciation of the fact that beliefs created in childhood are being reactivated, that we are accessing old learnings. Rarely do we realize we are suddenly looking into a mirror from such a long time ago.

Parents are not the only ones who reflect self-diminishing beliefs back to us. Children also see mirrors in other family members, friends, teachers and authority figures. The responses of all these people are taken in, as reflections of the developing self. When they are similar to the reflections from parents, children believe even more certainly that they are bad, or they are to blame, or they are inherently worthless. Or, when the reflections from those mirrors are consistently positive, good feelings about the self are enhanced and reinforced. Unfortunately, most people who grow up in dysfunctional families receive more self-diminishing than self-enhancing reflections.

I have heard clients describe the child within as if this part of them were a sponge, soaking up all the many messages conveyed by people in the environment. A common experience we have as adults relates to the compelling nature of the messages we took in as children. Think of a time you have had an interaction with someone, as an adult, and you felt strongly that something was wrong, or off, and you ended up feeling bad in some way. Then, almost as quickly as you recognized the feeling, you told yourself there really was nothing going on, that you were overreacting, or you were being paranoid or silly. Almost all of us fall into this trap, only to discover down the road that we were telling ourselves something worth listening to . . . that we *were* being devalued, abused, or disregarded. We learned, from an early age, *not* to listen, *not* to challenge. We learned to ignore our true, gut-level feelings. We learned to deny, diminish, and push away our deepest responses to what we were experiencing.

TRUE SELF/FALSE SELF

The idea of having "true feelings" about our experiences brings to mind an important concept in the development of the self: the relationship between the *true self* and the *false self.* In *The Drama of the Gifted Child,* [9] Alice Miller describes how the false self is created and the true self buried.

I remember a story a client told me about a special Christmas. Georgia had asked for a particular doll, one that was very popular at the time. When Christmas morning came, she discovered that her mother had bought her a puppet instead. When Georgia began to express her disappointment, her father responded with the following statement: "Is that all the thanks we get for taking the time to find you a special gift? We did the best we could. Why do you hurt us this way? Immediately, and unconsciously, Georgia pushed away her angry feelings and felt guilty for hurting her parents. She began to soothe them by acting pleased with the gift—a perfect example of the false self stepping in and saving the day. Of course, the price to Georgia of creating happiness for her parents was Georgia's loss of awareness of her real feelings of disappointment with the gift. She had to turn her feelings into self-criticism. How could she have been so selfish? This became a question that has followed her into many adult interactions. Time and again, the unacceptable disappointment felt by the true self has been submerged, leaving Georgia criticizing herself for being so selfish.

Many of us learn, early on, that our true feelings, our honest responses, are not acceptable and may bring about punishment or abandonment. Particularly in families where there is abuse—and in all dysfunctional families to some degree or another—daring to express the true self can have dire consequences and puts the child at risk of real injury. To protect ourselves from these potentially threatening outcomes, we learn to bury our true feelings and create a socially acceptable, psychologically lifesaving self: the false self. The false self allows us to survive. It also requires us to lose a certain sense of spontaneity, energy, and the ability to acknowledge and validate our own realistic needs.

Instead of pursuing our true desires, we create a self that is able to take care of those around us or to entertain others. We create super-responsible false selves or troublemaker false selves—whatever the environment demands. And often, we learn to hate our true self, because its honest, immediate responses to situations can get us into trouble.

In *The Emperor's New Clothes,* the child who finally declares that the emperor is naked represents the true self. The rest of the people represent the false, adaptive, survival self. In the story, the true self wasn't very popular, was he?

FAMILY MYTHS

One of the other ways children learn not to trust themselves and to bury the true self is when they experience the demand to maintain family myths. In a very basic sense, every family has myths. Some of these myths reflect the ways in which the family wishes to be seen or to perceive itself. Myths usually operate to cover up or reinterpret things that the family judges to be unacceptable. Often, these myths operate to protect the status quo. Children learn, all too often, that to respond honestly to what is going on may cause rejection, punishment or, worse yet, abandonment.

No child is *ever* going to risk abandonment by insisting on *his* version of reality. Children are magnificent survivors and will adapt in whatever ways are needed to insure they are safe. Because of this, when Uncle Al molests one of the young girls in the family, and she tries to tell someone, all too often she is met with a response something like, "That's ridiculous. Uncle Al was just fooling around," or "Don't talk like that! I never want to hear such nonsense again!" This child quickly learns to blame herself for being such a troublemaker.

Given enough of these interactions (remember what happens when a child's perceptions aren't validated), children stop listening to that special place in the pit of the stomach. Instead, they get angry at *themselves* for being off-base. They have to deny the basic truth of the self. As part of reconnecting with your true self, I encourage you to begin to listen to that very special place inside your stomach. It will warn you whenever a situation or person feels familiar in a bad way. It will signal you when you are involved in a situation that feels similar to times in childhood when you were abused or treated badly and couldn't acknowledge it consciously. Sometimes, it's scary and hard to tune into that place but it's worth it. It represents one of your best early warning systems, a part of you that lets you know something is out of synch, off-base, and possibly not good for you.

DOING TO OTHERS WHAT WAS DONE TO YOU

Alice Miller writes compellingly of the power of the patterns of abuse we internalize and bury as children. When we deny the reality of the true self, which *does* know it was being abused, we are likely to treat ourselves and others as we were treated.[10] I can recall the many times clients or workshop participants have experienced anger or indifference towards the child within. When I ask, "I wonder who felt that way towards you," often there are immediate tears. The tears signal a recognition that had been buried in the true self. They are a recognition of non-empathic responses received from caretakers and then pushed out of awareness.

A common experience is a feeling of a deep burden of responsibility for the child within and a wish not to take up that burden. I remember one woman who experienced a strong urge to ignore the child within. When we explored where that response came from, she became aware of her mother's ambivalence towards her. She realized that she was a burden for her already overwhelmed mother and that she had taken in those feelings and made them her own. With her new awareness, she could set them aside and discover, instead, the joys of caring for her child within.

Through becoming aware of the experience of the true self, which lives in the child you were, you have an opportunity to recognize how you have learned to abuse yourself and others. Such a recognition allows you to find a new, more loving and supportive connection with yourself.

And so, as children, we learn to smile when we'd rather cry, to say, "I'm sorry," when we'd rather scream with rage at unfair treatment. In time, we forget that the true self ever existed, as the false self becomes our *modus operandi* for surviving in a world where we fear rejection, humiliation, or punishment. We bury the true self deeply enough so that its murmurings can be dismissed as our own stupidity, insensitivity, or worthlessness.

LATER DEVELOPMENT

It's not only in early childhood that the development of the self can be either wounded or enhanced. We've been looking at early development, before the age of five. Throughout the school years and even into young adulthood, the development of a solid sense of self and of psychological resilience or rigidity continues. Teachers and schoolmates can have an important impact, one that is either reinforced or lessened at home.

I recall a friend, Faye, whose mother had a favorite saying, "Self pride stinks." This phrase tended to crop up whenever Faye came home from school excited about some accomplishment or another. One day in school, when Faye was six years old, a classmate was singing a song in front of the room. Faye was jealous of the attention this other girl was getting, and acted bored. She didn't applaud when the song was finished. The teacher noticed and, as a punishment, made Faye sing in front of the class. Faye was deeply humiliated. She was surprised by the teacher's anger at her and cried throughout the song. The teacher didn't relent. Faye had to complete the song, tears and all. To this day, Faye remembers this incident as a turning point in her school experience. From then on, she never volunteered answers in classes throughout her school years.

Faye's humiliation affected her more deeply than it might have another child because at home there was the attitude that she deserved to be humiliated for feeling superior. If her mother had been able to take more pride in Faye's accomplishments and had conveyed the idea that, "you're okay no matter what," this school experience might not have been so devastating.

During adolescence, as well, the young person's sense of who he is changes as hormones are released and the body goes through the transformation from a child's body to an adult's body. It is a confusing time when humiliating or abusive experiences can disrupt a solid sense of self and create the same internal feeling of being off balance that the younger child feels. Adolescence is also a time when positive, validating input from empathic caretakers—who understand the adolescent's need to be both dependent and independent (remember rapprochement?)—can strengthen an inner sense of balance and solidity.

Think back to when you were a teenager and remember how crucially important it was to make sense of your world and to find your place in it. One of the developmental tasks of adolescence is to discover who *you* are, what *you* believe, what values *you* want to hold. Often, this urge to find a separate sense of self creates conflict, as the teenager expresses lifestyle choices and values that are different from those of the family. Remember how you dressed when you were 16 or so? How about the music you liked? Was it the same as the music your parents liked? Take a moment to recall how your parents reacted to your favorite music or the style of clothing you wore.

Unfortunately, many of our parents didn't know that it's healthy—essential, in fact—to allow adolescents to be different. It's all part of learning to be a secure, self-confident adult—at least in cultures where individual autonomy and self-expression are highly prized. Of course, the challenge here for parents is to balance support for independence with reasonable, necessary limits. In families that are primarily functional, setting limits to ensure safety and teach responsibility is coupled with respect for the adolescent's point of view. The message to the still-developing sense of self is that you are worthwhile and worth caring about.

Often, however, you may have met with disapproval and a power struggle as you sought to define yourself during adolescence. In the empathic, functional family, parents remember their own developmental process and take some pride in the struggles of their offspring to define themselves. An atmosphere of agreeing to disagree, of respecting each individual's right to his or her own values and ideas nourishes the developing self and reflects back to adolescents that they are valued, that it is safe to have their own ideas and to express themselves in *their* own way.

When adolescents are met with responses that condemn, belittle or punish, they learn that it is *not* safe to be themselves—to really express who *they* are. Instead, they learn, once again, to smile when they would rather scream, or to get depressed instead of fighting back. Sometimes they fight back impulsively when what they really want is to receive an accepting response from people who are important to them. Again, the false self is buoyed up at the expense of the true self.

As adult development proceeds and the wounded child becomes a wounded adult, the false self attempts to find intimacy with another person. True intimacy requires us to be real. Unfortunately, all the messages over the years may have led to a belief that it's not safe to be real. This basic premise sets in place an acute sensitivity to rejection, humiliation, injustice—actual or imagined. Because of this, some people are able to engage intimacy only in its beginning, romantic stages. During this phase, they experience closeness and elation, and may think that *finally* it will work out for them. The problem is that, because they function from the stance of the false self, disappointments and imagined assaults inevitably happen. Their already wounded sense of self is further injured and the relationship ends.

It would be downright discouraging if we had to settle for the wounds we received growing up, to settle for living as a false self. Thankfully, as the disciplines of psychology and hypnosis mature, new approaches are providing additional opportunities to heal some of these wounds. We're learning new ways to allow the true self its rightful place in our lives. Now that you've explored some of the ways you got to be as you are, let's move on to deal with how you can heal these wounds and give yourself permission to have a better life than you may ever have imagined possible.

Chapter 3

SELF-HYPNOSIS: A TECHNOLOGY FOR CHANGE

An important step in the process of healing your wounds and creating a better life is to learn a technology that promotes this process. The technique offered in this chapter is a form of self-hypnosis that combines several approaches. First, it is Ericksonian in nature, which means that it is a *permissive* form of hypnosis. In permissive approaches to self-hypnosis, you allow yourself to accept whatever emerges into awareness during your hypnotic experience. You tend to give yourself open-ended suggestions, which allow your unconscious to fill in the specifics. For example, instead of telling yourself to be on a particular beach experiencing a particular event, you allow your unconscious to choose "some beautiful place where you can find ease and comfort right now."[1]

Also, from an Ericksonian perspective, it's important to avoid judging yourself or your hypnotic experiences. To use an Ericksonian approach is, above all else, to accept the uniqueness of the individual. It also affirms the inherent value of unconscious processes. To be caught up in judging what you experience while in trance interferes with the ability of the unconscious to communicate with you. Hypnotic trance is easier to attain when you approach it with a sense of playful curiosity, wondering just what you will discover and what it will mean to your healing process over time.

A second characteristic of the self-hypnotic work you'll learn here is that it focuses on creating safe places in your inner world. These are places where you can meet, and develop relationships with, many parts of yourself. In the safety of these inner environments, your healing process is enhanced.

THE BACK OF YOUR MIND AND THE FRONT OF YOUR MIND

Angel whskp II

You'll also learn to move into your experience from the "back of your mind." You can think of the back of your mind as that place where you connect with learnings, behaviors, responses and parts of yourself that are usually unconscious. Self-hypnosis connects with the wisdom that exists in the back of your mind and allows your conscious awareness, the "front of your mind," to become a passenger, an observer on your inner journey. Ordinarily, the conscious mind perceives and accepts what it knows already. When you hold an attitude of open curiosity, though, your conscious mind learns to be surprised by what the unconscious presents. Because of this shift in focus, you learn to trust what drops into the front of your mind from the back of your mind.

Many people are concerned that what they experience in trance is consciously created. There's no need to worry that you may be "creating" what you perceive in a hypnotic state. If you do find yourself consciously creating things, you'll soon learn to know the difference between this and unconscious awarenesses that suddenly become conscious. There's a different quality to each. Consciously created images tend to have a stilted quality. They reflect things you consciously know you want, rather than presenting you with new or different perspectives. Sometimes, when the conscious mind is actively trying to create your experience, there's a tendency to push aside impressions that don't seem to fit, that don't feel the way you wanted them to be. When impressions come from the back of your mind spontaneously, they have a quality of just suddenly being there, whether they make sense or not. Often, they are insistent and keep pushing through the images your conscious mind may be seeking to create in their place.

For most people, it takes practice to teach the conscious mind to become a passenger on inner journeys. If you find this is true for you, it's good to know that an Ericksonian perspective respects how learning takes place. When you first learned to ride a bike, roller skate or do any activity that required balance, it was essential to lose your balance at first. By falling down, or falling over, your body learned how to maintain its equilbrium. In your hypnotic work, it's the same thing. You need your conscious mind to interfere at first, so that you can learn how best to invite it back into the passenger seat.

EXPECTATIONS, FEARS AND HOPES ABOUT HYPNOSIS

Before continuing this chapter, it's helpful to take some time to explore your expectations and hopes about hypnosis, as well as any concerns or fears you may have. By doing so, you'll save yourself time when you begin to work with the exercises in the book. Remember to acknowledge everything you feel and think about hypnosis. It's all information that is valuable to have. Whatever you overlook now may surface when you have other things you want to do with your trance.

If you don't know self-hypnosis already, or if you've never experienced hypnosis with someone else, you may have some discomfort about it. You may have found a fear that says to be in trance means to be under someone else's control. A lot of people express this fear at first. It's important to know that hypnosis is a state of mind in which you are in complete control. In fact, you're probably more in control in trance than at many other times in your life. It's always up to you whether you remain in trance. It's up to you whether you follow a suggestion. It's up to you whether your eyes stay closed. It's one time when you can really depend on your ability to be in control.

It's also a time when you can experiment with holding on to that control and letting it go. Some people experience a great deal of pleasure when they discover that they can always choose whether or not to follow a suggestion. There's a certain sense of power in being able to let go of conscious control and be curious about what a suggestion might bring. As you explore self-hypnosis in this chapter, you might ask yourself how you feel about holding on and letting go, and how you experience your ability to control your own trance.

When I first learned hypnosis, it surprised me to discover that I would automatically come out of trance if someone suggested something I found uncomfortable. When working with other people, I now know that if I suggest something they don't want to do, they will begin to awaken themselves, or follow a suggestions of their own instead. It's comforting to know that a part of you constantly monitors your hypnotic experience and brings you back to an alert state if something is happening that you don't like.

Another common concern is that you might say something you didn't want anyone to know. That was a particular fear of mine. I recall the first time I was hypnotized. It amazed me to discover that my mouth didn't fly open and say the things I was afraid to let anyone know. In fact, I remember feeling a certain sense of surprise and pleasure when I chose not to share what I was experiencing during a trance and no one knew it.

Sometimes, the only exposure people have to hypnosis is through stage hypnosis. For these people, there is often a fear of doing something foolish—quacking like a duck, barking like a dog, or singing like Elvis. A woman once asked me why her husband had behaved in such a silly way on stage. I told her that it may be that stage hypnotists give us permission to perform and behave in ways that are delightful to a part of us but that are embarrassing when we're out of trance. A colleague has suggested that some people who perform on stage may be the same people who loosen up at parties after a few drinks and become the evening's entertainment. Also, there's the possibility that when you're on stage a certain pressure exists not to let down the audience. Whatever the reasons for people's varied responses to stage hypnosis, there isn't any danger you'll do anything you don't want to as a result of working with self-hypnosis.

Since there have been so many misrepresentations of hypnosis in the popular media, it would not be surprising if you had some misgivings tucked away somewhere inside. Because of this, take some time, as you begin this work, to allow your fears or concerns to surface. It's better to bring them into conscious awareness, where they can be explored, than to have them get in the way later.

The most important thing to know, as you begin, is that *all hypnosis is self-hypnosis.* Whenever you, or someone else, suggests that you enter a trance state, you do so because you *choose* to be there. When you follow the suggestions of a hypnotist, you do so because some part of you elects to go along with the suggestion. In self-hypnosis, it's the same thing. You follow your own suggestions because some part of you wants to go along with what you seek to accomplish.

In fact, when you're first learning self-hypnosis, it's a good idea to go along with your own suggestions, even if you only "pretend" as you begin. For instance, if you were to suggest to yourself that your eyes will close when you take a deep breath, go ahead and close your eyes even if you don't feel compelled to do so. By following your own suggestions, you develop a habit of going along with what you want to achieve.

Some people come to hypnosis with unrealistic hopes. They are looking for a magic pill that will fix things right away. Unfortunately, hopes for magic are destined to be disappointed. Hypnosis is a state of mind and provides a context within which you can discover and process new learnings. While trance, as an altered state, is relaxing and healing to the body, in and of itself, a hypnotic state doesn't provide all you need to promote a healing process. It's what you *do* while you're in trance that will create the differences you seek.

A WORKING DEFINITION OF TRANCE

At this point, it might be helpful to have a working definition of *trance* as the state of mind you seek when you go into hypnosis. For me, trance is a useful term to define the altered state of consciousness people enter during self-hypnosis. For the sake of brevity, I use the word trance to refer to any hypnotic state, regardless of its depth.

Something important to know about hypnotic trance is that it is a naturally occurring state of mind. Not only can you experience trance states with practice, but you are also in natural trance states all the time. Erickson knew this well and made an invaluable contribution to the field of hypnosis by pointing out that everyone spends a good deal of time in these natural trances.[2]

Trance is an altered state of consciousness that is especially characterized as *a focused state of attention.* You've had countless experiences of trance throughout your life. For example, have you ever been riding in a bus, train, plane or car and suddenly realized that you were staring out the window, eyes wide and glazed over? This is a trance state we all experience at some time or another . . . often in school or at a lecture! As your eyes defocus and seem to stare off into nowhere, your attention becomes absorbed in a thought, a memory, or a feeling of some kind. As this happens, awareness of your surroundings diminishes, becomes less immediate. During these times, you are in a naturally occurring trance, an internal state that has lots in common with hypnotic trance.

Another common experience of natural trance happens when driving a car. If you drive, think of a time you may have gone several miles without realizing that your mind was focused on some thought or reverie. When you suddenly became aware of the car and your surroundings, you may have wondered how on earth you got safely from here to there. You probably had no conscious memory of having driven those miles. The fact that you *did* get from here to there demonstrates that there is a part of you that deals with the external environment whenever you're in a trance state.

In fact, you may find that when you're in trance, even though you seem to care less about focusing on the external world, you are also acutely aware of what is happening there. It's just that you don't feel like bothering with external cues. It's important to know that your unconscious always takes care of you, always watches out for you. You can trust the part of your unconscious that maintains an awareness of your environment and activities, even when your conscious mind is off somewhere, thinking its own thoughts.

Other examples of natural trance abound. Have you ever listened to music and been so absorbed that someone was able to enter or leave the room without your being aware of it? How about those times you may have been watching television or a movie and became so absorbed in it that your surroundings faded from awareness? When the movie was over, you may have forgotten where you were and had to take a moment to reorient yourself. What happens when you're absorbed in a riveting book? Do you lose yourself in it? These examples of focused attention are identical to hypnotic trance.

Have you ever spent time daydreaming about someone special, imagining all the things you might do together? How about those times your mind may have drifted, not focused on anything in particular, and the solution to a problem just dropped into place? These are yet other examples of naturalistic trance.

What is often surprising when you experience hypnosis for the first time is that you are thoroughly aware of your surroundings when you're in trance. What you discover is, you're so focused on your internal experience that, momentarily, you *don't care* about what's happening in the outer world. Of course, if an emergency were to arise, you would immediately be aware of it. You would come out of trance automatically and be perfectly alert and able to deal with whatever needed your attention.

Even knowing this, it's not unusual for people to report that they weren't in trance because they were aware of what was going on around them. Sometimes, it takes time to learn how to know you are in trance. A colleague of mind was doing excellent self-hypnosis for four years before she finally realized that she was, indeed, in a trance. She would do self-hypnotic exercises but then say she wasn't doing them correctly. Her awareness shifted when she realized that she had expected to be totally unconscious during hypnosis. In her mind, any conscious awareness at all meant she wasn't really in trance, even if the experience felt good. Once she became aware of this expectation, she was able to let it go and begin to explore her unique, individual responses to being in a hypnotic state.

As the above example illustrates, it's important to know what your expectations and hopes are when you work with hypnosis. If my colleague had explored her expectations at the outset, she might not have had to spend four years questioning her process. She might have realized, right away, that she had some unrealistic assumptions. She might have gotten a more useful feeling of what trance would be like if she had been able to gather information ahead of time. Not having realized that she expected to be unconscious kept her from knowing the right questions to ask.

The degree of awareness of the environment that's possible when in hypnosis was demonstrated for me a number of years ago when I put a 13-year-old girl into trance. Her parents were in the room, sitting on a sofa, facing her. She went into trance easily. When I suggested she watch a balloon rise into the sky, her head moved as if she were actually seeing the balloon. At one point, she began to smile, as her mother looked at her with curiosity and some amusement. When she came out of trance, her first words to her mother were, "I heard you smile!" We all laughed, even as we were impressed by her ability to be so attuned to the external environment. While continuing to have an absorbing and enjoyable hypnotic experience of watching a balloon rise into the sky, a part of her was fully attuned to her external environment.

An interesting thing to note is that it's not at all unusual to be presented with paradoxical terms, such as "hearing someone smile," when a person is in trance. There are many ways of perceiving when in an altered state. If you know ahead of time that you may be able to "taste" a situation or to "see" with your sense of touch, you can allow yourself to accept the full richness of your unconscious process as you explore your inner world.

DEPTH OF TRANCE

It's not unusual for people to wonder how deep their trance needs to be to be effective. The surprising thing to discover is that depth of trance isn't really important when you're doing self-hypnosis.[3] Powerful and effective outcomes can be accomplished with light trances, as well as with those that feel deeper. The important thing to know is that depth of trance will vary, naturally, from time to time. There may be times when you focus easily and become so absorbed that you really do let go of any concern with what's going on outside. There may other times when you are aware of, and distracted by, every little movement around you.[4]

These variations are normal and to be expected. Again, the best thing to do is just to accept whatever quality your trance has at a given time. To be in a lighter trance one time and a deeper trance the next or usually to be in a lighter rather than a deeper trance is fine and won't get in the way of your process at all. Your unconscious knows what depth and quality of trance you need. Remember to let the back of your mind guide the process while the front of your mind allows itself to be surprised by what emerges.

Sometimes people discover that they come out of their trance not remembering anything. They feel as though they fell asleep. If this happens to you, which it may from time to time, simply

accept it. It's quite possible to process hypnotic experience totally outside conscious awareness with effective results. Chances
are good that you weren't actually asleep but that, instead, you
drifted into a type of trance that created amnesia for what you
were experiencing. One way to differentiate between sleep and
trance is your response to a suggestion that you come back. If
you reorient yourself in response to a suggestion to do so,
chances are very good that you were in trance and not asleep. If
you do fall asleep during trance, you'll awaken naturally, as you
would from a nap. If you find that you consistently have no
awareness of your self-hypnotic experience, give yourself the suggestion that you will remain in a light enough trance to be conscious of what you experience.

Your Unique Relationship With Trance

When using permissive techniques, the ability to work with hypnosis successfully is a skill most people have. As with all skills,
you get better at it the more you practice. If you start out feeling
you're not in trance, that you're too distracted, stick with it
anyway. There's no point in "trying" when you work with self-
hypnosis. Working hard to achieve an altered state of consciousness is a guaranteed way to stay in the front of your mind. "Allowing" is everything. If you feel distracted, allow the
distractions to be there first. Then, they will move on, outside
your awareness. If you resist thoughts, feelings, or noises that
intrude and distract you, you'll just strengthen your awareness of
them.

Whenever you feel distracted, you might think of the
thoughts, feelings or noises as leaves floating on a stream. You
can choose to watch the leaves float by, noticing that they move
on downstream and, eventually, out of sight around a bend in
the stream. You might want to watch particular leaves for a
while with real interest, focusing on their color and shape, until
they disappear. You may want to pick up one of the leaves and

set it beside you to consider later. You may even choose to look across the stream, at the other side, knowing that leaves are floating by without paying attention to them at all.

Another fallacy about hypnosis is that you have to be relaxed to be in trance. Nothing could be further from the truth. Hypnotherapists are familiar with how anxiety can quickly produce trance states. People who are frightened usually want to escape from the discomfort of the fear. Often, the most available escape route is into trance, into the comfort of someplace inside, away from the fear.

If you find yourself tense as you sit down to do your self-hypnosis, take a few moments and increase the tension. Allow it. Focus on it. By doing so, you give yourself an opportunity to acknowledge an inner state that has something to tell you. You may find that, after increasing the tension and listening to it, it settles down all by itself, with no effort on your part. In fact, you might even give yourself the suggestion that you may discover, after you come out of trance, that you had forgotten all about the tension shortly after beginning to focus on the exercise at hand.

A good rule of thumb is always to acknowledge whatever is in the forefront of your experience. Remember that to struggle to be where you're *not* rarely works and can only serve to create a sense of frustration or inadequacy. At the very least, it may take the fun, pleasure and sense of curiosity out of the experience.

There's a hypnotic state called a "bright-eyed, bushy-tailed" trance. Here a person appears to be fully alert and in a wide-awake state of mind, while actually experiencing a fully absorbing trance. If you find yourself feeling bright-eyed and bushy-tailed and yet absorbed in and interested by what you're doing, simply accept it. It represents one more variation of your unique way of being in trance.

The key to discovering your relationship with trance is to accept your own way of becoming absorbed in meaningful internal experiences. If you will allow yourself to accept whatever depth and quality of trance emerge at any given time, your work in self-hypnosis will be empowered. While a deep trance may be more comfortable or enjoyable because of a stronger sense of relaxation, nothing is served by striving for depth.

As you proceed with the self-hypnosis exercise in this chapter, it's helpful to remember that you are entering a terrain of your psychological landscape that is quite familiar. You may discover, sooner than later, that it's second nature to be in trance, like visiting an old friend with whom you've always been comfortable.

Time is another important element of the quality of your trance experience. Remember that the unconscious is timeless in nature. Whenever you're in trance, you enter a terrain in which time has no meaning, at least not as we know it. Time expands and contracts in trance. Five minutes of clock time may be experienced as hours and hours of inner time. Hours of clock time may seem but minutes when you're having an engrossing internal experience. Einstein is credited with saying something like, "One minute spent sitting on a hot stove feels a lot longer than an hour spent with a lover!"

You may have experienced this yourself in a wide variety of situations. For example, does time seem to fly when you're enjoying some activity and seem to drag when you're bored? When you were a child, did it seem like forever from September to June, when summer vacation would begin? Then, did it seem as though only a few weeks had passed when June became September again and summer was over?

Because of the inherent flexibility of time in the unconscious, even if you have only a few minutes some days to go inside and nurture your relationship with important parts of yourself, that's fine. You can give yourself a suggestion that you have all the time you need in the time you have. In those few minutes of clock time, you can experience as much as you need for this particular trance.

Space is also different in trance. There aren't the same constraints on movement from one place to another. All you need to do is think of a place you'd like to be and you're there. Even more different from the external, objective world is the ability of a part of yourself to be in one place while another part is elsewhere. For example, when some people do self-hypnosis for pain control, they leave their body in bed, with the pain, as the rest of them sits across the room, or in another room, watching television or reading.[5]

During hypnosis, it's possible to leave a part of you in the trance state as the rest of you comes back to do other things. In many of the exercises you'll do in the following chapters, there's a suggestion that you leave a part of you in your safe place as the rest of you comes back. This is possible because the unconscious keeps right on developing whatever you experience in trance, even as the rest of you returns to an alert state and begins to think about something else. What may be surprising to discover is that, when you return to trance next time, things *will* have developed in some way that has real meaning for you.

Having one part of you in trance while the rest of you remains in a conscious, alert state has lots of applications. One that is particularly helpful is when you are faced with a deadline on a work or creative task. I recall once when I was asked to do a book review and there wasn't enough time to get it done in the usual way. I decided to read the book while a part of me stayed in a light trance. I gave myself the suggestion that, as I read, this part would comprehend the material, organize it and write the review. I took notes each time I sat down to read and felt fully alert all the while. What surprised me was that I read the book more quickly than I usually do and that, as I sat down to write the review, it seemed to write itself. My unconscious appeared to know exactly where to put which notes and quotations and how to order points in the review. In fact, the whole project took less time than I was given and was of better quality than usual.

If you're interested in exploring more of the many ways you can use self-hypnosis, I've listed several books in the reading list in the appendix. They describe a variety of approaches to, and techniques of, self-hypnosis that have both personal and professional applications. For now, the exercises in the following chapters will focus on an internal process of going inside to develop relationships with parts of yourself, to hear the story of the child within, and to create a more empowered expectation of what you deserve. It's important to know, though, that this is just one of the many ways you can use your self-hypnotic skills.

TRANCE IMPRESSIONS, IMAGES AND FEELINGS

Another important aspect of trance is the difference between impressions and vivid images. When you are fortunate enough to have a vivid image or a vivid sensory experience, that's great. Sometimes, these come through so clearly that they leave little room to wonder about their meaning. They are clear to you and specific enough to keep your conscious mind from questioning their validity. Often, though, you'll probably find yourself dealing with impressions that may be more or less vague.

Impressions are those often subtle awarenesses that come from the back of your mind and nibble at the front of your mind. They may represent a vague sense of a color or the broad outline of a form. An impression may be experienced as a "sense of things" rather than as a clear outline or a specific, concrete awareness. An impression may be a smell, a sound, a color or physical sensation that develops into a clearer, more vivid image as you work with it.

It's helpful to follow vague impressions and allow them to develop in their own way without any conscious preconceptions or demands. Remember, the front of your mind is accustomed to being in the driver's seat; on your self-hypnotic journey it's a passenger. It can only know what it knows already. Your unconscious knows more and opens up *new* understandings and experiences for you, often beginning with some vague impression you discover in trance.

As you develop your own trance style and approach to your inner world, it's helpful to remember the richness and diversity of unconscious messages you may receive. There are an infinite number of possible responses you may have in trance. Seemingly inconsequential sensations may come to your awareness. They may include: fleeting glimpses of an image, a color, or a form; the presence of a fragrance or an odor; a faint sound, or any other sensory experience. These vague glimpses may be the beginning points of an unfolding, developing awareness. Allow yourself to follow the impressions that come to the front of your mind and just won't go away. They are likely to represent understandings your unconscious wants you to develop.

If your conscious mind wants to jump in and censor or edit what's happening, remind yourself, as often as you have to, that it is only a passenger on this journey. Allow yourself to have your experience, in whatever way it presents itself to you, with the assurance that you can analyze it later, if you want. Your conscious mind will have its time to go over what you experienced and help you decide what feels valid and what doesn't—after you've finished your trance.

It's all right, too, just to let what comes up during self-hypnosis be there without any further conscious understanding of what it means. Sometimes it's important to leave things, to let them percolate. Then, later, new, helpful understandings and responses may emerge in your daily life automatically and spontaneously, without much conscious activity on your part.

Remember, when you learned things as a child, you simply learned them. You didn't think about them ahead of time, or analyze whether you were doing them correctly, or fear that you were learning the wrong thing. When your unconscious prompted your body to crawl, you did so without realizing you were learning to walk. When you listened to people around you speaking your native language, you just took it in without wondering if the words were ones you wanted to learn. Your conscious participation came later, *after* you had already learned important lessons. Just as you did then, you can still trust your unconscious to get you where you need to be. Later, you can let your conscious mind become the tool that helps you along when it's time to create strategies in your daily life that utilize unconscious learnings in your daily life.

To allow this kind of process asks you to give up some of the control you've probably been taught is essential to successful thinking. We all learned in school to memorize and categorize, to follow one subject with another in a linear, orderly progression. In the unconscious, though, things can happen all at once, often in anything but an orderly fashion. Yet, *your unconscious process always has meaning that makes sense,* even when your conscious mind doesn't understand that meaning immediately.

For example, during a trance, you might experience yourself standing in the livingroom of the house in which you grew up. Using your hypnotic senses, you might discover that the room seems to be closing in on you. The walls themselves seem to be moving closer. Your first impulse might be to get out of the room, to get rid of the feeling. Give yourself permission to take a while to continue the experience anyway. Remember that the unconscious seeks to convey meaningful awarenesses and that you can trust that unconscious communications are intended to be helpful. After a while, you may realize that the feeling reminds you of how you felt as a child. It may remind you of how trapped you felt, of how there was nowhere to run to get away from family fights.

By accepting the first impression of the walls closing in, you discover that you were having *memory feelings.* Memory feelings represent awarenesses of things that have already happened. They can increase your conscious recall, they may even make you uncomfortable, but they can't hurt you anymore.

Continuing to imagine yourself in that room, your sense of family fights clarifies and you suddenly remember, vividly, how your parents argued there, all the time. As a child, you had nowhere to go, and it felt as if things were closing in on you. You wanted your parents to stop fighting, because you were frightened by their anger. You may also have been angry at them for getting so out of control. As an adult, the arguments had been forgotten, consciously. By allowing the vague impression of the walls closing in to develop, your unconscious brought it all back and created an opportunity to resolve residual feelings of helplessness or anger.

During trance, you may also tap into previously forgotten memory feelings of times when you felt particularly safe. Maybe you had a special place you would go when you needed to be alone. Maybe there was a wonderful day when you were with a friend's family at the amusement park, or somewhere else, and laughed a lot. Reliving the smells, sounds and other sensations related to these times and places can give you access to the good feelings, as well . . . and remind you that there *were* some good things back then.

SHIFTING PERSPECTIVES IN TRANCE

Another thing to know about self-hypnosis is that, even when you're looking at material or memories you've explored a dozen times before, you may discover new things while in trance. It's as though you turn a corner and look at something familiar from a slightly different angle. The difference in perspective allows you to see it in a new way. There's a moment of "aha!" where things fall into place differently. You can expect this kind of experience when you're in trance, so it's helpful to be willing to go back over old material, things you thought you'd put away for good.

A client named Ellie discovered this one day, as she worked with her child within. She remembered an experience she had recalled many times before, about being the youngest in a very large family. Her sisters were quite a bit older and weren't home very much. Her mother and father shared the house with two aunts and a cousin. Ellie recalls being a much-loved child in a home where her every whim was allowed. What had always puzzled her was how vulnerable she felt and how easily her feelings were hurt by friends. It didn't make sense to her that she had been so well loved and yet had such deeply felt insecurities around other people.

One day, in hypnosis, Ellie was reliving fond memories of how she was always allowed to be the center of attention and of how readily her demands were met by the adults around her. Suddenly, she gasped and said, "They couldn't stand to see me upset because it would upset *them.*" In one moment, she saw the entire scene differently. Now, she saw a little girl who was given total control over her environment because the adults couldn't stand to experience her distress if they said, "No." She discovered that there weren't any adults available who were able to draw reasonable limits. She experienced how overwhelming it was for a small child to have that much power, and that she was frightened, seeking limits with demand after demand.

What had always been experienced as a deeply loving environment suddenly became a place of chaos. What Ellie had always called love arose, in fact, from the discomfort in the adults around her. It wasn't that they didn't love her in the best ways they knew how. What was important was that Ellie's hypnotic perspective allowed her to realize that her current insecurity arose, in large part, from an early experience of being out of control. She had lived in a world where there were no adults who would set safe limits for her.

The kind of shift in perspective Ellie experienced represents an opportunity to heal the child within. If Ellie had pushed away these memories when they arose from the back of her mind, telling herself she already knew all about her loving family, she would have missed the chance to move closer to resolving her feelings of insecurity and vulnerability. Again . . . and again . . . and again, it's important to accept *whatever* the unconscious presents. There will be a good reason for it, which you'll discover in your own best time.

Two qualities in Ellie's experience are important to underscore. The first is that reviewing "fond memories" she'd thought of many times before opened the door to a new awareness. The unconscious often works this way, giving you something that is easy to focus on that can then develop into a realization you haven't had before. The second thing to note is that the shift in awareness came all at once. In a flash, Ellie knew things were different from the way she had remembered them consciously, and she knew exactly in which ways they were different. She had used her "hypnotic eyes, ears and feelings" to explore memories in a new way, and she registered new awareness in a hypnotic way—in a moment of realization.

As you work with your own self-hypnotic process, you will become familiar with the ways in which your unconscious sometimes gives you vague awareness that opens the door to deeper understandings. You'll also discover the ways in which your unconscious gives you instantaneous flashes of insight that answer questions you've never quite been able to resolve.

The important thing to keep in mind when learning the most effective ways to receive impressions the unconscious wants you to have is to avoid struggling with your conscious thoughts. Just let them be. The "monkey mind," as it's called in some meditative traditions, always seeks to be active. If you get caught up in a thought, eventually you'll realize that your focus has shifted. When this happens, simply refocus on your trance work. Everyone has the experience of becoming distracted by conscious thoughts. The key thing is to accept that you were distracted. There's no need to give any energy to the fact. Simply accept it and teach yourself to refocus whenever you realize you've been chasing the monkey mind.[6]

Another thing to be aware of before you begin working with self-hypnosis is that if, at any time, you find yourself blank, with nothing coming to mind, accept that, too. Blankness is a gift from the unconscious. You can call your blankness *the creative void*, and assume that your unconscious will draw from this infinitely full place just the right impression to give you when it feels you are ready.[7] It may be giving you an opportunity to realize that there *is* a creative void inside, a place where you may discover things you never before imagined.

POST-HYPNOTIC SUGGESTIONS

One final aspect of trance work may be helpful in making real the things you seek to achieve. Post-hypnotic suggestions are like powerful affirmations that you give yourself while you're still in trance. You can develop post-hypnotic suggestions of your own that meet your unique needs. They may range from a simple, "Throughout each day, I become more centered and secure," to "In the meeting I attend today, I am surprised to discover that my unconscious has created a more empowered state of mind than I thought possible. Whenever I reach for my cup of coffee, I am particularly articulate and calm."

I've used post-hypnotic suggestions often in my own journey with self-hypnosis. Early on, when I was still terrified of speaking in front of even small groups, I needed all the post-hypnotic suggestions I could muster. Before group meetings, I would go off to any place where I could be alone for a few moments. I would put myself into a light trance, just long enough to say, "As I begin the meeting, I am amazed to discover that I am nervous for only about a minute, or maybe two minutes, or maybe even three. After that time, I surprise myself by becoming increasingly comfortable, and I won't even realize until later that I've been speaking with more comfort than I imagined possible." The astonishing thing to me was that this kind of post-hypnotic suggestion really works. At some point during a meeting, I *would* find that I was comfortable and that my fear had left.

Sometimes, you may want to take your post-hypnotic suggestions and make them into affirmations that you can say to yourself throughout the day. There is no limit on how to deal with giving yourself suggestions. One thing that's nice to know is that, if you're ever thinking thoughts that pull you down, replacing them with positive suggestions can effectively shift your mood.

Use of language is also important when creating suggestions you give yourself. There are certain words and phrases that help you achieve your goals, and others that work against what you seek. For instance, avoid using suggestions phrased in the negative. The unconscious doesn't recognize the word "not" and will cancel it out of the suggestion, leaving the rest of the statement. When you say things to yourself like, "I'm not afraid," you inadvertently reinforce the fear. Imagine, for a moment, that someone said to you, "Don't think of a blue and orange striped zebra." You have to think of the oddly colored zebra in order to negate it. How many times have you heard a parent say to a child, "Don't spill your milk," only to have the milk topple over? Without realizing it, the parent was giving the child a hypnotic suggestion to spill the milk.

The word "try" is also problematical. Whenever you say "try" in trance, your unconscious hears an implication of failure. Imagine that you say to yourself, "This time, I'm really going to try to be on time." It's not hard to hear the underlying assumption that you probably won't make it, but you will try. Your intentions are good, but there's a real chance that your actions won't follow. Instead, make it a positive suggestion. "I surprise myself by being closer to on time than I realized was possible."

It's helpful to word your suggestions in the present tense, as something you have accomplished already. This way, your unconscious accepts the suggestions as fact and acts accordingly. Sometimes, you may want to include a future orientation. This is helpful when you're dealing with something that's particularly challenging, or with a development you want but are afraid to achieve. You might tell yourself, for instance, that you will recall an important, but traumatic, memory at just the time you're ready to receive it . . . "maybe tomorrow, or next week, or a few minutes from now."[8]

I often mention being "surprised to discover" certain things. Ericksonian hypnosis is filled with suggestions that give room for the unconscious to fill in the blanks and create whatever is needed most at any given time. Your travels in trance are adventures, above and beyond everything else. You are an explorer in a terrain that holds unrealized treasures. For any explorer, an attitude of curiosity and an ability to be surprised are invaluable assets.

REGULARITY AND THE SELF-HYPNOTIC PROCESS

Another valuable asset for an explorer is tenacity. A key element in any healing process is *regularity*. The approach presented in this book has an impact when you make time, preferably on a daily basis, to do self-hypnosis. The process of recreating yourself is ongoing and great benefits are gained when you attend to it each day, even if you have only a few minutes available for your inner work. Besides, you *deserve* to be the best you can be—and you deserve to have available a technology that will help you get there.

Developing a daily self-hypnotic process is a personal matter, and need not be overly time-consuming. Only you know the time of day when your concentration is best. You are also the final authority in deciding where you want to do this work. What matters most is the regularity of it. I encourage you to set up a daily routine of spending a period of time in trance, even if it's for two minutes. By attuning to your internal psychological terrain and centering yourself, you promote self-healing. Because the process provides a sense of connection and balance that can make all the difference in the quality of your day, I usually recommend doing self-hypnosis in the morning, before the day gets started. Remember, though, that this is only a general recommendation. If you are too fuzzy in the morning, or if your schedule is irregular, it's important to create what works best for you. In Chapter 10, entitled "Manifesting A New You," there are suggestions for structuring a daily self-hypnotic routine.

As you develop your own self-hypnosis process, let your creativity and personal style guide you. During trance experiences, allow things to develop in their own natural way. If you are doing some work with the child within, you may find that there are times when the two of you just want to sit together. There may be no need for remembering, no need for active interacting. You may just want to spend some quiet time. If you are having a more active trance, allow the spontaneous moment to develop and see where it leads. Often, it will take you where you hadn't expected and give you an insight or experience that meets your need at the moment. You may find, for instance, that you and the child want to play together, instead of focusing on other things. Let yourself follow these urges. They will always take you where you need to be.

Whenever possible, it's helpful to choose the same spot, and the same time each day, for your hypnotic work. Sitting in the same place each time you do your trance work creates an unconscious association between that place and the trance state. It will be easier for you to go into trance whenever you are there. Some meditative traditions teach their followers to have a particular place and time for meditation for this very reason. Unconscious connections between the place and the activity enhance the quality of your experience.

ABOUT THE EXERCISES

Each of the exercises in the book has a given time suggested to complete it. Most will take about 20 minutes or so. You may or may not choose to do one of these exercises as part of your daily self-hypnotic routine. Sometimes, you may want to set aside another time to do specific exercises and spend your morning time as a period where you connect with the child within and other parts of you to reinforce a sense of relationship. Even if you took only one minute each day to give comfort to the wounded child within, you would benefit greatly.

The following self-hypnosis exercise is designed to promote a trance state in which you can do your inner work most effectively. The induction presented here may be used as an introduction to your other inner work or it may be used, in and of itself, as a deep relaxation. If you use it for relaxation, simply set a time in your mind, say 10 minutes, that you would like to spend allowing your mind to drift without doing anything at all. As you review the induction, note the point where there is a suggestion to begin whatever inner work you've chosen to do. At this point, it is time to give yourself the suggestion that your mind will drift for a certain amount of time as your unconscious develops a deepening state of relaxation. You can also ask your unconscious to work on a problem for you during this time. As you allow your conscious mind simply to wonder, wander, or do whatever it would enjoy, there is no need to have to bother at all with what the unconscious is doing.

I recommend that you tape record this exercise so you can do the entire process without having to refer back to the book. Record only the sentences that are italicized. Use a soft voice, and speak naturally but slowly. Pause for several seconds wherever you see [pause] in the text. Of course, you may want to turn off the tape recorder if you need more time before moving on to the next step in the exercise. It's perfectly all right to move when you're in trance. Simply give yourself the suggestion that whenever you turn the tape recorder on or off, you will return quickly to whatever depth of trance you've been experiencing.

Before you begin your trance, find a place where you'll be undisturbed for 15 minutes or so. Have paper and pencil nearby, so that you can write down any impressions that may emerge. Decide ahead of time what you want to work on so that you'll be ready to go once your trance has developed.

I recommend doing self-hypnosis sitting up, unless you're interested specifically in stress reduction or deep relaxation. Often, people find that if they lie down while working with the child-within and other parts, they drift off and have no conscious awareness of their trance experience. It's often disappointing to reorient only to discover that you can't remember anything you did in trance. Of course, whenever you use self-hypnosis—yourself or with tapes—information is getting in, even if you're drifting or asleep. For developing healing relationships inside yourself, though, I recommend that you use a position that will enhance the likelihood that you'll remember what you've done.

Exercise #1   Self-Hypnotic Induction

Settle your body in a seated position, somewhere where there is support for your back. With your eyes open and your head facing forward, roll your eyes up toward the ceiling. Take a deep breath and, as you exhale, let your eyelids close naturally. Allow your eyes to roll down to their normal resting position. [pause][9]

As you take a second deep breath, hold it for a moment before you exhale. Notice how your body seems to know just how to settle, how to allow the support that is available right now to do all the work for you. [pause]

Take a third breath, now, and, as you exhale, notice that your body settles even further. [pause]

As you focus on the way in which the muscles in your body

seem to recognize the support that is available for you right now, allow your conscious mind to wonder . . . or wander . . . or do whatever it needs to do. Remember that your conscious mind is a passenger on this journey and that, whenever you're in trance, the really important work is done by your unconscious.

If any conscious thoughts float into your awareness, remember to just let them float on by. You can return to them later, when you're finished with your trance, if you want. Remember the leaves on the stream. There's no need to do anything but notice when the leaves move right on out of sight, around the bend. [pause]

If you notice any tension, or any other sensation or feeling, just accept it. Allow it to come with you and you'll be surprised to discover that, as you become more and more absorbed in your inner journey, your comfort level also increases. [pause]

Take a moment, now, to imagine that you are in a safe place somewhere. It may be a special room that is all your own. It may be a beautiful natural setting somewhere in the world. It may be a place you've been to before, or someplace in your imagination . . . or maybe a combination of both. [pause]

If you find that it's difficult to imagine a place that's safe, let yourself pretend. What would a safe place be like if you could imagine one? [pause]

As you become aware of impressions of your safe place, you might notice what the surface under you is like. If you're walking, notice the surface underfoot. Is it soft, or is it hard? Is it smooth, or textured? [pause]

If you're sitting down, can you run the palm of your hand over the surface that's supporting you and get a sense of how it feels? [pause]

And, if it's all right with you, perhaps you could take a moment to notice the surrounding environment in your safe place. Simply let an impression come from the back of your mind to the front of your mind that conveys the colors and shapes that characterize the environment around you. [pause]

Are there any natural smells or natural sounds that invite your attention . . . that convey the qualities of this place? [pause]

Do you notice a certain sense of comfort or ease that may be available to you here? [pause] *How does your body seem to respond to being here?* [pause]

You might also notice what time of day it is, what kind of day. As you continue to explore this inner environment, you might become aware of patterns of light and shadow . . . or of other things that attract your curiosity . . . that you may find interesting . . . maybe even pleasurable. [pause]

And how about a developing sense of safety or security that is conveyed in a way that's meaningful to you? [pause]

As your body continues to settle and your trance continues to develop, be sure to notice any areas of tension or discomfort that may continue to accompany you on your journey to your safe place. Remember that every part of you is welcomed on this journey and you want to be sure to attend to whatever is in your awareness now . . . perhaps by inviting any tension to let go, to be released whenever you exhale. [pause]

You may discover that, as your trance develops, a subtle experience of safety continues to develop, even if you're not aware of it just yet. [pause]

Notice now, if you will, how it feels to discover that, further in, there may be a perfect place where you can sit down and settle in for a little while, if you haven't found it already. [pause]

Remember, this is your safe place. It is a personal and private place. No one is welcomed here without your invitation. If there are things you don't like, or that make you uncomfortable, change them. Tell them to go away. This is your experience . . . it's your place. Here, in this safe place, you have the power to create what you want and need. [pause]

If you find that your mind is blank, and that no impressions have come yet, allow yourself to accept that the creative void has presented itself to you. Your unconscious will give you something from that void when it feels you are ready. In the meantime, just let yourself wonder what your safe place would be like if you could imagine it. [pause]

And now, having settled in, you might close your eyes and proceed with whatever inner work you've chosen for this time. If you simply want to have the quiet of some personal, private time, just let your conscious mind drift as your physical body and unconscious make their own best use of your trance. [Pause here for whatever exercise you have decided to use and for as many minutes as you have available this time. If you are using the induction for relaxation, or to allow time for your mind just to drift, continue with recording the following portion of the induction.]

Once you've completed your inner journey, you can leave a part of you here in this safe place to continue the work you've begun . . . to continue the learning you were experiencing . . . or to continue the exploration you began. [pause] *Remember to tuck away, in that safe place in the back of your mind, everything you've experienced, thought and realized. Here, your unconscious will continue the process of creating new understandings, new learnings and new responses which you may discover come into the front of your mind when you least expect them . . . and always when they are most constructive and you need them most.* [pause]

You might want to give yourself some post-hypnotic suggestions, now, as you come back. Perhaps you'd like to suggest to yourself that you feel relaxed and alert and refreshed, even as your unconscious continues to develop the theme you've just been exploring. Give yourself whatever suggestions you'd like, now, during this pause. [long pause]

To bring yourself back, simply count, mentally, from three to one. Tell yourself that, when you say the number "one," your eyes will open spontaneously and automatically and you'll be all the way back, ready to go on to your next activity.

Take a moment, now, to sit with the tone of your experience as you would the lingering tone of a bell just rung. [pause] *When you're ready, wiggle your fingers and toes to bring yourself all the way back.*

In time, you may find that you can put yourself into trance quickly and you won't have to go through the whole induction, unless you want to create a deeper trance from time to time. In fact, there will come a time when all you'll have to do is take a deep breath and close your eyes as you move into trance. The depth of trance will increase automatically as you begin to focus on your inner process, without having to use the step-by-step induction presented in this chapter.

Also, if you already have a self-hypnotic induction that works for you, great. Use whatever you find is most natural and effective. As you go along, it's important to allow yourself to modify your self-hypnotic exercises to suit your particular style and need at a given time, as well as your developing process. It's important to feel free to create your own ways to move in and out of trance, just as you will create your own best way to be in, and use, trance.

If you find that you are having trouble learning about trance or that you keep running into things that don't make sense, it may be helpful to find a professional therapist trained in hypnosis to assist you. Having someone else guide you into trance several times creates an internal learning set and awareness that you can then draw on when you do self-hypnosis on your own. Whenever you go into trance—and each time you seek an altered state—you can draw on your conscious and unconscious memories of what you learned before.

Sometimes, the issues that may arise during your self-hypnotic work are best addressed with the help of a professional. These are times it is most helpful to have an extra set of eyes along on your journey or another set of ears listening to what you experience.

Also, please give yourself time. Trance is a skill and skills take practice to develop. Avoid demanding a "meaningful experience" every time you go inside. Allow yourself to accept the variation in trance quality and awareness that inevitably accompany the process.

Most of all, enjoy your inner journey. A world of discovery awaits you. You will meet parts of yourself you didn't even know existed. You will have an opportunity to spend time with the child within, developing a relationship you may not have imagined possible. You will be joined in your journey by your future self, who has already been where you're going and is the best guide available to you. Allow yourself to be curious and courageous. The journey is worth it. So are you.

Chapter 4

~~

THE SELF:
PARTS OR WHOLES?

Vanessa is an incest survivor. As an adult, whenever she is in a room with other people, she becomes self-conscious and afraid of making mistakes. She reads disapproval in the faces of people around her as she struggles not to say the wrong thing. When she does say something she thinks is stupid or out of place, she experiences intense shame and agitation.

Vanessa's low self-esteem and her efforts to behave in ways that elicit approval from others are common responses in adult survivors of abuse. As children, adult survivors are faced with an impossible situation: the very people who love them are the same people who abuse and hurt them. Because this dual awareness is irreconcilable—and terrifying—children usually resolve it by blaming themselves for the abuse. They convince themselves that if their behavior simply improves those big, powerful adults will be kind and loving.

There is another way children cope with the dual messages of abuse. They push away the distress caused by the abuse side of the message by using an unconscious process called *dissociation*.

We'll look at this process in some detail in this chapter and explore how children create "protective parts" of the self using dissociation. When parts are dissociated, they "contain" and block from conscious awareness a child's traumatic feelings, memories and thoughts.[1]

Vanessa unconsciously created such a part to protect her from knowing, consciously, that there was nothing she could do to prevent her father from abusing her. This part was assigned the job of keeping the implications of this reality from Vanessa. To do this, it gave her messages that made her uncomfortable about *herself.* Experienced as a voice in her head, the part reminded her that *she* didn't deserve the approval of other people. It kept her *self-*conscious and *self-*blaming. This part was convinced that if it ever relaxed its vigilance, Vanessa would remember the truth. She might realize, consciously, that she had been victimized by someone she needed to trust, someone on whom she was utterly dependent. For a child, such a realization would be just too overwhelming to bear.

Like Vanessa, most adult survivors of dysfunctional families create protective parts. The function of these parts is to instill a sense of safety or a state of numbness. Protective parts allow us to fend off the terror that would come with full consciousness of an abusive, chaotic or neglectful environment.

Imagine, for a moment, a scene in which a little boy has had a fight at school. He runs home, seeking his mother's comfort. When he enters the door to the house, his mother takes one look at his bloody nose and begins to cry and wring her hands. On a different day, his mother might be tired and become angry and yell at him for being such a wimp.

Initially, this youngster came home seeking comfort. What he received, instead, was a response that required him to shift gears immediately. In the first case, he senses that his mother is frightened and needs reassurance. His own need for comfort must be buried as he seeks to calm his mother. It heightens his distress to see his mother this way. He needs her to be okay in order for him to be okay.

In the second case, he may be startled and humiliated by his mother's anger at him, particularly at her contempt for his inability to defend himself. By now, he is dealing with a whole new kind of distress.

When a child experiences these kinds of parental responses over time, he is learning something about trust. He may learn that it is dangerous to be vulnerable and open about his feelings. He may avoid seeking comfort from others. He may learn to be very careful of other people's feelings while submerging conscious awareness of his own. He may become an adult who is unwilling to confront a person who does something he doesn't like. He may be unable to tell bad news to someone he cares about. He may be unable to disappoint others by not going along with their requests. The one thing the child in him knows for sure is that *his* problems can be overwhelming to others. He knows for sure that to be in need may bring humiliation, or worse, violence or immobilization.

Alternatively, a child in this kind of situation may become increasingly unaware of her own feelings. She may not experience needs that are normal and essential for well-being: time to herself without fear of abandonment, comfort and closeness that are safe and nonabusive, the right to have her own opinions without fear of humiliation, and so many more. She has valid needs, but they are buried under the weight of her early learning: keep it safe, keep it quiet, keep it okay for the other person.

If you are an adult survivor, these responses are probably familiar to you in some form or another.[2] You may also be aware of a deep need—and ability—to be a caretaker. You may be able to express a great deal of compassion for others, but have little left over for yourself. You may carry a basic mistrust of others, along with the expectation that no one would be there if you were to allow yourself to be in need. You may have turned it around the other way and become someone who is unable to tolerate the needs of others. You may feel personally offended when someone you know seeks comfort or seems weak.

All of these are learnings that evolve when a child has to create his or her own sense of safety. These learnings are reinforced, continually, by the protective parts that operate to contain the child's true feelings of vulnerability, fear, despair, rage or helplessness.

ABUSE, DISSOCIATION AND PROTECTIVE PARTS

Let's look at the development and function of protective parts in a bit more detail. All of us use the mechanism of creating parts to some degree or another. In a very real sense, the process of dissociation is one of our best friends, psychologically speaking. It allows us to maintain the ability to cope with difficult or threatening situations. A colleague, Dr. Robert Mayer, talks about this process as "passing the hot potato."[3] Passing the hot potato means to dissociate—or split off—painful awareness. The dissociated part then "contains" the traumatic feeling and keeps it out of conscious awareness, as we saw with Vanessa. If the event is seriously traumatic and threatening to the psychological integrity of the child, if the "potato is too hot to handle," the part will split off a portion of the feelings and create more protective parts, each containing a portion of the experience.

For example, one part may hold the feelings, while another may contain memories of physical pain, while one more is created to hold rage or anguish—the child's response to being abused.[4] All parts cooperate in an effort to keep the child from being aware that she is at risk.

In essence, then, depending on the seriousness of the trauma, the "potato" may be passed numerous times so the child is thoroughly protected from any conscious awareness of her true situation. Because of this, the child might feel afraid but not know why. She may be able to describe being hit but have no feelings about it. Or, she may have no awareness whatsoever that anything at all has happened to her.[5]

This particular protective mechanism is often seen in children who suffer serious physical and sexual abuse. When taken to its extreme, the protective function of dissociating parts of the self creates multiple personalities, where the parts are so well sealed off from awareness that they take on complex and active lives of their own.

For most people, the parts of the self that arise from the process of dissociation fall into the interchangeable categories of *ego states* or *personality fragments.* [6] Throughout this chapter, these categories are called *protective parts* or, simply, *parts.* These parts fall along a continuum of being more or less within conscious awareness. Not all express as voices that tell us cruel, frightening or discouraging things about ourselves, as did Vanessa's. Some create impulses that we act on without thinking, or slips of the tongue that express a disowned feeling.

One of the most important things to consider as you begin to get to know your protective parts is that their activities often *seem* counterproductive or self-destructive. It's helpful to remember that they were created with a child's mind, which did not have many options available. Most importantly, without them, many of us would have been psychologically overwhelmed by early experiences. We could have curled up in a ball and withdrawn from the world. Instead, our innate ability to dissociate saved us, even as it created a challenge to be dealt with later, in adult life.

The challenge often involves the fact that our protective parts don't realize we've grown up. They are locked in time. To them, we are still children in a world of potentially dangerous giants. To relax their vigilance or change their strategies would mean to sacrifice the child. The exercises in this chapter focus on creating a more conscious relationship with your protective parts and helping them to realize you *are* an adult, now.

The continuum on which protective parts exist has two major characteristics. First, some parts are more autonomous than others. They are stronger, more defined, and seem to have a "mind of their own." These parts will have more influence on your thinking and behavior than weaker, less-developed ones. Secondly, some of these parts are well within your conscious awareness, while you're basically unaware of others. With some, you know their voice and their message. You're keenly aware when their message is influencing you.

For example, you may be quite conscious of the fact that

every time you have to deal directly with authority figures, you seem to become a little kid. Your voice changes, your body slumps and you speak more softly than usual. Even with this awareness, though, you may find that you can't seem to change this pattern of response.

Other parts may be much more subtle and it's only as you learn to monitor your responses that you discover them. You may also become aware of them when you can no longer escape the feeling that your life isn't working as you would like. Vanessa became aware of a protective ego state once she admitted that she was increasingly uncomfortable interacting with people and began to explore why. As with Vanessa, you may decide to ask yourself why a particular quality or pattern seems so prevalent in your life and then allow yourself to discover what protective parts might still be operating to keep you safe.

When we grow up, many of the protective strategies these parts developed tend to work against us. This is true of many effective and creative childhood ways of surviving. Often, the very things that keep a child safe are the *opposite* of what an adult needs to have an effective, healthy life.

For example, if you grew up in a home where physical or emotional abuse was present, you may have developed protective parts that operate to keep you invisible, out of the line of fire. The message from these parts may tell you that you have no abilities, that an opportunity isn't worthwhile or that there's no point in trying when you can't succeed anyway. This all makes sense when you're very small and need to be invisible, to avoid rocking the boat. Adults, on the other hand, need to be visible and active in the world in order to earn a living that provides security and self-esteem.

As you work with the protective parts that evolved to keep you safe, it's important to recognize they are viable, important sources of energy and protection. You may not like the ways in which they protect you at present. "Job retraining" is an idea to consider. You can allow your protective parts to become effective and valuable allies in your adult life. Because of this, I encourage you to be open to these parts, to respect and appreciate them for the ways in which they worked to keep you safe when you were young, even if you are aggravated with them in the present.

RESOURCE PARTS

It's important to know that not all ego states or personality fragments arise solely as a result of trauma or neglect. Some represent resources, states of mind in which you are highly effective and competent at some particular task or creative pursuit. The innate psychological ability to create parts can be a powerful asset when you are *conscious* of the roles certain parts play in your life.

A common example of a such a resource is the state of mind people enter when they have to perform in some way. For instance, you might find yourself in a job that requires you to make presentations. Perhaps you are a salesperson and part of your job is to approach people you've never met before and present your product. Maybe you're an entertainer and you have to sing or act for a living. You might be a teacher and find that you seem go into a special state of mind when you stand up in front of a class. Over the years, I've developed a particular part of me that is activated when I conduct workshops. It represents an internal state of mind that is especially suited to interacting in group settings.

Resource parts can also be developed around academic pursuits, parenting, hobbies or any other activity in which you experience competence. A resource part conveys a sense of being an empowered adult, capable of doing the task at hand. Take a moment, now, to bring to mind any resource parts you may have developed and draw on currently, without realizing it.

An example of a resource part came up in a session with a client named Fran. In trance, she discovered an elegant woman, calm and collected, sitting in a beautiful library. Fran focused on the hands of this woman. They were graceful and moved smoothly—qualities that were distinctly different from Fran's usual way of moving her body. As she got to know this part, Fran discovered that she could bring feelings of grace and ease into her experience whenever she had to do a task such as making a difficult phone call. She simply focused on how it felt to hold the phone with the hands of the resource part. Making calls used to overwhelm her and cause considerable anxiety. Since connecting with this resource part, she has discovered a new, more empowered way of experiencing herself.

You may wonder if you have this kind of part inside. Chances are that you do. As you explore the protective parts that were created when you were growing up, give yourself permission to discover resource parts, as well. The last exercise in this chapter gives you an opportunity to get in touch with these parts. It's important to know that your unconscious can create a variety of parts, including those that can become resources in your life right now.

A COMPLEX SYSTEM OF PARTS

Before beginning an exploration of how your protective parts may have functioned during childhood and on into adulthood, let's look a little closer at the idea that you are a complex system of parts rather than one stable, consistent, coherent "self."

In your mind's eye, imagine an orchestra for a moment. It can be any size orchestra. You are the conductor. As the conductor, you are in an "executive" role. You are essential for keeping order and direction in the performance. Because a conductor has the job of keeping the entire orchestra playing the same piece of music, you might think of the conductor as your "basic self."[7]

While the conductor sets the tone and pace of what is being played, he or she wouldn't get very far without the presence and cooperation of the musicians who do the actual playing. Each instrument has its own notes, its own quality, to contribute to the overall composition. Functioning together as a whole, *all* the parts of the orchestra have an important role in creating the total performance.

Continuing with the orchestra analogy, there may be times

when you, as the conductor, call upon a particular part to play a "solo." For instance, you may have a sales pitch you have to deliver and you want the part of you that is the accomplished salesperson to take center stage. Another time, you may want to do some rock climbing and so you call on the part of you that is comfortable taking risks.

A problem arises, however, when one of the musicians decides to take over and conduct for you, or to play a different piece of music, or to perform a solo when you haven't requested one. This happens most often when protective parts feel compelled to go into action without your conscious participation or intent. This dilemma is the focus of the work you'll be doing in this chapter.

For example, imagine that you are going for a job interview. As the interview evolves, you find a voice in your head that gives you a running commentary on how inept you sound when you speak, how untalented you are, or how no one could possibly be interested in hiring you. You leave the interview feeling miserable, convinced that you'll never get the kind of job you want. The part that was mobilized to protect you has done its job once again. It successfully convinced you not to try, not to bother getting yourself out into the world. It succeeded in giving you input that would encourage you to remain invisible, safe from abuse.

Some parts may seem hostile to you, as though they don't like you. Chances are that they are parts that "contain" experiences or feelings that were quite difficult or painful. As you get to know them, you may find that their hostility lessens.

You may notice that these parts are presented as if they were actual entities. In a sense, they are, even though they are not the same as multiple personalities. In multiple personality, the parts have become what are called "alters." Alters lead lives of their own, with histories, names, friends, events that are totally outside the "conductor's" awareness.[8] For most of us, the protective parts that are created in childhood are much less developed. Even so, they are autonomous in the sense that they operate unconsciously and with a great deal of power to influence our thinking and behavior.

The first step in working with these parts is to identify them and to recognize them as different from, although a part of, your basic self. For most of us, at least some of these parts are in awareness already. The focus of the first exercise in this chapter is to bring into conscious awareness the protective parts you haven't yet gotten to know and to develop cooperative relationships with all the parts of you.

At this point, if the notion of parts seems overly complicated, I wonder if you'd be willing to hold it as a "working hypothesis" as you go through the material in this chapter. It's a concept that provides a context in which healing is enhanced, particularly when there has been active abuse or passive abuse, such as neglect, in your history.

As you work with the material in this chapter, if you discover a protective part you dislike, or one that frightens you, remember that it evolved originally to keep you safe. Its underlying interest is in your well-being. It gets mobilized whenever it is afraid you are at risk. If you can keep this in mind, you may find that it's easier than you think to develop new and constructive relationships with all the parts of you, even the ones that seem to be uncontrollable monsters.

THE STRENGTH OF PROTECTIVE PARTS

Many of the people I've worked with have been deeply moved and surprised by the intensity of the protective urges these parts express. Sally, a middle-aged woman, grew up in an environment in which physical violence could erupt between her parents at any time. Objects might come flying across the room, creating a very real danger that Sally might be hit. Her parents might get in a fight that terrified her because she didn't know if one of them, or both, would end up dead.

Sally came into therapy complaining of her tendency to become increasingly rigid and angry whenever members of her family would do things in ways that were different from her usual routine. As we explored her discomfort with things being out of place, we discovered a protective part that held the "hot potato" of her terror of chaos and unanticipated violence. This part appeared as a stern schoolteacher. The schoolteacher was a pillar of unbreakable rules. Although Sally consciously disliked the teacher, when she explored the teacher's protective function, it became clear that someone this rigid was needed to create an internal sense of control and safety. Whenever Sally's present environment seemed to be out of control, which could be caused by something as simple as her son's leaving dishes in the sink, the stern teacher would come to the fore. In a sense, the adult Sally would move into the background as the stern teacher "took over." Once a sense of safety was restored, or something allowed Sally to become aware of her behavior, the schoolteacher would recede and things would settle down.

As is true with most protective parts, the schoolteacher didn't realize that Sally had grown up to become a competent, effective adult. As is also common, even the slightest hint of chaos was enough to mobilize the schoolteacher into action.

Working on the assumption that even as adults we need to be able to protect ourselves and create internal states of safety and comfort, Sally and I set about updating the teacher's function. We agreed that the role, if not the style, of this part needed to be maintained.[9]

Mostly, you will find that it is unlikely in the long run that you would want to totally eliminate any part of yourself. You might combine several parts, and certainly update them, but it's important to remember that they are part of your psychological life and have energy and consciousness to contribute to your basic self.

Sally began by defining the teacher's function during childhood. This protective part was created unconsciously primarily in response to two factors: first was Sally's inability to get the violence and terror to stop and second was her inability, as a child, to leave home and live elsewhere. As a child, she adapted as best she could to an overwhelming situation. The "hot potato" of terror that she couldn't let herself experience consciously was dissociated and the teacher was created.

Next we explored what the protective part might be like if its skills were updated to serve Sally in more appropriate, adult ways. Sally's unconscious presented an updated image of the teacher as a wise medicine woman. This woman had a natural power that felt much more positive, much more in line with who Sally felt herself to be, in contrast to the stern teacher. Instead of creating rigid rules to protect Sally from feelings of chaos, the medicine woman can help her become conscious of developing feelings that things seem out of control. Sally is then able to take steps to change things, to say no, or to walk away. The medicine woman reminds her that she does have the power and the wisdom, as an adult, to leave any situation that feels too chaotic or threatening. She also has the power to learn to tolerate the positive and inevitable chaos that is sometimes present in an active family. With an awareness of her feelings, Sally has a choice of whether to act on them. Instead of automatically assuming that the chaos is dangerous, she can differentiate whether she's really at risk.

Now, whenever Sally feels that old, familiar rigidity, she immediately locates the schoolteacher, thanks her for her concern, and reminds her of the medicine woman. The process of becoming conscious of the rigidity and immediately engaging it in a constructive dialogue helps Sally remain in an adult state of mind.

As you begin to work with your protective parts and explore the ways in which they operate to protect you, there's an important thing to keep in mind, which I mentioned earlier. Underlying the strategies and posturings of these parts is their *fear*. Just about every protective part with which I've interacted has had, at its core, a basic fear for the safety of the child it was created to protect. In working with these parts, it's important to acknowledge their fear, to let them know that you understand. The simple act of recognizing the fear these parts feel creates a greater willingness in them to cooperate in learning new responses to adult experiences.

This was particularly clear with George, a man in his early 40's who had been struggling with depression much of his life.

He had a history of suicide attempts—quite dramatic ones, at that—which left him feeling that he was truly a failure. He couldn't even kill himself successfully.

George had grown up with parents who didn't have the time or inclination to pay attention to his needs for attention and acknowledgment. They abandoned him emotionally and were particularly unavailable when he tried to get attention by "showing off," crying, or just being in the way. Most children respond with fear and distress when parents withdraw emotionally and George was no different. He was desperately afraid of losing his parents altogether and had to protect himself from pushing them away.

He dissociated the rage and despair that arose every time his parents withdrew from him and created a protective part that looked like a timid field mouse. This part felt its job was to keep George as invisible and low-key as possible.

During his trance, George continued dialoguing with the mouse and discovered that it had an even more important mission: to keep the rage and despair hidden from George and others. The mouse was afraid that if George felt the feelings, he might express them. Even in the present, the field mouse feared that if George were too expressive, he might accidentally say or do something that would cause people to withdraw from him.

In adult relationships, George prevented himself from revealing his own interests and needs. He became, instead, a good listener. People liked him. The problem was that he couldn't develop friendships that were nurturing for himself. The people he chose tended to be like his parents. They were caught up in their own interests and had nothing to give him on those rare occasions when he allowed himself to ask for support.

When he began to work with the protective part that encouraged him to think about suicide, what emerged was a fierce warrior with a sharp sword and a sharper tongue. The warrior would tell George how worthless he was and encourage him to kill himself whenever he began to feel better and venture out into the world. George hated and feared the warrior and yet felt powerless to resist the pull of those words.

As we explored the purpose of this part, its underlying protective function was revealed. The warrior was another part that prevented him from expressing himself openly and spontaneously. This part was a deeper version of the mouse. The warrior's task was to protect George from the devastating feelings of abandonment at all costs, even if that meant getting rid of George. It's easy to see the "child mind" at work here. When encouraged to consider their stance, many suicidal parts discover that they really seek safety rather than death.

In trance, George continued to communicate with the warrior and offered the idea that there were more productive means available for protecting George. The warrior agreed to listen. He also agreed that he didn't really want to be dead, he just wanted George to be safe.

The three of us then looked at how, until now, this protective part had kept George from expressing a good bit of himself. The warrior was introduced to the idea that many kinds of self-expression are not only safe in adulthood but essential to success and internal well-being. The key was to help the warrior discover that it had developed an elegant sensitivity that could be used to prevent George from expressing himself inappropriately, rather than not expressing himself at all.

As of this writing, the warrior has agreed to hold off urges towards suicide as George and I work with other parts that will help make his self-expression safe and appropriate. By acknowledging the warrior's protective function and addressing its underlying fear, we created a bridge of understanding from past to present.

Another client, Alice, was raised in a physically violent home and experienced a most distressing part of herself that emerged only when she was involved in intimate relationships. It was what she called "the witch." This part of her lashed out consistently at her lovers with a degree of viciousness that made her extremely uncomfortable. She was often puzzled at the intensity of her response to what seemed to her conscious mind to be minor infractions and irritations.

As she explored this protective part, it emerged as a gray-brown cat, large, with claws extended, back arched, snarling, tail thrashing. It would lash out with its claws even when no threat was apparent. When Alice asked the cat its function, it said it had to fend off people, to create distance, so that Alice would be safe. Certainly, the tongue lashings delivered by this part succeeded at creating distance between Alice and her lovers.

I asked the cat if it would be willing to update its function, to become more effective in adult terms. It wasn't thrilled with the idea. It preferred, instead, to continue snarling and lashing out. It was expressing a quality that shouldn't be any surprise when dealing with protective parts. It didn't trust me yet, which is a sensible response when you recall that the adults in Alice's childhood were anything but trustworthy. It would take time to build a relationship with the cat; that was acknowledged and accepted.

The next step was to allow the cat to get a glimpse of how it would look if it were willing to change. To do this, Alice allowed her future self (see Chapter 5) to enter the picture. Her future self provided an image of the cat as it would look once it learned to protect her in ways appropriate to an adult. What Alice saw was a beautiful, sleek, jet-black jaguar, filled with a powerful, comfortable strength. The snarling gray-brown cat also saw the jaguar and liked what it would become. This glimpse of its potential to no longer be driven by fear was appealing. Most important, it got to see that it wasn't going to be destroyed. It had an ongoing role to play in Alice's life.

DEVALUING/FEARING PROTECTIVE PARTS

One word of caution. For those of you who were physically, sexually, and/or emotionally abused or neglected, there will be a strong tendency to devalue the protective parts that evolved to keep you psychologically intact and physically safe. There will also be a strong tendency for these parts to devalue you, to put you down, to tell you that you deserved what you got. These parts sometimes seek to create a strong sense of futility once you begin to work with them. It helps to remember that the more "monstrous" or abusive a part seems to be, the more frightened and threatened it probably feels. It fears that you will be left unprotected if anything changes.

Also, you may discover that you begin to get in touch with feelings that seem as though they will be more than you can handle. Actually, this was true for the child. For a child, feelings are experienced without the cognitive overlay we have as adults. If you find yourself afraid of being swept away by the intensity of feelings that may come to the surface, remember that they are *memory feelings*. You, the adult, now have the cognitive and emotional sophistication to experience and deal with them effectively.

Also, when working with self-hypnosis, you can trust the fact that your unconscious will give you only those awarenesses you're prepared to handle. It might be nice to know that you can't force a memory that you're not really ready to have.

It may still seem paradoxical that something that puts you down so viciously could conceivably be acting on your behalf. It's true, though. When you were young, drastic steps were necessary. It was *essential* that you remain invisible, were compliant or behaved in whatever survival mode the situation warranted. The means of survival we adopted as children often leave us feeling bad about ourselves. Remember, children usually have to blame themselves for what is happening. If they were able to understand that it actually was the *adults* who were out of control, that realization would be too overwhelming. It would make too real the fact that they really *were* unsafe in a world of chaos.

It bears repeating to say that it is positive and healing to learn to respect the survival mechanisms that kept you alive, mechanisms that have enabled you to be here, now, reading this book. You *are* a survivor. We all are, and we got here because certain parts of us made sure we adapted to the demands of our early environment.

OTHER ORIGINS OF PROTECTIVE PARTS

So far, we've focused on situations that were actively or passively *abusive* to the child. These aren't the only ones in which protective parts evolve. Children also dissociate unmanageable feelings as a result of experiencing natural disasters, social catastrophes such as mass murders, and other kinds of experiences that arise within the larger environment. Also, in homes where there is physical illness, where children are required to take on adult tasks or are ignored because of the concern and attention required by an ill relative, protective parts are also needed.

Imagine that you are a child in the home of an ill parent. You would probably have some natural and automatic feelings in response to your environment. These feelings might include neediness, anger at being ignored, anger at having to take care of someone, inadequacy at not being able to make things better, or even fear of the ill person. If you were to express these feelings openly, you might risk rejection or disapproval. The adults in the home are already overwhelmed. They simply do not have the time or emotional resources available to attend to the needs of their healthy children.

A child living in this kind of situation is likely to develop a protective part that functions to keep such feelings buried, to internalize them and turn them on the self. This kind of part can easily develop into an internal critic with harsh standards and strict rules for expressing and dealing with feelings. Another possibility is a protective part that works as a caretaker, focusing on the needs of others while lecturing you not to be so selfish.

These are some examples of the many ways in which protective parts develop. It is nearly impossible to grow up without them. As you begin to explore the internal relationships you developed as you grew up, it's helpful to remember that having protective parts isn't an indictment of your family. Instead, these parts are evidence of the rich heritage of human consciousness on which we all draw as we adapt to the necessities and demands of our environment.

If you feel at all uncomfortable about the idea of protective parts operating in your unconscious, you may want to think of them as attitudes and beliefs, learnings and understandings that you seek to change. You can begin that process of change by accessing a deeper awareness of their existence through the use of the self-hypnotic exercises that follow.

THE CARETAKER

Before moving on to the exercises that follow, there is a resource part that deserves special attention. It is called the *caretaker*. Almost everyone has a caretaker part inside. It operates to look after the parts of you that were created as a result of hurtful or traumatic experiences.

The caretaker may appear as a man, a woman, or as an undefined, formless presence—or voice—that is experienced as supportive and reliable. The caretaker may be represented symbolically as a wise old person or an animal. The *form* of the caretaker doesn't really matter. The important thing to know is that you can connect with this resource part and depend on it to help you develop an internal experience of safety—and to regain a sense of yourself as an adult during those times when you may be thrown off balance by an interaction or event.

While the caretaker usually has a relationship with all of the protective parts, special emphasis is placed on the vulnerable, frightened parts that appear as aspects of the child within. Remember that the protective parts were created to help the child; keeping the "little ones" safe continues to be the prime motivator for activating these parts in your current life. Calling on the caretaker to "take the little ones inside" whenever you feel vulnerable, enraged or at risk can deactivate protective parts and allow you to reconnect with your adult awareness. In fact, a major benefit of getting to know the caretaker is developing the ability to shift into an adult state of mind more quickly.

For example, think of one of those times when you may have

felt frightened by something and couldn't shift back into an adult state of mind. Remember that during those times you were experiencing a protective part that had been activated. It's the responses of the protective part that left you feeling too small to manage in the adult world or too powerless to help yourself. Next time you feel this way, call on the caretaker to come and take the protective part to a safe place "inside." "Inside" is safe because it is removed from the world "out there" where protective parts automatically use childhood strategies to cope with adult issues.

The safe place inside can be anything that comes to mind for you. During trance, Elizabeth became aware of a protective part she experienced as an angry teenager. This part had been activated in an interaction with her mother that had left Elizabeth feeling thwarted and powerless. The caretaker took the angry part inside to a horse corral. The teenager loved horses and was glad to be in the corral instead of ineffectually venting her anger out in the world. Once this angry part was safely inside, Elizabeth was able to reestablish her adult sense of competence and balance.

Another person, Teri, imagined a beautiful cave with special alcoves for all the parts. In the cave were many helpers who would take over when the caretaker brought frightened, vulnerable or angry parts inside to safety. Whenever she thought of the cave, Teri reported a special feeling of ease. She felt more in control of her world because, if she were to find herself shifting into feeling small and vulnerable, she could call on the caretaker for help.

Your own caretaker can help you create a safe place inside. For many people, the safe place is a special, private room. It may be a room that is decorated with colors, furniture and other items that emphasize a sense of security and comfort. Whatever qualities suggest safety to you are the ones to build into this special place. You may find somewhere outdoors that feels safer than any indoor place ever could. Whether indoors or out, remember that your safe place exists *inside,* in your own self-hypnotic world, away from the demands and perceived dangers of the adult world.

ABOUT THE EXERCISES

There are two exercises. The first focuses on discovering and developing cooperative relationships with protective parts that still operate as though you were a child, using childhood coping strategies. The second focuses on connecting with resource parts. For each of these exercises, you'll need a place to write down what comes to mind—not only to keep a record of what you discover, but also to provide the processing and integrating time that comes when you write down inner experiences. If at all possible, I recommend that you tape record the following self-hypnotic inductions so you can play them back to yourself as you do the exercises. *Record only the sentences that are in italics.* Speak slowly and softly, and leave a few seconds of time whenever you see the word [pause] in the induction. As you work with the exercise, remember to shut off the tape recorder whenever you need, to give yourself enough time to complete each step.

If you don't have a tape recorder, read over the following inductions several times to get a feel for where you are going. Then, use the short form of the exercises at the back of the book as a reference point to remind yourself of the steps involved.

In the first exercise, a protective part may come to your awareness as a voice in your head, a feeling in your body, or an image. Whatever form it takes, you can let an awareness of this part of you come from the back of your mind to the front of your mind without any conscious preconceptions. There's no need to "work at" getting this awareness. Your unconscious knows which part to bring to mind.

Before you begin either exercise, find a spot where you can sit down without being disturbed for about 20 minutes. Remember that it's helpful to use the same spot each time, as the unconscious begins to associate the self-hypnotic trance state with that place and this will enhance your inner journey.

Exercise #2   Identifying Protective Parts

[Use the *trance induction* found in Chapter 3 to put yourself into trance, or choose another approach/method that suits your personal style and needs. The most important thing is to allow yourself to develop, over time, a place in your inner hypnotic landscape that is *safe*.]

Once you have moved into a safe place inside, bring to mind a way in which you limit yourself through fear or immobility, or talk to yourself in abusive ways. Even though more than one may come to mind, allow yourself to work with the one that keeps pushing to the front of your mind and stays there. [pause]

Allow yourself to imagine, if you will, now, a person, animal, object, creature or other kind of being that represents the part that uses the kind of protection you're exploring. If nothing comes to mind right away, that's fine. Let yourself imagine what the image would be like if it were to come to mind. [pause]

Also, you may have a feeling or a symbol or a color, instead of an image. That's fine, too. Simply allow anything that the wisdom of your unconscious brings from the back of your mind to the front of your mind.

If you find your mind is blank, think of the blankness as a creative void, a place in which your unconscious takes its own time to give you whatever awareness it wants you to have, when it wants you to have it. Simply allow something to come in its own good time.

Now, I'd like to ask you to explore the qualities of that impression. What kind of person, animal, object, creature or essence comes to mind? [pause] *How do you respond to its qualities? Are you frightened? Disgusted? Indifferent?* [pause] *What other qualities does this part convey to you?* [pause] *Simply accept whatever comes to mind. Everything is information you need.* [pause]

Recall that this part evolved for a good reason and provides some function in your overall psychological life that was, at one time, perceived to be essential to your survival. With this in mind, allow yourself to imagine that you are that person, object, thing or essence. Really give yourself an opportunity to experience that part from the inside, as if you actually were that part. [pause]

As the part, what do you feel like way deep down inside? [pause] *Do you seem one way on the inside and another way on the outside? Are you surprised at any of the qualities you're experiencing?* [pause]

Ask yourself, as this part, "What is my function?" What do I do to protect [your name]? [pause] *You may be surprised at what you hear, or you may already have a clear sense of what this part does for you.*

Allow yourself to notice, now, that nearby somewhere there is a special place where you see a home movie projector and screen, or a VCR set up. There is an important piece of film ready to be viewed. It reflects a childhood memory or some other awareness of the time and place where this protective part was created. [pause]

You may find yourself observing a childhood memory, or a memory from some other time in your life, prior to the present. Allow the experience to unfold as you become aware of what was going on . . . remembering that you're observing this on a screen, as the adult you are today. It's safe, now, to remember whatever you need to know because you've already survived it and reached adulthood. [pause]

And I wonder if your unconscious would be willing to take a few moments to give you an overview of the ways in which this early learning has affected your life . . . all the way from back there up to the present. [pause] *You were learning something about yourself and the world when this part was created, something you have an opportunity to think about differently now.* [pause]

And I wonder if you might feel some sense of appreciation at the work this protective part has done to keep you safe, now that you see where it came from. [pause] *Be sure to give yourself permission to take whatever time you need to feel comfortable with this. Remember, this is an opportunity to practice being gentle with yourself, to give yourself all the time you need to come to an understanding of, and an accommodation with, this part of you.* [pause]

Become aware, again, of the image that represents the part. Take a moment to check in with this part and ask it if it is willing to update its function and change the way it protects or helps you. [pause]

If you find it isn't willing to change right now, that's all right, too. Allow yourself to be patient, reassuring the part that you are sincere in wanting to have it as an ongoing part of your life. And, be patient with yourself as well, if you aren't yet ready to acknowledge that this part is a potentially valuable resource. You may be surprised to discover that tomorrow, or next week, or at some time when you least expect it, you'll have arrived at a new feeling about this part . . . a feeling that is positive and much more empowering than what you've been experiencing.

Take a moment to point out to the part that you're now all grown up. In fact, point out the difference between how you look as the adult you are today and how the child you were looked in that remembered scene. All too often, protective parts just don't realize that you've grown up. They look at you and still see a child. [pause]

Allow your unconscious to present you, now, from the back of your mind and without any preconceptions, an impression of what this part can be when its skill and energy become a resource in your adult life. [pause]

Remembering that whenever you hear negative messages from this part, or have a response of dread or rage or some other feeling in your body, you'll know that this part of you is concerned for your safety. Allow yourself to appreciate its concern and know that its input allows you to recognize that the child in you needs your attention, protection or validation. At the same time, you can encourage the part to focus on its new style of being a resource for the adult you. [pause]

Take a few moments, now, to sit quietly with what you've experienced, allowing it all to find that safe place in the back of your mind where new learnings, new responses and new awareness are created and developed even as your conscious mind goes on to other things. And, you can bring to mind the fact that even as you begin to reorient to other things that your conscious mind must do, your unconscious keeps right on developing the new things you are learning so that they will be available to you when you need them most. [pause]

When you're ready, return to an alert state by opening your eyes. Wiggle your fingers and toes to bring yourself all the way back and jot down a few notes about your experience.

As you work with the second exercise, *Identifying Resource Parts,* you may be surprised to discover that it can be difficult to allow yourself to acknowledge parts of you that you really like. If you find that you're hesitant about accepting the good parts of you, it may be because there are protective parts operating to keep you from expressing too much of yourself. As with the first exercise, allow yourself to accept *whatever* you experience. Everything that comes to mind during your inner work is information that is helpful to have. It all plays a part in how you experience yourself and the world. Whatever awareness comes provides a means of accessing those parts of you that protect you by keeping you less fulfilled and empowered than you have the ability to be.

You may also find that some of your resource parts spring easily to mind and that you feel very good about them. Great! Give yourself an opportunity to really bask in the pleasure of that feeling.

Exercise #3   Identifying Resource Parts

[Again, use whatever self-hypnotic induction works best for you.]

Once you have settled in and are in a safe place, allow a part of yourself you really like, a way of being that is particularly pleasing to you, to come to mind. Or, bring to mind a quality that you'd really like to develop as a resource, something you have felt fleetingly or have imagined in your fantasies. [pause]

Once you're aware of the quality, skill, or feeling that you consider a resource, allow an impression of a person, animal, object, creature, color or sensation that represents this part to emerge. [pause]

What qualities are conveyed by this part? [pause] What feelings arise as you explore these qualities? [pause]

Give yourself an opportunity, now, to become that part . . . really to feel what it's like to be that resource from the inside. [pause]

Discover a sensation in your body, or a special feeling or state of mind, or a supportive voice in your head, that encompasses this resource part. [pause] Give your body, your feelings and your mind time to learn how this resource feels. You are providing time for nonverbal learning that you will draw on unconsciously as you bring this resource more and more into your life. [pause]

And, you may be surprised to discover that whenever you're in a situation where this skill or quality would be particularly helpful, the image or thoughts or sensations you've just experienced will spring into your awareness. As you recall how it feels to be this part, you'll automatically draw on its qualities even more.

In fact, take a moment, now, to imagine yourself in a situation where you are using this resource. Use all your senses—your hypnotic eyes, your hypnotic ears, your hypnotic feelings—to experience yourself as drawing on and successfully using this resource. [pause]

Take a few moments, now, just to enjoy exploring and acknowledging this positive resource part, conveying your pleasure at having it in your life, perhaps encouraging it to increase its activities on your behalf. [pause]

Also, remember to accept whatever other feelings or awareness you might be having. Everything that comes to mind is important and provides further opportunities to work on parts of you that may be frightened of moving forward.

When you're ready, bring yourself back now, with the thought in mind that it's nice to know, isn't it, that even as you come back to an alert state your unconscious keeps right on developing the important learnings and awareness that you touch each time you go inside.

Be sure to wiggle your fingers and toes, to open your eyes, and to jot down some notes about your experience.

As a closing thought to this chapter, let me share with you the metaphor of the kaleidoscope. One of the wonderful things about a kaleidoscope is the way in which all the pieces of glass are rearranged into new and unexpected patterns when you turn the cylinder. The important thing to keep in mind is that *all the new patterns are created from the same old pieces,* even when those patterns are entirely different from what came before.

As you engage the many parts of yourself in a dialogue and begin to develop a more conscious, accepting relationship with them, you never know just how the old protections and defenses may be turned into helpful new skills. The creative part of your unconscious takes care of the process of turning things around and giving them a chance to fall into place in a new way. What your conscious mind can know is that self-acceptance and an attitude of willingness to allow change to occur give the creative unconscious permission to shift the patterns without losing any of the parts.

When you change the pattern without losing any of the parts, you discover one of the very real and tangible benefits of recreating your self through developing cooperative relationships with all the parts of you: You begin to experience, both consciously and unconsciously, the ability to give yourself permission to be everything you have the capacity to be.

Many of us received messages as children that told us to hold back, hold off or to be less than we are. As you come to know parts of yourself that both protect and support your development, you have an opportunity to create greater harmony in your internal orchestra. You have an opportunity to change the quality of your life and affirm your right to express yourself effectively in your adult world.

Chapter 5

THE FUTURE SELF

Among the many parts you have available in the unconscious, perhaps the most versatile and useful is the future self. This is a part of you that has accomplished things you have yet to discover—a part of you that's right around the corner, living in ways that are not yet evident in the present. It is a part of you that exists several years ahead of where you are presently; it can become a beacon, showing you where you are headed. The future self can teach you how to get from here to there, how to become what you seek to be. You may experience the future self as a guide, a protector, a friend. If you have abuse in your background, your future self will be an invaluable companion as you resolve the effects of that abuse. Most important of all, the future self, as you will learn to contact it in this chapter, is your *optimal* self. It is one of the most powerful resources in your healing journey. It represents the *best* you can be.

The concept of the future self fell into my life quite by accident a number of years ago. I had just moved from Los Angeles to the Berkshire Hills in Massachusetts. It was a big change from urban to rural living, a time of real transition. A recent divorce had left me open to change. I left my known world of California to move into an untried and unknown experience of codirecting a transpersonally oriented center in Western Massachusetts. The task ahead was unfamiliar, as was the area of the country. It was a time of high risk-taking.

During the two years I spent in Massachusetts, my focus was on meditation, therapy, and self-hypnotic activities. There was time for inner journeys, not only with clients, but with myself as well. My time was spent getting to know intimately the terrain of the unconscious. Sometime in the beginning of the second year there, one inner journey produced a rather surprising image of me standing in a corporate conference room, wearing a navy blue business suit. I was at a flipchart with a pointer, speaking to a room full of executives.

It's hard to describe just how far this image was from the reality I was living at the time. I couldn't imagine what meaning it had. Not only was I in a rural setting doing rather alternative, psychologically oriented work, but I was also terrified of public speaking, which I did under duress from time to time. The thought of standing and teaching at the front of a room was horrifying. What I experienced when I *became* this future self, though, was the power of the person in that navy blue business suit and the ease with which she talked to the group of executives.

I spent the next months imagining "her" every morning, either visualizing the image or experiencing the feeling of *being* her. From the standpoint of outward time and space, nothing much seemed to be happening . . . except that the center was failing financially. It looked as though I would have to begin seeing clients part-time in New York City in order to earn needed income.

As it happened, the center folded within two years of my arriving in the East and forced a move to New York City full time. Soon after I moved to the city, a friend introduced me to a management training group at the Stern School of Business, New York University. I began consulting as part of a management-training team. The trainer's role was to observe managers run a fictitious company for a day and, then, the next day, facilitate an extensive group feedback process. A year or so after beginning the process, I was conducting a feedback session and realized that I was, indeed, standing in a conference room using flipcharts to teach executives . . . and that I was doing it *comfortably*. Although I never got the navy blue suit, I *did* become the essence of that future self.

A year or so later, I was studying Ericksonian hypnosis. In one of the classes, we were introduced to what was called "pseudo-orientation in time."[1] To my astonishment, I found myself face to face with the Ericksonian concept of the future self. I was amazed and delighted.

Since that time, I have come to know and respect the power of the future self in healing early trauma and creating a more viable, empowered life in adulthood. I have also discovered that, as you become the future self you've envisioned, a new one emerges that represents next steps in your development. At times, you may even want to look ahead a decade or more and get a feeling for where things are headed in the overall process of recreating yourself.

TAPPING THE FUTURE

You may wonder how it is possible to go into a future that hasn't yet happened. It may make more sense if you think of the future self as an impression that becomes a self-hypnotic suggestion fed into the unconscious over and over, creating a self-fulfilling prophecy. You may prefer, instead, to conceptualize the future self as an actual part of you, as alive in your experience as the child within and any of your protective parts. It may be that, because the unconscious is timeless, it *is* possible to tap into as-yet-unrealized ways of being that you'll develop in a time that has yet to become the present.

As you work with the material in this chapter, you might give yourself permission to leave open the question of whether or not it's really possible to tap into the future. What is most important is that you allow yourself to experience the future self as a *living* part of your internal world.

Many examples of the empowering qualities of the future self come to mind. Janice came from a violent, physically abusive home. When we began to work with the child within, she discovered early on that she needed some extra support and help in order to look back at her history. The possibility of having to go back into that abusive environment, hypnotically, to reclaim the child felt too big a task to be handled all by herself.

In their first meeting, Janice and her future self responded to one another immediately. Janice felt that her future self was like an older sister, supportive and able to give important guidance. She described her future self as a bit taller than her present-day self, with a straighter back, head held higher. When she *became* the future self, experiencing this part of her from the inside, Janice described a feeling of solidity right down the middle of her body. It was a feeling that conveyed a sense of being grounded, firmly planted and balanced.

Whenever Janice felt vulnerable, either during her work with the child within or when functioning in the world, she would call on her future self to show her what to do or to help her feel strong. The mere presence of her future self conveyed a sense of greater strength. This strength allowed Janice to know that she didn't need to face difficult or frightening situations alone. Instead, she could recall how it felt to be grounded and balanced. Her body remembered the hypnotic experience and drew on the qualities of the future self automatically. Janice described her relationship with the future self and the child within as her new "family," as the most important relationships in her life.

During trances in which Janice went back in time to rescue the child from abusive situations, something you'll read more about in the next chapter, she often took along the future self. In one experience, she discovered that she was too frightened to confront her abuser until the future self had taken the child within to a safe place. With the child protected in this way, Janice found that she had all the power she needed to deal with her abuser.

Tatiana, a workshop participant, had another kind of experience with her future self. She was feeling stuck in her job and was seeking to connect with the part of her that had developed professionally beyond where she was at that time. The future self emerged as a blonde woman dressed in more expensive clothing and jewelry than Tatiana had been accustomed to wearing. Tatiana's hair was light brown at the time, and her clothes, while presentable and professional, weren't of the fine quality she experienced in the impression of her future self.

Tatiana had a hard time imagining that she could become the kind of woman she saw in her trance, more sophisticated and elegant than she felt in the present. Over time, though, as she consistently imagined how it would feel to be her future self, things began to change, almost in spite of her. Tatiana lost her job and decided to become self-employed. It was a high-risk move that created a good bit of anxiety. Without really knowing what her professional life would look like down the road, Tatiana began "following her nose" and putting herself out in the marketplace. She also continued to attune to her future self, realizing that her unconscious somehow knew what it was doing. She trusted that she would be guided toward where she needed to be. For Tatiana, her hair was the focus for connecting with her future self. By recalling the blonde color and the style, she could access how it felt to *be* that future self. Her hair became the door that opened Tatiana's mind to the new potentials inherent in her future self.

In time, Tatiana found herself not only with blonde hair, which she had highlighted at the urging of a close friend, but also with a successful consulting career. She had, in essence, become the future self she had been visualizing for several years.

For Kenneth, the future self became a resource for soothing himself. Kenneth was high-strung and prone to anxiety attacks. He would easily "lose his cool" in tense or stressful situations. For him, the qualities his future self conveyed were wisdom and a certain equanimity in the face of unexpected events. He developed the ability to access a memory of how his future self seemed to let difficulties roll off his back. In stressful situations, Kenneth learned to remind his body of how it felt to be his future self. He would imagine that the future self was there with him, with a hand on his shoulder. It was consistently reassuring to imagine the steady presence of that hand.

THE FUTURE AS QUALITY, NOT CONTENT

Because the process of getting in touch with the future self deals with an as-yet-unrealized future, it is an activity that needs to take place in the back of your mind. When the front of your mind gets involved before you actually meet your future self, there is the possibility that you are creating, consciously, what you *think* you would like to be. The problem with this approach is that *the conscious mind can only know what it knows already.* The future self embodies learnings and developments in your life that, often, you haven't anticipated or even imagined are possible. As you work with the exercise in this chapter, it will help to let yourself be surprised, to allow impressions of the future self simply to drop into the front of your mind from the back of your mind. If you do this, you'll find that you really can trust what comes to you.

Whenever you're working with the future self, it's the *quality* of the impression, rather than the concrete imagery, that conveys the essence of what you need to experience. People often get bogged down in the front of their minds when they seek specific content or a clear idea of exactly what is going to happen to them. If you focus on the quality and essence of the impression of your future self, you'll avoid the pitfall of getting anxious or concerned about whether or not you're getting an "accurate" representation of your future.

You can also focus on specific *aspects* of your development when working with the future self. There may be certain changes you want to make, particular psychological wounds you want to heal. In this case, your emphasis will be on a given *part* of the future self. For example, you may discover that you have no idea how to be kind to yourself. When you go inside to deal with the child within, you may find yourself at a loss for words.

Angel

At a time like this, you can call on your future self and experience, specifically, what it's like to know what to say. As you *Let yr Angel* connect with how the future self feels about the child within, you automatically become aware of responses that are more loving, more accepting.

Another time, you may discover that, when starting towards a particularly challenging goal, you run into fears that block your forward movement. You may want to access a part of you that has already accomplished the goal so you can explore how you will feel *after* you have achieved it. When you do this, you have an opportunity to learn how success feels. Your mind, emotions and body all learn the sensations associated with succeeding. You can draw on these memories as you go forward and meet the challenge.

In each of these cases, you have an opportunity to experience ahead of time what it is like to be the person you want to be. This kind of experience promotes unconscious efforts to bring about what you seek. A process of *regularly recalling* the feeling or image conveyed by the future self also empowers the unconscious to do its work of bringing you and that future together in time and space.

PAYING ATTENTION TO BODILY SENSATIONS

It's important to focus on how your body feels when you experience the future self. When your body learns the sensations associated with new states of being, it's possible to recall these body states often to enhance your journey into your optimal future.

Sensations may be experienced in any part of the body. You may discover that you feel a certain openness in your chest. There may be a strength in your jaw. Perhaps your hands feel powerful, your feet more firmly planted on the ground. You may experience your eyes as more focused, your neck as stronger, your head held high. Wherever you experience new body sensations that feel empowering and positive, focus on them. Recall them

often. They will help you create the states of mind and emotion ~~ASK~~
that automatically accompany them. ~~angel~~

The important thing is not where the sensations are but *that
you feel them.* Your body needs to learn where it is going. If you
don't actually feel any sensations, imagine what they *would* be
like if you could feel them.

One client, Jim, used his ability to draw on an experience of
the future self to create important changes in his life. When he
first began to work with his future self, he felt his life was on
hold, stuck. He faced a major decision about whether or not to
relocate and couldn't find a comfortable choice. Essentially, he
was caught between wanting to remain in an urban area, with
access to people and work he didn't enjoy but felt compelled to
do, and moving to a rural area to follow a lifelong wish to experience a slower pace. The conflict was tearing him apart, literally
consuming all his waking thoughts.

In his first session with the future self, Jim connected with an
impression of himself in a rural setting. He was surprised by this,
as his conscious mind thought that moving to the country was
foolish. The impression that came from the back of his mind
that most captivated Jim's attention were the shoes worn by his
future self. They were shoes he couldn't imagine wearing in his
current life. As he became the future self and experienced himself in those shoes, the quality he reported was one of feeling
grounded, solidly planted inside himself and in his decision to
live in the country.

Connecting with his future self in this way didn't ease Jim's
internal conflict about the decision he would have to make. His
conscious mind was convinced that he needed to remain in an
urban area, but his feelings were crying out for a new lifestyle.
He kept recalling and connecting with his experience of the
future self, even as he doubted that it had any validity. He kept
recreating the sensation of feeling solidly planted inside himself,
allowing his body to remember what he had experienced as his
future self.

Around the time he discovered his future self, Jim changed
jobs. He began a consulting career that allowed him to work out
of his home. He discovered that he didn't need an office in the

city. Because he flew to his clients, he could live anywhere he wanted. A year or so after starting his new career, Jim surprised himself when an opportunity arose to buy a house in his favorite country setting. He responded with what seemed to be a snap decision to put down a deposit and buy the house.

After he moved, I didn't see him for a number of months. One day, he was visiting Manhattan and came by my office to say hello. As he entered my office, I was struck by Jim's appearance. He was wearing the shoes he had talked about in his first contact with the future self. He had become the man he had described.

A more specific area of healing was experienced by Laura when she connected with her future self. Laura came from an alcoholic home in which everyone had to be very careful not to disturb her father. To make noise would mean to risk a scene that could range anywhere from a sullen look and sarcastic comments to a full-blown tantrum, with household objects flying through the air.

As she worked on healing her tendency to be painfully careful around other people, Laura discovered a future self who was able to laugh out loud. This part of her future self was astonishing to Laura. As the future self, she was able to experience herself laughing out loud in perfect safety and comfort. She felt particularly strong in her arms. She described the sensation as having the ability to reach out and connect with her world, able to express herself if she wanted to. Now, instead of automatically holding in her feelings, she had a new option. She could remind herself that she was safe and that she could share her feelings if it felt appropriate to do so.

THE UNFAMILIAR FUTURE SELF

There are times when the future self isn't experienced as a welcome change. For many adult children of dysfunctional families, chaos is the rule, intense emotions the norm. If you are accustomed to the super-charged ups and downs characteristic of many dysfunctional families, it's no surprise that a future self who has a more balanced, coherent style might feel alien. Often, this kind of future self is described as "cold, detached, disinterested."

At first, it's hard to imagine that it's possible to be loving and connected with others without that old pattern of emotional intensity. It's as though you've suddenly been put on a no-salt diet and can't imagine enjoying food without the kick salt adds. If you've ever had to change your diet in this way, you've experienced the fact that after a while your taste buds reawaken to the rich subtleties in food. Suddenly, you are able to recognize flavors that were covered over by the salt and a new relationship with food evolves. You are more conscious of nuance. You have actually enriched your experience rather than dulled it.

In the same way, the chaos so many of us experienced in dysfunctional relationships with our families has dulled our awareness of the richness available in our emotional lives. If you discover a future self that feels cold or detached, give yourself time to explore what the qualities of that self feel like over time. You may discover, as you become your future self, that what you thought was coldness is actually a healthy shift away from emotions that were part of dysfunctional patterns of interacting.

You may also find that the future self has outgrown ways of relating and behaving that were developed in childhood and that didn't mature as you entered adulthood. At first, it may not feel like good news to discover that you may eventually relinquish a personal style you now consider to be most genuinely who you are. Sometimes, this creates a feeling of real loss and reluctance to connect with the future self.

Stephen comes to mind. Stephen always thought of himself as a particularly witty and entertaining kind of guy. He described the ways he liked to joke around with women. He always had a good time. The problem was that the women he dated often experienced him as insensitive and he was surprised when they stopped seeing him. As he connected with the future self, Stephen experienced a man who was much more serious and conscientious than he felt in his present-day self. The future self was, as Stephen described him, "an adult." To Stephen, as is true with many people, the idea of becoming an adult felt decidedly unappealing. To him, adults were boring, burdened people. He certainly had no desire to fall into that trap.

Because of his notion of what it meant to be an adult, Stephen didn't want to give up his witty style, which he associated with the boy in him, even though it cost him relationships. It represented energy, liveliness and an interest in living. For Stephen, the only models of adulthood he understood emotionally were his parents, who had been hardworking immigrants. In no way did he want to grow up and be like them. As is true for lots of people, Stephen didn't realize that he *was* an adult already. Even more important, he didn't realize that to be an adult meant he could be serious *or* playful, depending on the situation in which he found himself.

As Stephen worked on letting go of his fear of becoming an adult, the future self became less threatening. In fact, Stephen was eventually able to feel the powerful difference between his previous way of being and his future self. The change became something positive he wanted to achieve. The image of the future self became a lifeline to grab hold of whenever he had those old urges to be the clever, entertaining boy he had always been when that response was inappropriate.

All change brings with it gains and losses. The process of becoming your future self will probably involve some losses along the way. What's important to keep in mind is that you *will* be comfortable as that future self by the time you get there. That's certainly been true for me, and I encourage you to trust your unconscious to take you in directions that will be healing and empowering.

THE OPTIMAL LIFE PATH

There are a number of ways to access the future self. One of my favorites is the image of an *optimal life path* along which you travel everyday of your life. The path symbolizes the process or journey encompassed by whatever it is you are seeking to heal or to develop. Along the path, on down the road where you haven't yet traveled, you can meet the part of you that has already made the journey. This part, who knows where you are going and how to get there, becomes your guide. The guidance needn't be conscious at all. In fact, the future self can fill the back of your mind with all relevant "memories" of how you got from here to there and your unconscious can do the rest. The memories of the future self become supportive and positive urges, inspirations and responses to unexpected opportunities in the present.

Another way to connect with the future self is to imagine yourself moving forward in time toward a given event or situation and meeting the future self there. As I did with the future self in the navy blue suit, you can experience what it's like to be there already.

It's also helpful to find a quiet place in your internal hypnotic terrain where you can meet with the future self and simply spend time together. During these quiet times, you might allow yourself to feel some kind of contact with your future self. The sensation of hands solidly planted on your shoulders or of holding hands with the future self is often both reassuring and empowering.

The reason I generally choose the optimal life path is because it enhances an unconscious urge towards movement forward. It reminds you that each day you are presented with numerous choices and steps that make up your ongoing life journey.

If you ever find that the future self seems antagonistic, judgmental or in any way negative towards you, or if you find that your way is blocked on your optimal path, it's helpful to wonder about what beliefs or family myths may be in the way. A sense of negativity coming from your future self usually means you are projecting unresolved issues onto this resource part. Accept your experience and *use* it. Often when you begin to move forward, family rules and injunctions against becoming empowered may prompt your unconscious to create images that seem to be unfriendly or unhelpful. In fact, they may reflect your own feelings of shame and unworthiness. What begins as a journey into the future becomes an opportunity to let go of something from the past. Remember that everything is information to work with to further the process of recreating yourself.

It has been my experience that the optimal future self, ultimately, is *never* truly disapproving or abusive towards the present-day self or the child within. The future self has learned a great deal about loving you, about self-acceptance. Consistently, you will find that your future self offers support and encouragement, rather than criticism or "shoulds."

Joan, a successful professional, had this kind of experience. When she described her first contact with the future self, she talked about a woman who was cold and looked at her with disapproval. The future self she described closely resembled prior descriptions of her mother. I suggested that Joan use her hypnotic eyes to look more closely at the future self. I also suggested that she might find that there was a quality of love in the future self that she simply hadn't recognized before.

After a few minutes, Joan began to cry. Allowing herself to recognize the support and acceptance available from her future self tapped into an area of pain she felt deeply. She had always looked to her mother for approval, but saw only disappointment reflected in her mother's eyes. As she experienced her future self, she discovered a reflection of herself that was what she had always sought. The tears expressed both sadness and gratitude. They were tears of healing, tears that allowed Joan to open to something she hadn't really believed was possible.

I cannot emphasize it enough. Your future self will never actually feel negatively toward you. Anytime this happens, go deeper, look more closely for projections of your current attitudes about yourself, including feelings of shame, guilt, or self-hate. Give yourself permission to come back to your future self later. There is no need to settle for anything less than a future self who understands, supports and accepts you. You have a right to know what it feels like to love yourself.

BRINGING ALONG THE CHILD WITHIN

When you take the journey on your optimal path to find your future self, it's helpful to bring along the child within. The child is the seed of your potential, the place where your talent is held, awaiting the time you embody it in adulthood. There is a certain affinity between the future self and the child within. Because the child is the seed of your potential, and the optimal life path is the blueprint for the best you can be, the optimal future self represents someone the child often recognizes and responds to eagerly.[2]

You, as the present-day self, are *the point of power in the present,* the part living in time and space that can make actual what is potential. You have the ability to reach into the past and touch the child, as well as to reach into the future and tap the memories of the future self to guide you. It is within *you* that both come together.

Sometimes, at first, the child within is shy around the future self. With patience and acceptance, though, the child usually responds quickly to the self-acceptance and love conveyed by the future self. If you will allow yourself to give the child permission to get to know the future self slowly, over time, you will probably discover that the child's inherent excitement and curiosity soon emerge.

You needn't take the child with you every time you meet the future self. There may be times when you just don't *want* to include the child within. If this happens, take a moment to ask yourself why. You might find that you really will have a more powerful experience with the future self if you're alone. You may also discover that you are having a reaction to the child that's worth knowing about, a reaction you'll want to explore further using some of the other exercises in the book.

Since every part of you is touched by your present-day self becoming the future self, it's important to invite *all* the parts of you along at some point or other in your journey. In fact, you really can't leave out any of the parts of you as you move forward on your optimal life path. Whenever protective parts seek to block the way, you need to deal with them. As mentioned in Chapter 4, the future self is an invaluable and powerful helper in convincing protective parts to participate in "job retraining." By looking through the eyes of your future self at changes you need to make, you connect with a source of inspiration and awareness. When you are able to sense what a protective part becomes when it has been updated, the process of change is promoted and hastened.

ABOUT THE EXERCISES

There are two exercises in this chapter. Before beginning them, remember that it is best to tape record these exercises. Have your journal or notebook handy, also, so you can jot down anything you may want to keep in mind. Record the italicized sentences and leave pauses where you see them indicated. You can always turn off the tape recorder between steps if you need some extra time for any part of the exercises.

In the first exercise, you will be walking on a path. The induction refers to it as your optimal life path. When you use this future-self exercise to explore healing processes or developments you would like to achieve, allow yourself to create other optimal paths. For instance, you can explore your optimal path of healing, your optimal path of career development, or your optimal path of learning some new skill or developing some new attitude. There's no limit to the applications of your future-self work. Let your creativity and whatever need is paramount be your guides.

As a reminder, I want to encourage you to seek *essence* and *quality* rather than content. Looking for specifics is likely to get you bogged down. If specifics come to mind, fine. They can be something interesting to think about from time to time as you continue to concentrate on the essence of what you have touched. Remember, I never went out and bought the navy blue business suit, but I *did* focus on how it felt to wear it and to be the person inside it.

Exercise #4   Discovering Your Future Self

[Before beginning, find a quiet place where you will be undisturbed for about 30 minutes. Use whatever self-hypnotic induction works best for you. Once you have shifted gears and begun to go inside, begin the tape of the exercise that follows.]

From the back of your mind to the front of your mind, allow an impression to emerge, now, of a path. It represents your optimal life path, or whatever journey you're undertaking now.

Imagine yourself walking along this path. Notice the surface underfoot. Is it hard? Soft? [pause] *What color is it?* [pause] *Become aware of the feel of that surface as you move along.* [pause]

Is the path a straight path? Can you see ahead in the direction you're going? Does the path curve? Go uphill? Downhill? [pause] *Simply become aware of the nature of the path and accept whatever comes to mind.* [pause]

And, how about the surrounding environment? Notice the colors, shapes and textures around you. [pause]

Are there natural sounds and natural smells that come to mind? [pause]

You might notice whether you're in sunlight or shade. Are there patterns of light and shadow that capture your attention? [pause]

You may find that there is a special feeling in the air itself. There may be a sense of anticipation, or curiosity, or even a kind of magical sparkle in the air. Simply notice how it feels as you walk along. [pause]

This is your optimal path. It represents an important journey in your life, a journey you have decided to take.

Remember that your conscious mind is a passenger on this journey. Allow it to wonder what you will discover as you go along.

Allow the child to join you now. Remember that this is the child's path as well. If you have mixed feelings about having the child there with you, just accept what comes into your experi-

ence. It's all important information about the quality and current state of your internal relationship with the child in you. [pause]

You might take a moment, now, to become aware of the state of mind of the child who has joined you. This might be a child within you've met many times, and whom you know very well. Or, it may be a child who is new to you, a child who is ready to emerge now and become part of your healing process. [pause]

Whatever the child's state of mind, simply accept it. You may be surprised to discover that there will be times when the child is even more eager than you are to go down the path. The child is perfectly safe here, so you can allow that child to run or explore, or to stay close.

If you discover that you or the child are reluctant to go forward on your optimal path, give yourself permission to wonder about what beliefs or fears may be holding you or the child back, now. [pause]

If there is a protective part that is frightened by the prospect of going forward, make a note of it. Later, when you have time, you might want to work with the protective part to resolve any fears or beliefs it may have that it is dangerous to go forward. [pause]

For now, move ahead a bit along the path, simply noticing how it feels to go forward. [pause]

Take a moment, now, and look back and see how far you've come. You might also become aware of the quality of the environment you've left behind . . . of what it used to be like to be there. You might be surprised at how far you've come. [long pause]

And now, look forward again and begin to move ahead on your optimal path. Be sure to keep the child in your awareness, offering encouragement if it's needed.

Remind yourself that every step you take on this path is a step towards something you seek to achieve . . . towards healing, empowerment, recovery. Let yourself know that each step along the path represents an affirmation to your unconscious that you want to move forward in your life, that you are moving forward. [pause]

Notice, now, that coming towards you from on up the path, from where you have yet to travel, someone is approaching. That someone is your future self, the part of you that has already made this journey. [pause]

Simply let some impressions come from the back of your mind to the front of your mind as the future self comes nearer. Give yourself permission to just let the impressions come, with the thought that you can analyze them later, if you want.

Take a moment, now, to notice . . . what kind of person is this? [pause] *What is this person wearing?* [pause] *What do you notice about this person that is different from your present-day self?* [pause] *What do you think of this person?* [pause] *Are you comfortable or uncomfortable with your experience of your future self?* [long pause]

Take a moment, now, to become that person. Notice how it feels to be inside your future self. [pause] *What is it like to be that person?* [long pause]

Take a moment, now, to experience where, in your body, you feel the power and the stability of that future self most strongly. [long pause] *Your body is learning something important about how to create this experience as a reality in your present-day life.* [pause]

Once your body learns to recognize the feeling of being the future self, you can recall that feeling often. Your body will remember.

If you were able to look at the world through the eyes of the future self, what would you see? [pause] *How would the world be different from the one you experience as your present-day self?* [long pause]

Now, from the perspective of the future self, take a moment to look at the present-day you, standing there. What feelings do you experience as you look at your present-day self through the eyes of this wiser, more mature part of you? [long pause]

Remember, the future self has learned much more about love and self-acceptance than you know in your present-day consciousness. You may discover a feeling of love for yourself that is richer than what you've experienced before. [pause] *Or, you may have some other experience that is deeply meaningful for you at this time in other ways.* [long pause]

For a moment, now, become aware of how the child responds to the future self, and how the future self responds to the child. [pause]

Simply allow the response to be whatever it is right now. Use every opportunity to convey acceptance to the child. It's okay for that child to have honest feelings.

Perhaps for a moment, now, you might allow the future self to convey to the back of your mind anything that would be helpful for you to know about in the present. Perhaps the future self would be willing to convey to you an impression of the next step you need to take in healing or resolving a situation, or in promoting a particular development. Remember to leave this alone consciously. Simply let the back of your mind receive whatever the future self wishes to communicate. In your own best time and your own best ways, the unconscious will convey to your conscious mind whatever impressions are most helpful.

The memories of the future self become the blueprint for your journey, the map that you will follow unconsciously to get you from here to there.

Take a minute or so of clock time, now, to let the future self give you whatever impressions may be available. That minute of clock time can be all the time you need to receive whatever will be helpful for this journey. [long pause]

As your present-day self, now, perhaps you could ask your future self to become your guide. [pause] *Each day, you face many choice points. You might want to ask the future self to guide those choices so that each takes you more surely towards your optimal future. And, if you like your future self and feel positive about your experience, you might want to say to the future self, often, "I want to be you."* [pause]

For now, it's time to come back, so leave a part of you on that path, moving forward with the future self and the child within. As you come back, remember that there is a part of you always on that path, always moving forward on your journey, no matter what your conscious mind may be doing, no matter what your day-to-day demands require of your attention.

Give yourself the suggestion, now, that by the time you open your eyes, you'll be as alert as you need to be for whatever is next on your agenda. Take a moment to wiggle your fingers and toes and come all the way back, now, and take a few minutes to write down your experience.

Remember, in order to become aware of your future self, it's not essential always to experience yourself on an optimal path. You can also find the future self with you anywhere, at any time. Just as the child within accompanies you wherever you go, so does this most important part of you.

Also, you may find that the statement, "I want to be you," changes as you move along your optimal path. After getting to know the future self, and walking a ways along the path, you may discover that you find yourself saying, "I *will* be you." Then, after some more time, you might say, "I *am becoming* you." Allow yourself to progress at whatever pace, and in whatever way, feels natural to you. The main point is to remember that you are *becoming* the future self, that in your own good time you *will be* that person.

In the second exercise, you'll be focusing on the power of the *connection* that exists between the future self, your present-day self, and the child within. You'll need about 15 minutes for this exercise, or whatever brief amount of time you may have available. It's primarily an exercise that is used to reinforce the intensity and immediacy of your connection with these important parts of you, rather than to work with any unfolding content or process.

Exercise #5   Your Thread of Connection

[As before, use whatever self-hypnotic induction best suits you at this point in time. As you enter trance, focus on finding yourself in a safe, private place.]

As you settle in and become aware of all the sights, sounds and smells of your private, safe place, become aware, if you will, of a certain quality of comfort or support in the very air itself. This is a place where you come to connect even more deeply with parts of you that live in your timeless unconscious. [pause]

It may surprise you to discover that the child is present nearby. There are many children within you, many different ages that may be sources of your potential or wounded and in need of healing. Allow whichever child within needs you most right now to emerge in your awareness. Allow it to be the child within that automatically comes forward from the back of your mind. [pause]

Also become aware of the fact that your future self has approached and is there with you, now. Notice the feeling you get when the future self approaches. You are with a part of you that provides important support and guidance. [pause]

Take a moment to notice, now, a thread of some color that emerges from the chest of the future self, in the area of the heart. I don't know what thickness the thread will have, or what color it may be. It may be golden, or silver, or some other color that has meaning for you.

Notice that the thread reaches out and connects with your chest, in the area of your heart. There's nothing to do with this . . . just become aware of it. [pause]

The thread represents a living, vital connection between you and the future self. It reinforces for you the presence and availability of the future self. Along this thread, the future self feels what you feel, is aware of your needs. Also along this thread, you are aware of the presence and response of your future self. [pause]

Now, notice that a similar thread emerges from your chest, in the area of your heart, and connects with the chest of the child. [pause] This thread is a continuation of the one that comes from your future self. It is your connection with the child within, and affirms your awareness of the child's feelings and needs. [pause]

Simply be aware of the continuous thread . . . of how it connects you with both the future self and the child within. Remind yourself that you are the point of power in the present. It is through you that healing, recovery and achievement of your goals take place. The thread affirms you as this point of power and reinforces the relationships you are building with your future self and the child within.

The thread is also a magnetic link. It automatically draws you toward the future self. You might take a moment and imagine the feeling of being drawn forward, inevitably, into your best future. [pause]

The thread connecting you with the child within is also magnetic and draws that child inevitably into your present, into a time and a place where a healing process is occurring. The thread reinforces the fact that you are the child's promise that the child makes it, just as the future self is your promise. [pause]

When you're ready, begin to reorient yourself, holding onto the feeling of being connected with these parts of you. Allow yourself to keep in mind the magnetic quality of the thread. Remind yourself that you are being drawn forward into your optimal future every moment of every day, with every step you take.

And, as you return to fully alert consciousness, wiggle your fingers and toes to bring yourself all the way back.

You can recall the thread often during the day. It will remind you that you are on a journey into your optimal future, that you *will* get there in your own best time, in your own best way. Remember that your inner journey is empowered when you allow yourself to *feel* the pull of the thread in your body.

I want to underscore again the importance of the future self in your life. During the day, whenever you have a free moment, recall your impression of the future self. This will empower your unconscious journey towards change. Remember that often, throughout the day, you can say to the future self, "I want to *be* you," or, "I *will be* you," or "I *am becoming* you. You might even want to say to yourself, "Now, I *am* you," and imagine a sense of deep gratitude and satisfaction that you have become a wiser, more mature person, a person you like being.

The desire you feel when you repeat these statements is a powerful reinforcer for unconscious programming. The more you can *feel* your wish to accomplish your healing journey, to become much more than you have ever been, the more strongly your unconscious will guide you in that direction.

Chapter 6

THE CHILD WITHIN: RECLAIMING THE SELF

During a hypnotic journey, Beverly discovered her child within hiding at the back of a hallway, against a closed door. It was dark back there and the little girl, about four years old, was huddled in a tiny ball. In trance, Beverly imagined herself walking slowly down the hallway. She talked in reassuring tones as she approached cautiously and with respect for the child's fear. She didn't know how the little girl had come to be there, but she *did* know the child was terrified. Slowly, Beverly sat down on the floor near the child, carefully inching closer. Then she reached out her hand and touched the little girl on the head. It nearly broke her heart when the child flinched. It became clear, at this point, that it would take time for this child to be able to trust *any* adult, including Beverly.

Over several sessions, the child began to respond to Beverly's calm and steady presence. Eventually, the child allowed herself to be carried from the dark hallway. In time, she began to let the numbness lift. At first, she felt profound relief. Then, the terror and pain began to come into Beverly's adult awareness. The child had begun to feel safe and could now reveal her story.

As the child shared her story over time, various protective parts were activated and needed to be reassured. Beverly had to remind herself that protective parts are originally created to keep the child safe from potentially abusive adults. In the present, she, too, would be experienced by these parts as an adult who might abuse the child—until she proved herself trustworthy. Because of this, as Beverly listened to the child's story, she also listened for input from protective parts. As the relationship with the child developed and Beverly proved herself reliable, the protective parts consistently allowed more of the story to be revealed.

Every child within, even yours, has a story to tell. It's a story that lives deep inside and has been hidden from everyone, usually including you. To have told the story honestly would have been to risk possible abandonment, rejection, ridicule, or even retaliation from adults in the child's environment. In order to keep the story hidden, the child buried his or her *true* feelings and created the *false self.*

THE TRUE SELF AND THE FALSE SELF

For me, the false self is a *concept.* It encompasses all the protective parts and maladaptive strategies you developed as you survived impossible childhood situations. You can think of the false self as the totality of your dysfunctional responses, which arose by *necessity* when you were young. Your protective parts are all aspects of the false self. Rather than seeking to define a single false self, think of the false self as the fabric of which the protective parts are threads.

It was the false self that adapted to the demands of the early environment.[1] With the development of the false self, you learned to be numb or to appear always to be okay. You learned to express whatever emotions were acceptable in the family and to hide all the others.

The truth Beverly buried was of an alcoholic family where sexual abuse, neglect, humiliation, and verbal abuse were all elements of the child's experience. Piece by piece, she recalled what it had been like. Bit by bit, she reached inside to touch the child's true feelings. She cried with the child, felt terror with the child, held the child when there was just too much pain for any other response. Beverly's false, numb, *nice* self was giving way to an inner, forgotten self filled with difficult feelings and memories.[2]

The major work of reclaiming the self is to hear the child's story *from the perspective of this forgotten, often-buried true self.* This means being willing to experience pain that was never expressed openly. It means letting into conscious awareness the terror that may have arisen during abusive experiences. It also means allowing grief and rage and a whole range of other feelings that the child didn't dare show or even realize, consciously.[3]

Reclaiming the self also means allowing the protective strategies of the false self to begin to drop away, and that can leave you feeling vulnerable and exposed. As old ways of coping cease to work, you discover your true self, and you begin to experience and express your true needs and feelings in new, and sometimes frightening, ways. Also, it involves discovering and experiencing, perhaps for the first time, the *life,* energy, and joy of the child. When the pain is buried, so, too, are the wonder and enthusiasm that are so much a part of a child's way of experiencing the world.

Listening to the child's story also means acknowledging and validating both the true self *and* the false self, loving and accepting the importance of each. For several reasons, this can represent a significant challenge. First, the false self automatically rejects the true self. To the false self, the true self may seem a troublemaker who has honest feelings that could get the child in trouble. The false self has worked hard to ignore and dismiss these feelings. The false self may also have some ways of behaving and feeling that create shame and guilt.

Also, as you reach inside to validate the true self, you may find it hard to accept the child's story. You may find yourself angry at, or impatient with, the child. You may discover that you don't want to know things that the true self has to show you. Or you may be deeply moved and respond with profound love and compassion. You may experience the need and vulnerability of the child's true self and understand vividly why the creation of the false self, with all its protective strategies, was essential to your survival.

For many of us, the ways of being that emerge from the false self are all we've ever known. As children, false-self strategies allowed us to feel on top of things. In reality, though, these strategies contributed to a diminishing sense of self-esteem as we attempted to accommodate unmanageable situations. The false self also kept us from knowing how bad it was and helped us behave in ways that would minimize mistreatment. During childhood, the false self allowed us to survive.

The problem is that the false self is created in a crisis situation. On the surface, it *seems* to be strong and safe. Actually, though, operating from the false self often leaves you feeling attacked, rejected, or defensive when interacting with others. It may have been that, as a false-self strategy, you had to become chronically depressed to keep from feeling what was really going on inside.

We depend on the false self without realizing that it is but a thin shell of who we really are. It's made up of protective parts that allow us, if needed, to be the cheerleader in the family, always bright and ready to help. It allows us to cook dinner when we're only nine years old because Mom is out at the bars looking for Dad. It keeps us from knowing how overwhelmed we really feel. Often, the false self has learned to feel nothing, to become numb instead.

REDISCOVERING YOUR TRUE FEELINGS

One of the things Beverly reported early on was that she didn't know what she was feeling. Something stressful would happen in her life and she then would develop a pressing need for sex. She had no idea that she had experienced distress, fear, or anger and was seeking to soothe it. She didn't know how to listen to her body and recognize her feelings.

Beverly isn't alone in not knowing how to recognize her feelings. Early on, when the true self put a feeling in the pit of your stomach, the false self often squelched that feeling with numbness. If you've ever had an arm or leg go to sleep at night, you know how it feels to have a wooden, numb, useless appendage. You literally have to carry it if you want to move it. You can touch it and feel nothing, as if it belonged to someone else. You know it's there, you know it's yours, but you're not connected with it. Imagine going through a day with a leg or arm that's asleep, as if it were paralyzed.

In order to reclaim the use of the limb, it must be awakened. If you've ever had a leg or arm fall asleep, and then had to move it, you probably know how painful those moments can be when sensations begin to return. Even with the pain, though, this must happen if you hope to reconnect with that arm or leg as a part of you that's useful. Until you begin to move beyond the numbness in you and hear the child's story as it was experienced by the true self, you are like the limb that's asleep. Your resources, the depth and range of your feelings, are numb and not available.

It's important to know that, within the numbness, there isn't only pain—there are also your joy, your life energy, your enthusiasm. As the child's story unfolds, you not only experience the strong emotions that reflect the bad times, but you also tap into the boundless energy and liveliness of your true self.

The process of discovering your true self and leaving behind the protective mechanisms of the false self allows you to reclaim the totality of your being, *all of you.* You create, in the present, an empowered, integrated experience of self. As you listen to the child's story, there are moments of discomfort along the way. There are also moments of deeply moving intimacy when you learn to love yourself unconditionally, as you accept and embrace the entire range of your humanness.

The story the child has to tell may contain uncomfortable truths. Many children have learned to convert fear into courage, or terror and confusion into depression, because their true feelings would have created even more abuse or distress. There are those who became seductive, acting out sexually as adolescents, recreating unacknowledged sexual abuse. Feelings such as these stay under the surface of conscious awareness and often become the basis for self-destructive behaviors.

Think, for a moment, of feelings you may have carried since adolescence that still have the power to embarrass you. As you imagine that teenager, how do you feel towards her or him? What do you think of that youngster's behavior from your vantage point as an adult? Would you find it easy to show affection or support for this part of you?

THERAPEUTIC DISSOCIATION

You may notice my reference to the teenager as "her" and "him." An important part of learning to listen to the child in you is to create a "therapeutic dissociation."[4] This means that you—as the adult you are today—get to know the child as a separate part of you. For too long, the child has been alone. He or she needs and deserves to have a relationship with a reliable, trustworthy adult. *You* are that adult.

You may be one of those people fortunate enough to experience yourself as an adult most of the time. Only occasionally do you find yourself feeling small, incompetent or helpless in a world that suddenly feels too big. More often, adult children of dysfunctional families struggle with feeling vulnerable, at risk or overwhelmed on a more ongoing basis. It's as though something happens and you suddenly shift gears into a child's state of mind.

For example, things may be going along fine at work and you feel pretty good about what you're doing. Then, in an interaction with your boss or a colleague you suddenly find yourself feeling anxious, depressed or enraged. It's as though you switched channels and tuned into an entirely new program. When this happens, most often you've switched from an adult-part to a child-part. Your thinking may have shifted to black-and-white, either-or terms that limit the range of your response options. You go on autopilot and begin to respond from the vantage point and feelings of the child.

At times like this, there's a child who suddenly finds herself on the firing lines and desperately needs an adult's reassurance and comfort. If you think about it for a moment, you may realize how helpful it would be to be able to switch back into your adult self and soothe that frightened child. Think of how much safer it would feel if the child could depend on you to take center stage and handle things competently, an adult who could calm and care for her.

The purpose of this chapter is to teach you how to become that adult.

THE FEBRUARY MAN

My work with the child within is derived from the teachings of Milton Erickson. Ericksonian hypnosis has received much attention in the psychotherapeutic community in recent years. This approach promotes a respect for the richness and healing potential of the unconscious. One of the most creative of Erickson's approaches, and there are many, is called the "February Man" technique. The technique demonstrates the inherent flexibility and resourcefulness of the unconscious.

Many years ago, Erickson developed a reputation of being something of a miracle worker with difficult problems, and many people sought his expertise. At one point, the wife of a colleague asked Erickson to help her.[5] She was pregnant and concerned that she wouldn't be a caring parent. Her childhood had been spent in a home where she had interacted primarily with her spinster aunt. Her mother "never had any time for her" and her father was caught up in his business. As a result, she spent a great deal of time alone. She grew up feeling that she wasn't important to her parents and was concerned now that her unhappy childhood would affect her ability to be attentive to her own child.

Erickson put her into a deep trance and regressed her back to a special time in February when she was very young. That special time was her birthday and, while she was in trance, Erickson "visited her" as an old friend of her father's. He made numerous "visits" during trances, engaging her over the years at different ages, always entering her trance experience as the same friend, as someone who cared about her very much. Erickson became someone she could talk to about her fears, curiosities and other things of interest and importance to a child.

Essentially, Erickson's hypnotic work with this woman created new memories in her psychological history. These were memories that hadn't existed before. How was this possible? It's possible because the mind seems to experience vividly imagined events as being as real as actual events. Both produce "memories" to draw on and learn from. It's this ability of the mind that promotes the powerful effects that are possible with visualization and self-hypnosis exercises.[6]

After Erickson entered this woman's unconscious world and shared experiences with her in trance, she drew on these new, unconscious memories as if they had really happened. She had learned from her interactions with her father's "friend" how it felt to be cared about, what it was like when her experiences and thoughts were regarded as important. She internalized a set of responses in her trance experiences with Erickson that became the basis for positive, unconscious responses to her child.

BECOMING YOUR OWN FEBRUARY MAN

When this technique is translated into a self-hypnotic approach, you become your *own* February Man. You can enter your own psychological history and become a supportive presence that wasn't there before. As you explore the approach offered in this chapter, you'll have an opportunity to discover ways to take care of the vulnerable child in you.

It's not unusual, in this process, to have some ambivalent feelings, or even reluctance, about taking responsibility for the child. Sometimes, people resent that *they* have to do the caretaking they have been seeking from other people. They'd rather get what the child didn't have: support from someone outside, from someone else. It's an understandable response and an understandable goal. The problem is that it doesn't work in adult relationships, no matter how hard we try or how many people we attempt to enlist.

Think, for a moment, of times when you may have tried to get someone else to take care of you or to be emotionally and materially supportive in ways you always imagined a good parent would be. How successful were your efforts? Did you end up receiving the things you thought you wanted?

Inevitably, when there is an underlying demand that other people take care of you or make you feel worthwhile or happy, you will be let down. Other people get tired of the constant demands, move on to another phase of their life where they don't have the same amount of time to devote to your needs—or they may even die. It may also be that, over time, small disappointments build up as people fail to live up to your expectations and demands. You may get so disappointed with their inability to meet the level of need you feel inside that you move on to someone else, still searching for what the child never got.

I recall how I felt when I got married. There was an underlying sense of relief, as I secretly told myself, "Thank goodness. Now *he* can take care of me, now *he* can earn enough money to make it safe." What a surprise I got when things didn't turn out that way. Divorced and once again on my own, I discovered that the security provided by another person is a tentative thing, at best. Ultimately, we have only ourselves to give support and comfort to that place deep inside that has such need. Having significant people in our lives is important, but we have to begin with the *most* important relationship of all: the relationship we have with ourselves.

Meeting the Child Within

The best place to start is at the beginning, with an introduction between the present-day adult and the child in you. At this point, you may be saying to yourself that you already know the child—perhaps far too well for your taste! You may have done child within work before, or perhaps you are more than familiar with the responses you experience when you switch channels and *become* the child. You may be one of those people who wish you could just put the child away once and for all and forget the whole thing. Whatever your response is to the idea of getting in touch with the child in you, it's helpful to let yourself experience what follows as if it were for the first time.

Anna's first meeting with the child illustrates the value of allowing yourself to be surprised by, and to accept, whatever arises when you meet the child within. When she went into trance, she was convinced that she and the little girl in her already had a reliable, loving relationship. During her trance, she found herself, unexpectedly, with the child as a baby. She hadn't connected with this aspect of herself before. What surprised her was how uncomfortable she felt holding the baby. She didn't like the feeling of being responsible for such a small, helpless being.

After a few moments, I suggested that the feelings of discomfort might reflect how her mother had felt when Anna was born. Almost immediately, Anna began to cry. She described a deep longing to be held by her mother, something that hadn't happened often when she was young. Along with the longing, she also felt, in herself as the adult, her mother's intense discomfort in the role of caretaker.

Anna's negative reaction to the baby allowed her to get in touch with an internal experience that had always remained unconscious, but had operated in all of her intimate relationships. She often felt terribly needy and then would withdraw with a conviction that the person would let her down. Once she was able to feel how her mother seemed to be overwhelmed by the baby's dependency and ongoing need, she could also acknowledge the deep pain, confusion and longing she felt as a child.

This acknowledgment allowed Anna to discover strong feelings of love and support towards that tiny, helpless baby. She was able to reach out to the child's need with warmth and tenderness.

BECOMING A SUPPORTIVE ADULT

The process of getting to know the child within hypnotically is focused on one primary goal: giving the child access to a supportive adult who is reliable and empathic. As in Anna's experience, it's valuable to pay particular attention to any *negative* feelings that may arise. Becoming conscious of these feelings allows you to listen more deeply to the child's story, and to learn how caretakers felt inside and responded nonverbally.

You may discover, unexpectedly, that you dislike, or feel a wish to punish, the child. You may find yourself wanting to withdraw from contact. Often, negative responses to the child within come as a real surprise, something you may not know about until you experience the child self-hypnotically. Always, such responses represent information that is most helpful to bring into conscious awareness.

Alice Miller addresses the kinds of internalized responses we take in from adult caretakers in two of her books, *The Drama of the Gifted Child* and *For Your Own Good*. She points out that, if you are abused and humiliated as a child, it is possible that as an adult you may respond to yourself and others in the same ways. In the next chapter, you'll spend a good bit of time exploring how to discover internalized messages you received from caretakers and how to give them back. For now, it's helpful to know that most of us have unconscious, unrealized negative feelings about ourselves that can become conscious as we develop a relationship with the child within.[7]

As you get to know the child, you may be surprised at how different your responses are at various stages of the child's development. Often, people find they have little trouble loving and nurturing the younger child within. As they meet the older children, though, it sometimes gets harder to be really loving. In fact, some people find it's hard even to *like* the child as he gets older.

Joe had this experience. He loved the infant and young child. He enjoyed playing with the toddler. As he began to get to know the 11-year-old, his enjoyment began to fade. In fact, he actively disliked the boy he was getting to know. It was at this age that his self-esteem plummeted: his body looked scrawny, he felt awkward and his face broke out. It was difficult for Joe to imagine that there could ever come a day when he would feel anything positive for this boy. He thought of the boy as pathetic, a wimp, a real loser. Initially, he wanted just to leave the boy alone, to ignore him, hoping that this part of him would simply fade away. He forced himself to continue to relate to the boy. As he did, he remembered the cruel taunts from his schoolmates. He got in touch with the pain of being 11 and having other kids exclude him. He discovered that he had learned to reject himself just as they rejected him. Realizing all these things, he began to experience young Joe differently. He found himself giving the boy lots of positive, loving responses. Now, he could tolerate the boy's pain because he had faced it head on.

Getting in touch with negative feelings toward the child is a powerful way of moving toward loving yourself. By connecting with these kinds of feelings, you open the door to remembering how it was for that child. Once you feel things from the child's perspective, it's almost impossible to continue being cruel to yourself. It's awfully hard not to empathize with someone whose pain you've experienced. Once you're no longer afraid of the child's vulnerability, you can open up to the closeness and caring that you, and the child, have always deserved.[8]

Another important experience may occur when the child doesn't like *you* and doesn't want to have anything to do with you. There may be issues of trust. The child may have been abused and have learned never to trust an adult. This is important information; I encourage the child within to keep a safe distance until the adult has proven herself to be trustworthy. It would be crazy-making to ask the child within of an abuse survi-

vor to ignore all of that real-world learning and simply feel trust-
ing. That child's actual experience deserves respect.

Also, people sometimes find that they draw a blank when they
go inside to meet the child within. If this happens to you, accept
it. Remember the creative void. Remind yourself that you have
temporarily entered that void and your unconscious is still deciding which awareness of the child to give you.

There is also the child within who is eager and ready to be
held, soothed and comforted. Often, when people meet the
child for the first time, there are tears of recognition and sadness,
as well as joy and relief. Whatever your experience, accept what
comes. It's all important information to have available in the
process of recreating yourself.

ASPECTS OF THE CHILD WITHIN

As you may have discovered in other child-within work, there are
many aspects of the child in each of us. At each age, the child
represents a different stage of learning, experience, and development of a sense of self. Some of these stages may be characterized by feelings that are positive. Some may be characterized by
experiences that injured your sense of self. *All* are valid. All play
a role in the totality of who you are, now, and how you experience the world. Accept and embrace the wounded, cautious children inside with the same enthusiasm and commitment as you
do those who are playful and loving.

Throughout the exercises in this book, it's crucial for you to
be the *observer* of the child's story. It's terribly important that
you do this from the perspective of the adult. The child has been
alone for too long already. While it takes some practice to experience reliably the difference between your adult self and the
child within, once you do, you'll be keenly aware of the benefits.
It is deeply healing to have a sense of what the child is feeling,
experiencing it vicariously yourself, while you maintain your
"observing ego" as the adult. You can then decide, as the adult,

what the child needs and be able to provide it. Remember, if you feel confused or anxious about what the child may need from you, call on the future self to help. Also, ask yourself how you would respond to this child if the child were someone else's. In this way, you'll draw on a response that is more likely to be clear of any mixed feelings you may have towards the child within.

I never cry alone anymore. Now that I have an ongoing relationship with the child in me, I'm aware of her feelings. If I'm upset, angry or depressed in a certain, vulnerable way, I know that all I have to do is look inside and find the child. Usually, it is *she* who is upset, angry or depressed. As soon as I am able to locate her and acknowledge what she's feeling, things begin to ease. She knows that she is no longer alone. She recognizes my presence as a signal that she'll be taken care of, that things will be all right.

ABOUT THE EXERCISE

The following exercise is designed to help you connect with the child in you. If you have done child within work before, you may want to use this exercise to discover a child within you haven't met yet, perhaps at an age you haven't explored before. If this is your first experience with the child within, the exercise provides an opportunity to take a look at how you feel about the child *at this time.* It is the first of two exercises in this chapter and can be done occasionally, once a month or so, as your relationship develops with the child within. You can use it as a "diagnostic" experience to see where you may have unrealized negative feelings or increased empathy for the child. The second exercise builds on the first and allows you to respond actively to past experiences in which the child was wounded.

Before you begin the exercise, find a quiet spot where you can sit without being disturbed for about 15 minutes. Remember that if you sit in the same place each time you go inside, you enhance your ability to develop a comfortable self-hypnotic state. As you continue to return to the same spot, you also create an increasingly reliable place of *safety*.

You may also want to have paper and pencil handy, or a journal, to record your experience when you've finished the exercise. Writing down what came into awareness can be a real help in processing this kind of inner work. You may surprise yourself by writing down an insight or thought that hadn't come into conscious awareness until you discovered it on paper. It's worth the few minutes it may take you to do this integrative activity just after you come out of trance.

Also, remember to record the following exercise into your tape recorder. Record the *italicized* sentences in a soft voice, pausing for a few moments whenever you see the word [pause].

Exercise #6   Discovering the Child in You

[Use the trance induction in Chapter 3, or one you have developed yourself. The important thing to keep in mind is to create that place of safety *inside*, a place you can go to connect and communicate with various parts of yourself. Your safe place is a place where *no one* may come without your invitation.]

As you settle in to your safe place, take a moment just to be there, aware that you have come here today seeking to meet the child in you. Discover how you feel about this possibility. Does it excite you? Frighten you? Just be aware of whatever you are feeling. [pause]

Now, allow an impression of the child to come from the back of your mind to the front of your mind. It may be an old photograph that you recall seeing. It may be an impression of the child that you haven't ever thought of before. Allow your conscious mind to be an observer and, perhaps, to be surprised at the impression that emerges now. [pause]

If your mind is blank, you might ask yourself what the child would be like if you were to be aware of that child.

Now, ask yourself the following questions, pausing for a moment after each:

What do I think of this child?
What kind of child is this?
Would I call this a "good" child?
If not, then what kind of child is it?
What do I feel in response to this child?
Am I happy to see this child?
Am I angry?
Am I indifferent?

Remember, there is no right or wrong response for you to have. What's important is that you allow whatever needs to emerge to come to mind.

If you haven't done so already, allow the child to come to life, now. You may imagine that you and the child are in your safe place together and that you can interact with each other in whatever ways feel natural to you.

If it's all right with both of you, perhaps you could reach out to the child, offering your hand, a cookie or a toy. You may discover that the child seems to be shy and withdrawn and doesn't respond easily to your overtures. Simply observe and accept whatever comes. [pause]

Remember to allow the child to have whatever responses are natural right now. This child may always have had to smile when he or she would rather have cried, shouted or run away. You give the child a profound gift when you allow the child just to be. [pause]

Notice how you feel about the responses you sense in the child and in yourself. Do you find it difficult just to let it be, to be open to whatever your unconscious wants you to know? [pause]

If you discover ambivalent feelings, irritation, fear or some other uncomfortable response, remember that your unconscious may be giving you an awareness of subtle or direct messages you received from important caretakers when you were a child.

If you and the child come together easily, you may find that there is some sadness, or perhaps deep relief. [pause]

Take a few moments, now, just to be with that child in whatever way is right for this time. Give yourself all the time you need to explore the various responses you and the child may be having.

If the child is willing, and hasn't already, you might invite the child to crawl into your lap. Notice the weight of the child on your legs and against your chest. Feel the difference in size between your hands and the child's hands. Imagine how it would feel if you were stroking the child's hair. [pause]

Whatever you choose to do, be sure to listen to what the child wants and allow that, whatever it is. Remember to call on the future self, if you feel you need help in relating to the child.

When you're ready, take a moment to remind yourself that a part of you stays in relationship with the child in your unconscious, even as your conscious mind begins to come back to the everyday world and other activities that demand your attention.

It might be nice to know that the process begun in trance continues to develop into new responses and awareness in both you and the child. You may be delighted to discover that, over time, both of you deepen your connection with each other, as your ability to listen to the child develops. You may also have the deeply meaningful experience of having the child learn to trust you in a new way. [pause]

When you're ready, now, come all the way back with the knowledge that part of you does stay with the child in that safe place inside. Let yourself remember that everything you thought, felt and became aware of finds its way into that special place in the back of your mind where new learnings and understandings are created that emerge as surprising and positive new responses when you least expect them and when they matter most.

Wiggle your toes and fingers to bring yourself back all the way, now, and go on to the final step in the exercise, which is to write down your experience.

Remember, this is only the beginning. By accepting whatever emerged in this exercise, you begin to develop a foundation of self-acceptance and self-awareness that will create a new climate inside. Most important of all, be gentle with yourself and with the child. Relationships take time. As you discover the true self in the child, you may well find yourself facing feelings and responses you don't like or that make you uncomfortable. That's fine. It's normal to have mixed feelings. Often, it takes time to develop the ability to tolerate and accept the child's true feelings. Allow yourself to accept this fact of human nature. Most of us have a lifetime of learning that says we must deny, repress and reject the truth in us. Give yourself permission to arrive at a feeling of acceptance in your own way, at your own pace.

I encourage you to do the above exercise before going on with the next one, *even if you've done child-within work before.* An assessment of your current relationship with the child is helpful to what comes later. You won't need to do this exercise often. You can use it from time to time to check on how you are feeling about the child at different ages. You may find that your feelings change in a decidedly positive way as you work with the exercise that follows and those that appear in other chapters.

CORRECTIVE REGRESSION

The next exercise is called *corrective regression.* [9] It is a technique that draws on Erickson's February Man approach. In it, you reach back through time and enter the child's experience as a supportive adult who wasn't there the first time around.

As far as we know to date, it's not possible to move back through objective time and change physical reality. What you *can* do is reach into the timeless unconscious and create new psychological learnings and new psychological history. You can add things that weren't there before, and still honor the truth of what the child experienced, without having to deny that it happened or how it affected you.

Let me share with you some examples of how clients have used corrective regression in beginning to reclaim the child and create a new internal reality.

One client, Denise, had a father who was particularly brutal.

Denise had memories of being in bed when her father would come into the room and beat her. What always troubled Denise, though, was that she couldn't remember why she had been beaten. She only knew that she was often anxious at night and had difficulty falling asleep.

During a corrective regression dealing with this memory, Denise found herself back in the bedroom, looking at the little girl. For the first time, she was fully aware of the terror the child felt. She had never before realized or acknowledged the depth of fear in the little girl. It was deeply moving to share Denise's pain as she sobbed over the tremendous burden the terror had caused the child.

As she allowed the feelings to come, so did the memories of what occurred before the beatings. Watching from the perspective of the observer, Denise saw the little girl call for her mother. She wanted a glass of water and a kiss goodnight. If her mother came to the door, all would be well and she could go to sleep in safety. The problem was that she never knew whether her mother or her father would come. When it was her father, she would be beaten for crying out and disturbing him.

To create a corrective experience, I asked Denise to sit on the edge of the bed as the adult and to have the future self there, too. Both adults were to reassure the child with their presence. Denise then told the child that whoever came through the door would have to deal with both adults first. As it happened, Denise's father was the one who came. She stood up and discovered that her father didn't seem so big to her anymore. Her father was surprised to find other adults in the room. Denise told her father to leave the child alone and, as is so often true with adults who abuse children, her father seemed intimidated by Denise's adult presence. Denise explained to her father than the little girl was no longer fair game for brutality. She further explained that *she* was now in the child's life and that the child was now safe from this kind of abuse.

All the while the child was listening, frightened that anyone could or *would* stand up to her father. She was certain she would be beaten, despite the reassurance from the adult Denise. To the child's surprise, her father turned and left the room. I asked Denise if it would be all right with both her and the child if she were to bring the child to the present. It's helpful to bring the child to the place where you live today, to reinforce the fact that the child now lives with *you*, that you are the now the important adult in the child's life. Rather than being stuck alone in the past, the child now lives in Denise's conscious awareness. Whenever there is a fear that someone will hurt her, Denise can feel the child's terror. She knows, now, that the terror is a signal to reach inside and comfort the child, perhaps to reach back across time and have another corrective interaction with her father.

BRINGING THE CHILD TO THE PRESENT

Bringing the child to the present is an important part of the process. In the timeless unconscious, the child continues to experience the original childhood environment as if it were the present. When current situations link back to that dysfunctional environment, the child doesn't realize that he or she lives with you, now, in a different place.

Another client, Kim, went back to explore the child's environment hypnotically, seeking a sense of the true self that child experienced on a daily basis. She was aware that she had been physically abused as a child, but much of the feeling of that time was absent from her memories.

The first thing Kim discovered was that the home in which she grew up felt cold and dangerous. She began the experience by "listening" to the rooms in that home with her hypnotic ears. She felt the very air of the place with all her hypnotic senses. Whenever you attune to your hypnotic senses, you create a keen awareness of what the child really experienced, opening up channels of unconscious memory, providing access to the child's buried truth. This is what happened to Kim.

She discovered a little girl at about the age of five. The child was in the bedroom, huddled under the bed. She was terrified of her stepmother, who would punish her with little cause and great enthusiasm. She was particularly frightened of her stepmother's harsh and grating voice, which conveyed the feeling of being beaten with a baseball bat.

During this particular experience, Kim's stepmother wasn't present in her room. It felt to Kim as if the little girl were perpetually hiding, seeking a safety she couldn't seem to find anywhere. I asked Kim, as the adult, if she would step into the scene and encourage the little girl to come out from under the bed. This took some doing. Because the child was bright, she wasn't about to trust an adult without some reassurance. What reassured her turned out to be a stuffed dog, a cuddly companion she had had for a number of years.

With some coaxing, the little girl came out from under the bed and sat next to Kim on the floor, holding on to the stuffed dog. As they sat together, Kim became increasingly conscious of the unpredictability of the abuse she experienced as a child. She felt how that unpredictability made everything feel so dangerous. She could never know when things might erupt and she would find herself in the middle of something she hadn't anticipated.

After a time, the little girl allowed herself to be brought to Kim's apartment. Kim sensed that the first thing to do was put the child to bed for a nap. Sitting on the edge of the bed stroking the little girl's hair, Kim realized that the child had lived a lifetime without ever really relaxing, without ever really letting go. As she continued to stroke the child's hair and speak soothingly, she noticed that the little girl's muscles began to loosen up. The child's breathing slowed and she fell into a deep sleep. Kim was struck by the realization that the child was having the first sound, secure nap she'd ever experienced.

Now that the child was safe, Kim and I took some time to explore how she was feeling as the adult. She became aware of a profound sadness that the child had lived her life in such a state of alertness and readiness, never having enough sense of safety to let down and relax. She felt the grief people often feel when they realize they have been robbed of the innocence of childhood.[10]

Kim also felt the ease and comfort the child was experiencing for the first time.

The impact of the child's experience on Kim is characteristic of the corrective regression work. As the child has new experiences of comfort, safety and support from the adult, the adult's internal experience shifts as well. Corrective regression is a powerful way to get back memories that are buried within the true self of the child, memories you may not be aware of at all.

For Kim, the corrective regression work she did with this abused child created a place of safety inside where this part of her can learn to let go and relax. For Denise, a place was created inside where she knows she can stand up for herself. As you might imagine, these internal attitudes and resources can be quite useful to draw on in your adult life.

Whenever you work with corrective regression or with the child in any context, you weave back and forth between past and present. Because the child experiences the present as if it *were* the past, the more you go back and intervene on the child's behalf, the more your present-day life will feel empowered and safe.

An important point to realize is that there will almost always be a particular physical feeling you get when you are identified with the child, experiencing some past pattern of interaction. When you learn to recognize the signals that are unique to you, you can use them to alert yourself to the fact that the child has been mobilized and feels at risk or is in need. You will have a tool that allows you to handle current situations in new ways, right on the spot.

So often, we get caught up in old patterns without realizing it. Once the signals are made conscious, we can reach inside and find out what is being triggered instead of playing out old patterns. With the adult's power and awareness, the child in you can be soothed. You can shift gears and respond to the situation in a more constructive, functional and self-protective way.

ABOUT THE EXERCISE

As you work with the following exercise, remember to allow yourself to accept whatever comes. Use your hypnotic eyes, ears, and sense of touch, taste and smell to increase your awareness of the child's truth. Sometimes, your hypnotic senses may convey subtle, barely noticeable qualities. At other times, you may receive vivid impressions. Whatever emerges fills in the blanks of the child's story.

Also, if you find yourself experiencing something that is difficult to believe, allow yourself to go along with the experience anyway. When doing hypnotic work, it's helpful to save the analyzing for later. Everything that comes to mind will either fit into the larger picture at some point or become a curiosity that may remain unresolved. It doesn't matter. What does matter is that you are taking the time and effort to connect with and help the child in you.

You will need from 20 to 30 minutes for this exercise. Remember to tape it, leaving pauses or turning off the tape recorder when you need more time between steps. Have some paper and a pen or pencil on hand to record your impressions when you've finished.

Exercise #7 Corrective Regression

[Use whatever self-hypnotic induction you'd like to begin the exercise.]*First, allow yourself to go to a safe, comfortable place where you can sit down for a while.* [pause]

Notice that nearby, much to your surprise, there's a scrapbook you haven't seen before. This scrapbook holds mementos of all the important events in your life, big and small, remembered and forgotten. It has inside it all the interactions and learnings that have had an impact on who you are and how you relate to yourself and others.

On the pages of the scrapbook, you may find photos, words, vague images and impressions, or blank spaces that seem to speak to you in a way you don't understand consciously.

Let yourself turn the pages, now, and discover that you seem to stop at a particular page with a scene or impression on it. You may or may not be conscious of it immediately. The main thing is to let yourself turn to whatever page your unconscious has chosen for this time. [pause]

Gently and easily, now, allow your mind to drift back across time, across space, to a time and a place depicted by, or related to, whatever you have discovered in the scrapbook. [pause]

Remember, you are going back there as the adult. You are going back as an observer to discover what you need to know about the child's truth. If you find yourself uncomfortable or afraid of going back alone, bring along the future self. [pause]

Allow yourself to observe where the child is and what is happening to the child. Let yourself watch the scene run through once or twice, observing what happened in whatever detail your unconscious gives you. As hard as it might be, let the scene unfold in exactly the way it happened back then. [pause]

If you begin to have intense feelings about the experience, allow them just to be there in your awareness, as you remain the adult. If the feeling seem to be too strong, just take a step back mentally and be the adult watching as if you were watching a movie. You'll have other opportunities to be aware of the child's feelings. Right now, the child needs you to be the adult. [pause]

Once you have a sense of what happened to the child and what the child felt, step in as the adult and do whatever is appropriate to protect the child. If you have difficulty knowing just what to do, imagine that the child is somebody else's and see what comes to mind. [long pause]

Remember to call on the future self if you find yourself afraid or uncomfortable about confronting the situation.

Take a moment, if you will, to become particularly aware of how the child is feeling with you there as a support. Is the child relieved? Is the child frightened that now things will get worse? Whatever the child is experiencing is fine. Allow yourself to accept that child's feeling. [pause]

When you feel you've done what is needed, bring the child back to the present with you. You may choose to bring the child to the safe place you are creating in your hypnotic world, or you may want to bring the child to your current home.

If the child has difficulty leaving the old environment, or if you feel guilty taking the child away, allow the future self to help you with this, also.

Give yourself permission to accept mixed feelings. Inevitably, you and the child will come together in the present. You are and will always be the most important person in the child's life. It's only a matter of time before the child experiences that fully. [pause]

Once you've brought the child to the present and you've spent some time together, notice how you're feeling and how the child is feeling.

Give the child permission to let you have a signal when the child needs you. It may be a certain body sensation . . . a tight stomach or nausea . . . a headache or just a feeling of dread. Take a moment, now, to discover what the signal is. [long pause]

Leaving a part of you there with the child to continue developing the relationship you are creating, bring yourself back to a fully alert state when you're ready.

Take a moment, now, to write down your experience.

As you do the corrective regression work, you'll find that you can go back to the same, or similar, experiences many times. There will always be new things to discover as you move beyond the child's false self adaptations and explore more of the child's truth. You can create many opportunities to add positive new learnings to your psychological history, learnings you will draw on in your adult life as resources you didn't realize you had.

In the next chapter, you'll have an opportunity to address two especially important aspects of the child within: the infant and the shamed child. As you work with these particularly needy and vulnerable parts of you, it's helpful to draw on some of the new, more positive and affirming responses that have emerged in your prior experiences with the child-within.

Chapter 7

~~

BONDING WITH THE INFANT AND HEALING THE SHAMED CHILD

The ability to self-soothe is a fundamental aspect of psychological well-being.[1] Because of the chaos and mixed messages inherent in most dysfunctional families, many adult children lack the ability to self-soothe adequately. When life presents challenges, they often experience an intensity of distress that feels excessive and out of control—or a depth of hopelessness and futility that seems overwhelmingly powerful.

Two aspects of the child within are especially related to self-soothing. Their need is such that I'd like to give them special attention.

First, there is the part of you that, as an infant, may have entered a world filled with emotional turbulence, interpersonal chaos, parental neglect, anxiety, rage or fear. Calm reassurance and a timely response to an infant's needs are essential to easing the distress that often accompanies cries for caretaking. Instead, you may have been left to cry or responded to harshly. This may have left you even more distressed and overwhelmed.

The second child within who needs special attention is the

part of you that experienced, and continues to feel, deep shame. This child cannot bear to be exposed. To do so would risk humiliation, which feels too painful. This is a child who feels he or she is inherently a bad person. If you have a shamed child inside, you probably know it. You may have compulsive behaviors that serve as attempts to soothe the shame, behaviors that can take the form of addictions to alcohol, drugs, shopping, sex, reading, work or other activities that focus you outside yourself. When you are with other people, you may find that you feel defensive or deeply vulnerable when criticized.[2]

These children in us cry out for soothing. They cry out for someone to take care of them and love them just as they are. Their cries can be recognized when you, as an adult, find yourself in an escalating, seemingly uncontrollable spiral of emotions. Someone may hurt your feelings and you just can't let go of your anger or sadness. You may experience fears you can't quell. No matter how often you promise yourself you'll eat well, you may ignore your basic needs and neglect yourself. You may find that you experience a repetitive pattern of getting close to people and then feeling hurt or angry when they let you down. Are you a person who defends herself at all cost, always having to find someone else to blame? Maybe you avoid conflict and risk altogether, feeling that the cost of being humiliated is too high. Or you may have become a perfectionist, refusing to do anything until you can do it perfectly or blaming yourself harshly when you make mistakes.

Because self-soothing is so important as an internal, reliable regulator of feeling states, developing this ability can be invaluable. Most of us have had times when we've felt out of control, times when our emotions seemed to run away with us. It's like the tail wagging the dog, and it can be extraordinarily uncomfortable.

As you learn to self-soothe, you develop an unconscious mechanism that can respond when you're triggered. It operates to calm you, even when you're not consciously aware of it. By developing the ability to self-soothe, you learn to love yourself even when you make mistakes, even when you're not perfect. You may even learn to laugh at yourself when you do something ridiculous, or when someone else points out a flaw in your performance.

If the infant in you experienced neglect, rather than chaos, you have an opportunity to create an unconscious expectation that you count, that someone will be there for you when you have needs. Remember, *you* are the most important person in that child's world. *You* are the one person who can promise that you'll always be there when needed.

You can learn to listen to your needs and honor them. If you're one of those people who ignores your body's signals to rest, you may discover that you can learn to enjoy quiet time. You can be less afraid of missing out on something and realize that your well-being is as important as anything else. If you're a person who always gives away whatever money you have, leaving yourself in debt in the process, you can learn that it's all right to use your money for your own needs.

SOOTHING THE INFANT IN YOU

Let's look first at soothing the infant in you. For a moment, recall the two infants in Chapter 2. One had a mother who was calm and able to deal with her child's needs and demands. When her baby cried, she responded appropriately and took care of whatever was required. The other mother was anxious and insecure about how to take care of her baby. When her child cried or became distressed, she felt increasingly anxious, sometimes even irritated or angry. Because of the mother's response, the baby's distress also increased, leaving the child in a heightened state of anxiety.

One infant learned to self-soothe by internalizing the calm, reassuring responses that came from a caretaking adult. The other infant experienced escalating distress, with no soothing available from outside. When there's no soothing from the outside, the infant has no opportunity to internalize it for self-soothing later in life.

Some people, when regressed hypnotically, return symbolically to an experience of being in the womb, prior to birth. Using the retrospective awareness of their adult perspective, they experience their mother's state of mind and feelings about them before they were born. While metaphorical, these experiences often create a means for understanding and resolving unconscious conflicts, as well as uncovering patterns of interaction that were too subtle to identify consciously.

An example of this kind of retrospective, imaginary experience occurred with a client named Theresa. Theresa had always felt abandoned by people who were important to her. Whenever she felt that someone preferred another friend to her, she became angry and depressed, and seemed unable to stop her spiraling reaction. From early on, Theresa felt that her mother didn't really love her, that her mother was detached from her. Many times, she would be left in a playpen alone for hours. Her mother worked and was often gone from home. Theresa was well-fed and well-dressed as a child, but she had a pervasive experience that her mother didn't care about her.

When she went back in trance, she found herself experiencing a time before birth. She became aware of her mother's fear around the pregnancy. She sensed that her mother was constantly afraid of the upcoming birth and approached it with dread. In trance, Theresa realized that her mother was frightened about the possibility of losing another child.

Theresa explained that it had always been known in the family that her mother's first child was a stillborn daughter, whose birth occurred two years before her own. What she hadn't known, though, was how this event had colored her mother's anticipation of another child. As she explored the feelings she'd uncovered in trance, Theresa realized that her mother was so terrified of losing another child that she couldn't allow herself to bond with her second child.

As the trance progressed, Theresa reexperienced her birth and then, as the adult, reached out to the newborn infant. She was deeply relieved by what she had experienced. With her relief came pain and compassion for her mother's loss. As a grown woman herself, she could realize fully how devastating it must have been for her mother to lose a first child in that way. Theresa also realized how impossible it would have been, as a child, ever to have gotten her mother's love in the ways she needed.

Now, in response to this "memory," Theresa spent time with the infant each day, holding her, talking to her, paying attention to her. A priority was to make eye contact and to bond with the infant, to let the infant know that Theresa was present and available. Over time, Theresa developed an increasing ability to calm herself when she felt abandoned. At times when she couldn't break free of her reaction, she would feel that old, familiar anger and depression. What she also discovered, though, was that the reactions were of much shorter duration. She began to bounce back more quickly—another indication of her more effective ability to self-soothe.

Suzanne's experience was different. She presented as an individual who was highly fearful. Almost anything made her afraid: the dark, other people, new situations, and change of almost any kind. She spent a good deal of time feeling anxious. As she went back in trance, she found herself, as the infant, in the delivery room at the hospital where she was born. She was extremely distressed and had a sensation of being dropped and caught roughly. She seemed to be experiencing a "body memory" of hands around her ribs, grabbing her. She felt startled by such rough handling.

When Suzanne took on the adult's perspective and looked at the infant in the delivery room, she described a child who was crying loudly, gasping for breath between cries. As she reached out for the infant, she was immediately aware of the tension in the baby's body. She described the infant as red and wrinkled, and very distressed. She began to massage the baby's arms and legs, focusing on how small the infant was in comparison to her own adult body. She had learned somewhere that newborn infants respond positively to gentle, and yet confident, stroking. As Suzanne massaged arms and legs, the infant's muscle tension began to ease. Suzanne also began to talk to the infant in soothing tones and to rock her. It took time, but after a while the infant stopped crying. Her color became less intensely red and she began to relax. Eventually, the infant looked at Suzanne and contact was made.

Just after this regression, Suzanne had another intriguing experience, which other people have reported as well. She found herself laughing in a new way. It was a laugh that just bubbled up from somewhere deep inside. People at work told her she seemed somehow "lighter." She felt it, too, but she couldn't explain it. She also found that she tended to smile more after she had spent time with the infant, whenever she was able to help her relax and feel comforted.

Over time, Suzanne reported a lessening of her anxiety state. She began to feel less fearful and discovered, after several years of working with all the children in her, that she had developed an ability to soothe herself that had been totally lacking in the past. She attributed much of her newfound ability with self-soothing to the work she had done with the infant. Such basic insecurity had required her to go back to the very beginning.

For Glen, the experience of connecting with his infant brought up feelings of a different sort. His first reaction was anger. The infant represented the beginning of a long history of abuse. He wasn't pleased to be reminded of how small and vulnerable he had been when it all began. Deep inside he had always blamed himself for the abuse. It felt safer to tell himself he could have made it stop if he had only figured out how to be good enough.

By accepting the anger and exploring its meaning, Glen eventually was able to connect with, and tolerate, the infant's helplessness and neediness. As he developed a relationship with the infant, he began to recognize and resolve the terror he had always had whenever he felt needy or vulnerable with other people.

Glen's experience underscores, again, how important it is to accept whatever your experience when you contact the child within. If you feel anger—or any other negative emotion—as you meet the child, allow it. Explore it. It has something important to tell you. If you find yourself blaming—or wanting to attack, hit, or ignore—the child, allow yourself to explore these feelings. Ask yourself who may have felt this way toward you when you were young. Ask what feels so unacceptable about the child. The answers that come to mind may well reflect messages you took in growing up.

Sometimes, it's hard to define exactly what you're feeling when you react negatively to the child. All you may know is that you're not comfortable, or you wish you were anywhere else. The last thing you may want to do is respond with caring and tenderness. If you find yourself in this kind of situation during the following exercise, it's helpful to call on the future self for assistance. This part of you is a reliable resource and can help you if you get stuck and don't know what to do to soothe the infant. Also, remember that, if you can't seem to get beyond a negative response, you can imagine the infant as someone else's and discover what you would do then. You may find that a more empathic response becomes possible.

ABOUT THE EXERCISE

In the next exercise, you'll have an opportunity to meet the infant in you. You may find that, after using the exercise several times, you won't need to follow all the steps. It may be enough simply to be with the infant for a period of time each day, perhaps even just a few minutes. After a while, you may not need to contact the infant so often. What this exercise offers is a means to create a foundation of connection and self-soothing that will, in time, be available to you in an ongoing way. Once you have built it into your unconscious repertoire of responses, you can connect with the infant for the pure pleasure of having contact, rather than for the healing work of developing self-soothing.

As with the other exercises in the book, it's best to tape record this one. Remember to speak slowly and softly when you record the exercise, leaving space for inner work when you read the instruction to [pause]. Be sure to have your paper and pencil handy so you can jot down notes about your experience.

Exercise #8   Bonding with the Infant

[Put yourself into trance in whatever way is best this time. Find yourself at your safe place.]

Once you've settled in, allow your mind to begin to drift back . . . across time . . . across space. Allow yourself to drift all the way back to the beginning . . . to a hospital . . . or a home . . . or somewhere else where there is a newborn infant waiting for you. [long pause] *Just allow impressions of moving back in time to come to the front of your mind. You may just suddenly be there, with no awareness of movement at all.* [pause] *The infant that awaits is you on the first day of your life.* [pause]

You may discover how easy it is to just keep drifting right into that infant . . . to become the infant. [pause]

As that infant, where are you? [pause] *Are you warm . . . or cold?* [pause] *Is there noise, or is it quiet where you are?* [pause] *Are you being supported in some way?* [pause] *Are you lying on some surface? Is it hard . . . or soft?* [pause] *If you have any difficulty experiencing yourself as the infant, allow yourself to wonder what that experience would be like if you could have it.* [pause]

As you continue to be the infant, you may have a sensation or some other awareness that invites you to notice it. Simply let yourself be aware of whatever is there.

And now, if it's all right with you, become the adult you are today. Notice your surroundings and how you feel as you look at the infant. [pause]

What responses arise in you spontaneously, without thought? [pause] *Remember to allow whatever comes into your experience. Every response has meaning and is a gift from the unconscious.* [pause]

It may be helpful to ask your future self to join you, now. Perhaps you could reach out and pick up the infant. How do you feel about that? Does it feel good to imagine holding the infant? Does it make you uncomfortable? [pause]

If it's all right with you, take the infant in your arms, now. If you don't feel comfortable with that, you might allow your future self to hold the child, instead. If your future self is holding the child, give yourself an opportunity to observe how the future self responds. You might even become the future self for a moment to experience how it feels to respond positively to the infant. [pause]

Is the infant agitated, or sleeping? [pause] Remember that the birth process is extremely stressful. It might be soothing to massage the infant's arms and legs, with your fingertips, gently and with confidence. Imagine how this would feel if you were actually experiencing the touch of skin on skin . . . the movement and pressure of your fingers on small, tight muscles. [pause] Notice the difference in size between your hands and the baby's hands, between your arms and the baby's arms. [pause]

You may also find an alert, eager infant . . . a child ready to be held, ready to relate to you. If this is the infant you discover, it's nice to know that you can give yourself permission to enjoy the infant's fresh energy and curiosity. This is an infant who has yet to experience the stress that may live in its future. [pause]

If you find that the infant is sleeping, you may discover that contact with you will awaken the child. Become aware of the infant's internal state when awake. If the baby becomes distressed, use a soothing tone of voice and a soothing touch to offer some comfort. [pause]

Notice that there may come a moment when the infant looks at you and makes eye contact. Remember that you are the first, and most important, mirror in this infant's life. Allow yourself to wear a face that reflects your love and acceptance. [long pause]

Whenever you have contact with the infant, you are a mirror. Your tone of voice, as well as your face, convey needed messages of welcome and love.

When you're ready, bring the infant back to your safe place. Remember, you are the most important person in this infant's life. The infant lives with you now, in your present. [pause]

It's helpful to give yourself the suggestion, now, that you will notice a physical sensation, or a thought that drops into your mind, that is a distress signal from the infant . . . a way you can know that the infant needs you. [pause]

For now, take a moment to let your unconscious gather together all that you've experienced and tuck it away in that safe place in the back of your mind where new responses are created. [pause] *And, let yourself wonder, for a minute, just how surprised you may be to discover that you are learning to soothe yourself, that you are becoming calmer than you ever thought you could be.* [pause]

Be sure to leave a part of you there with the infant. This is the part of you that is always connected with the infant, the part that listens to that child's needs and lets you know when self-soothing is essential. [pause] *If your future self has accompanied you on this journey, you can let that part of you also be aware of the infant's need . . . and be available to help you discover the best ways to create soothing responses.*

When you're ready, bring the rest of you all the way back to a fully alert state, now. To be sure you're all the way back, wiggle your fingers and toes and realize that the nice thing to know is that you can return to your safe place anytime you want.

THE SHAMED CHILD

The presence of a shamed child inside is painfully common among adult children of dysfunctional families. The impact of the shamed child is so profound that developing a positive, loving relationship with this part of you is a core piece of reclaiming yourself. To have a shamed child inside creates the potential for feeling alienated from yourself. It promotes the experience of disliking yourself, of feeling that you are a bad person, or of having a part of you you don't want anyone else to discover. Sometimes, you may not even know that the shamed child exists. You only know that you can't bear to be alone with yourself or to have quiet time where you would have to listen to that still, small voice inside. You may only know that you have an irresistible urge to fill your time with activity, with anything that takes you outside yourself. It would be too painful to have to look, to have to see.[3]

The shamed child is a part of adult children that is hidden away, deep inside. It's a part of us that is frightened of humiliation and is painfully vulnerable to exposure, disapproval—to any kind of psychological injury. It is a part of us that we dare not see. We are convinced that, were we to look the shamed child fully in the face, we would see the terrible person we fear we must be. Often, the shamed child is buried as far away from conscious awareness as we can push it. Instead of consciously knowing how bad we feel about ourselves, we engage in self-destructive behaviors that demonstrate our underlying feelings of shame.

Developing a relationship with the shamed child creates a context for increasing self-esteem. The process involves remembering, listening to and acknowledging the child's story. It asks you to look deeply into yourself and accept what is reflected there. You have an opportunity to experience, for yourself, that children aren't born feeling ashamed of themselves. They learn to label themselves as inherently bad as a result of interactions with other people. Getting to know the shamed child within allows you to know that your basic humanness, with all its frailties and strengths, is worthwhile, rather than something flawed and humiliating.

Dysfunctional families create a fertile ground for the seeds of shame. If you were abused as a child—physically, emotionally or sexually—you know shame. If you were humiliated, "teased," criticized or made to feel guilty when you expressed needs of your own, you know shame. If your parents demanded that you meet their needs, telling you that you were selfish or ungrateful whenever you attempted to meet your own, you know shame.

Frank knew shame all too well. His father had a need always to be right. Whenever Frank had a different opinion, his father became enraged and demanded that his son respect him. He called Frank "stupid," "ungrateful," "full of pride" for thinking he knew so much. Frank would blame himself for disagreeing with his father. He couldn't figure out why had felt so compelled to say "no" or to say anything at all. When his father told him to eat spinach, which Frank hated, why couldn't he just eat it instead of saying "no"? Why did he have to dislike some of the things his father wanted for him? Why, when his father said the pool water was warm, couldn't Frank just take his word?' Why did Frank have to feel cold in the water . . . and say so? These things were hard to figure out and all Frank really knew was that he was totally unacceptable in his father's eyes. Because he was like most children, he blamed himself and felt terribly guilty for making his father angry. Frank had no way of realizing that his father also had been a shamed child and couldn't tolerate the humiliation of being wrong.

As Frank explored and accepted the fact that he was never able to get his own needs met, he softened towards the shamed child. He realized that it is natural for children to have their own opinions and wishes. It is natural for them to want to do things differently from the way their parents want them done. He began to see the shame in his father and was able to let go of his self-blame and his guilt for being a bad son. He accepted his true self, with all the imperfections that exist in any human being, and developed a greater ability to state his needs clearly without feeling he was being selfish or insensitive.

He also was able to overcome an urge to blame his father. An important part of freeing yourself from shame is to realize that blame of any kind perpetuates more shame and binds you to a feeling of being a victim. For the child within, nothing is served when you, the adult, also feel helpless and powerless to change things.

I often describe the shamed child as a part of us that lives in a closet, hidden away where no one can find it. Most of us go to great lengths to keep that closet door closed. The false self is created to keep the door locked. If you have such a locked place inside, and if it is ever opened even slightly, you may feel extraordinarily vulnerable, embarrassed, guilty, or ashamed. You may find that you feel compelled to defend yourself whenever anyone criticizes you. It's as though someone has to take the blame. If that someone turns out to be you, it painfully confirms the bad feelings you already had about yourself.

As you explore the exercise for contacting the shamed child, you may find that your first encounter is with a symbolic representation of this part of you. The characteristics conveyed by the symbol are, of course, unique for each individual. There are some common symbols, though, that you may discover. The shamed child can appear as a worm-like creature that is shaded, dark, or pale, like an earthworm. Another possibility is to discover a lifeless form of some sort. It may be a rag doll with no energy or animation. It may be an emaciated child who is folded over, unable to move. Sometimes, people get enraged when they meet the shamed child. A few have wanted to harm the child or get rid of this part of themselves altogether. At times, the self-blame is so strong that it's hard even to look at the shamed child.

When you engage the process of getting to know the shamed child, it's helpful to remember all the things you've learned about accepting whatever comes as important information. The resulting relief of coming to terms with the shamed child and learning to love this part of you is real, lasting, and well worth the journey.

It's also helpful to remember that your future self is an important resource here. A nurturing relationship exists already between the future self and the shamed child. You can draw on the ease and self-acceptance your future self has already developed in response to this part of you. Remember, the underlying purpose in creating more conscious relationships with all the parts of you is to increase your level of self-acceptance, your ability to love yourself. As you embrace the shamed child, you will take many large steps towards accomplishing this purpose.

CONTACTING THE SHAMED CHILD

When Jennifer first contacted the shamed child within, she found, lying on the road in front of her, an armadillo without its shell. The armadillo was badly bruised and terribly sensitive to being touched. At first, Jennifer didn't know what to do. Then, she realized that she had to pick up the armadillo if the healing process were ever to begin.

Carefully, she cradled the armadillo in her arms, and she began to cry. All at once, she was aware of a part of herself that was frightened and in deep pain. It was a part of her that felt she was a terrible person, convinced that if anyone ever really saw inside her they would find her hateful and disgusting. The depth of this conviction surprised Jennifer, although she recognized the feeling as a familiar one.

The bruises on the armadillo that were so deep, and so dark, represented the depth of Jennifer's psychological wounds. She had always known that she was acutely sensitive to criticism. She always seemed to react with rapid defensiveness whenever anyone implied that she might have done something wrong. She tended to feel judged and blamed when someone pointed out that she seemed to be angry or hostile. Even so, it shocked her to realize that she was this deeply wounded.

Jennifer held the armadillo for several minutes of trance time every day for several weeks, opening herself to the pain in that wounded part. In time, the armadillo became a little girl, about four years old. She had a darkness about her face, as if she were in shadows. It was difficult to see any of her features. As time passed, and as Jennifer kept her contact with the shamed child, things began to happen. Forgotten childhood memories began to surface. Most of the memories dealt with sexual abuse she thought she had worked through. The more she related to the shamed child, the more able she was to accept memories that were locked away with that part of her.

In time, the child's face became lighter and Jennifer could see her features. The child began to relate more actively. Because she was willing to remember and to accept the origins of her shame, Jennifer reclaimed a part of herself that had been unavailable all her life. She also got in touch with rage she hadn't been able to accept before. What liberated her most was the level of self-acceptance she developed after working with the shamed child. Her ability to tolerate criticism increased. She even learned to be less defensive in her interactions with others. Instead of feeling a need to explain herself, she gave herself soothing comments. She would tell herself she was okay, that it was normal to make mistakes, and that she shouldn't expect herself to be perfect all the time.

An important aspect of Jennifer's self-soothing was to remind the child that other people have a right to have, and sometimes a need to express, their own reactions. If they are critical or angry, that's okay, too. The shamed child had always experienced people's negative reactions as having something to do with her, as further evidence that she was bad. Now, Jennifer could reassure the child, telling her she was safe and that she didn't have to make it better when other people were upset. Jennifer's soothing presence allowed the child to rely on the adult part of her to handle difficult interactions. She was no longer alone. She no longer had to take it on herself.

ANOTHER SHAMED CHILD

For Bruce, a busy, up-and-coming salesman, the shamed child was a surprise to discover. Growing up, Bruce had been encouraged to be good. In his family, explosive, conflicted or angry feelings were never allowed. In fact, Bruce presented himself, always, as polite and eager to please.

When we went back to find the shamed child, Bruce found him sitting in a chair, curled up in a ball. The child wouldn't respond to words or touch. He just curled up even more tightly. As Bruce explored what the shamed child felt, he found himself aware of anger and disappointment that he'd never before acknowledged. In his family, these feelings would never have been validated. In fact, they would have been totally unacceptable, so Bruce had never learned to accept them as normal. Instead, he felt like a bad person whenever these kinds of feelings bubbled up into his awareness. As with most children from families where conflict isn't allowed, Bruce hardly ever even let himself know he had such feelings.

Over time, Bruce's presence began to change the posture of the shamed child. He uncurled, but still hid his face. What surprised Bruce was that another child within, one with which he had built a reliable, ongoing relationship, showed up in his work with the shamed child. The presence of this other child helped, giving the shamed child more confidence in Bruce as a trustworthy adult.

Eventually, the shamed child lifted his head and looked at Bruce. As the relationship developed, Bruce experienced more memories of his childhood and got in touch with feelings he had buried long ago. Most importantly, he began to accept himself in a new way. No longer did he experience mistakes or embarrassing moments with shame. Instead, they became part and parcel of a normal adult life, part and parcel of the ups and downs that comprise healthy, active living.

ABOUT THE EXERCISE

As you work with the following exercise, be sure to allow any mixed feelings that may emerge towards the shamed child in you. Some people find that, as the shamed child begins to come to life, they feel uncomfortable. They've become accustomed to the shame, the guilt, the feelings of being bad. They buried the energy of that part of them a long time ago. Sometimes, when the shamed child expresses curiosity, or energy, or a sense of well-being, at first it doesn't feel safe. If you have feelings like this, acknowledge them. It may actually have been potentially dangerous for this part of you to realize its own power when you were young. The fact that it's safe now, with you, will dawn on both of you in your own best time.

Developing a relationship with the shamed child occurs over time, with regular contact. At some point, you'll have an inner sense that the healing work has been done. The child within that previously held your shame will become a resource, a reservoir of energy and creativity you'll draw on unconsciously. You'll discover, also, that remnants of the child's shame will emerge only occasionally. When they do, you can respond by reaching inside with reassurance and soothing comments.

As with the other exercises, I recommend that you tape record this one. Also, be sure to have your paper and pencil available to note aspects of the experience you want to remember.

Exercise #9 Healing the Shamed Child in You

[Put yourself into trance in whatever way works best for you. Discover a special area in your safe place that is particularly private, particularly quiet. Let it be a place that feels especially supportive and healing.]

As you take a nice, deep breath, now, and settle even further, allow the shamed child to be there, in front of you. You may find that this part of you initially reveals itself in symbolic form . . . or as a child within. [pause]

If you find that your mind is blank, recall the creative void. Accept the blankness as a message from your unconscious that it is still searching for just the right impression to give you. You might wonder, for a moment, what the impression would be if your unconscious were to present it to you now. [pause] *Maybe it's nice to know that, right now, there is nothing to do, nothing to change. All you have to do is be receptive to what your unconscious wants to give you.* [long pause]

Once an impression does drop into your awareness, let it be as vivid or as vague as it appears to you, now. Remember, even vague awarenesses develop clarity as you explore them. [pause] *What does the shamed part of you look like? What main characteristics or qualities of that shamed child invite your attention first?* [long pause]

If the shamed part of you appears as a creature instead of a child, what are the characteristics of that creature? [pause]

What is your first response to the shamed part of you? [pause]
Accept whatever comes. [pause]

What is your second response? [pause] *Are there any other
feelings?* [pause]

*If it's all right with you, take a moment, now, and become the
shamed child. Perhaps you are curious about what it is like to be
this child. Or, maybe you have some other responses to experiencing the shamed part of you from the inside.* [pause]

*Do you notice any difference when you look at the child from
the outside and when you become that part of you?* [long pause]
*Sometimes, the experience of being inside the shamed child can
be different from what you expect. You might wonder just what
the unexpected awareness may be that come to mind as you
explore the internal experience of this part of you now.* [long
pause]

*After you've experienced this part of you from the inside,
become your adult self again. What do you feel, now, in response
to the shamed child in you? Are you moved? Do you feel compassion . . . sadness . . . discomfort? Simply accept whatever is in
your experience now.* [pause]

*If it's all right with you, reach out in some meaningful way to
that shamed part. If you need help with this, ask your future self
to show you, or tell you, what to do.* [pause]

*If you can, at this point, give yourself permission to open your
heart to this part of you. Even if it's painful, or elicits mixed
feelings, imagine, for a moment, what it would be like if you
could let yourself open up in this way to a part of you that has
been buried for so long. Accept whatever comes as you do this.*
[long pause]

*Realize, from somewhere way in the back of your mind, that
this part of you has a story to tell about how it came to be this
way.* [pause] *Let yourself wonder how it will feel to remember
. . . to embrace the story of the shamed child.* [pause]

*Take whatever amount of time you'd like, now, simply to be
with the shamed part of you. Give yourself permission to explore
the entire range of feelings you have right now.* [long pause]

*Allow yourself to realize that each time you reach inside to
embrace the shamed child, you open yourself further to remem-*

bering . . . to bringing into your conscious mind an awareness of how the shame came to be there.

Ask your unconscious, now, to guide the process in whatever way is healthiest and most positive for you. Remember that way back there, in that safe place in the back of your mind, your unconscious creates new learnings, new understandings and new responses that are positive and constructive in your life . . . responses that will emerge in your own best time, in your own best ways, and always when they are best for you. There is no rush . . . no hurry. The process of healing the shamed child will unfold in your own best time . . . in your own best ways. [pause]

When you're ready, allow a part of you to remain there, with the shamed child. The healing process continues, even as your conscious mind focuses on other things.

And, you might tell yourself that whenever you feel the old, familiar responses arising from the shamed child within, allow yourself to reach inside and reassure that part of you. Notice that the more you soothe and reassure this part, the more self-assured and comfortable you feel in daily interactions in the world. [pause]

It's hard to say just how soon you'll notice the first shift. Will it be right away . . . or will it surprise you by seeming to come out of nowhere just when you need it most? [pause]

Also, you might wonder just when you'll first notice changes in the shamed child as the healing process takes place. And, what changes occur in you as the healing process continues. If you have any discomfort as the child's energy increases, acknowledge that. The old family myth that you are a bad, shameful person is being dismantled . . . and, this sometimes touches new, different, and maybe even strange feelings. [pause]

When you're ready, now, bring yourself back, with the suggestion that your unconscious will keep right on developing the healing process you have engaged. Wiggle your fingers and toes to bring yourself all the way back.

It's important to realize that, for most of us, deep wounds and old vulnerabilities create areas in our response repertoires that may always have some sensitivity to certain kinds of events and interactions. The nice thing to know is that, once you're aware of these "rocks in the road," you are prepared to deal with them more effectively. Ultimately, you are the only person in the world who can give the wounded parts of you the validation, love and acceptance you have always deserved. When you stub your toes on rocks you thought you'd moved out of the way, be kind to yourself. Discover that there may come a time when you respond to your vulnerabilities with amusement and gentle humor, and learn to laugh with yourself when familiar rocks in the road unexpectedly resurface in front of you and demand your attention.

The shamed child and the infant are central elements in your process of reclaiming the self and healing old wounds. As you work with each of these parts, you give yourself the gift of an internalized sense of well-being that wasn't available when you were young. It is the most precious of gifts, and I wish for you the inner calm, ease and confidence that come when you know you are a good, worthwhile person—even when you do things you wish you had done differently.

Remember that you are constantly available to yourself—all the time—and you have an innate ability to go inside and be with yourself whenever the need or desire arises. You really *can* provide the kind of support you have always deserved, no matter how powerful the family myths and early learnings you were given, subjects we'll turn to next.

Chapter 8

THE POWER OF FAMILY MYTHS

When we are children, the creation of the false self is necessitated, in large part, by a need to conform to the myths the family holds about itself. All families create myths. Some myths are positive and give you a warm, supportive feeling when you think of them. Good feelings may come when you recall certain family stories about seas of adversity that were navigated successfully. They may come when you think of a certain saying a family member had that always made you feel better.

Some family myths seem positive when you're young and are only called into question as you develop your own sense of self, with your own preferences. In fact, part of the power family myths exert on a continuing basis is that they are presented as positive, when, actually, they create problems for you. For instance, imagine that your family has a myth that defines you as a tight knit group. You have no reason not to believe the myth. If you have brothers or sisters, maybe you were all dressed alike.

This seemed proof positive that you were close—you looked the same. Maybe you were told that you came from a long line of musicians, and your parents started you with piano lessons as a very young child. The only problem is that no one asked you if you liked piano and, in reality, you detested it. In fact, as a young child, you much preferred building model airplanes to playing piano.

As this child, you might have quickly discovered that having a different preference was interpreted as being disloyal to the family. With your child's mind, you couldn't know that the family myth of closeness reflected other people's likes and dislikes, values and beliefs. Instead, whenever you met with disapproval, it felt like you were being a bad person. You had no way of conceptualizing the fact that your likes and dislikes might just have been different. With this scenario, you could grow up continuing to think that your family was very close, rather than realizing that your family had difficulty dealing with difference. In fact, you might still value the myth of closeness and experience deep guilt whenever you want to do something that someone else may not want to do.

By the time you were 11 or 12, you may have felt compelled to question family myths about privacy. You may have never before felt such a need to have your parents not know everything about you. At this point, you may have realized that you had learned a major myth about closeness: to be close meant your mother had the right to read your mail or listen in on your phone calls. It may also have meant that you still had to leave the bathroom door unlocked.

If you expressed your discomfort with these established forms of closeness, you may have been surprised to discover that your parents were unhappy with you. You may have learned, whether through overt punishment or quiet disapproval, that you had to push away your own wishes if you wanted to be acceptable and fit in with the family. You had to support the family myth to avoid being rejected . . . or engage in a struggle for autonomy that may have left you feeling like a troublemaker, or bad in some other way.

THE FUNCTION OF FAMILY MYTHS

Family myths, for all the potential problems they may represent, serve important purposes in all families.[1] They create a shared world view, which promotes harmony among family members. They enhance conformity to norms and values. They transmit beliefs about the world and self. They control family members through loyalty, guilt, humiliation, or punishment whenever norms and values are transgressed. Family myths are a way to pass along traditions and a sense of togetherness across time. They define a context of acceptance and belonging, as well as conveying a sense of what is normal.

FAMILY INJUNCTIONS AS HYPNOTIC SUGGESTIONS

Combined, all of the expectations, attitudes, values, norms and beliefs of a family create powerful *injunctions* that become, in some ways, inescapable post-hypnotic suggestions. These injunctions act on you unconsciously and create shared *perceptual filters* through which each family member experiences others and the world at large. Your perceptual filter is the "lens" through which you take in and interpret experience.[2]

Each of us has a lens that has been shaped by growing up in our particular families. You can think of this lens as if it were a large tapestry. All of the elements that are embedded in family injunctions are like threads in the tapestry. Part of the process of recreating yourself is to examine your perceptual filter and change it, to reweave the tapestry with new threads to form a new pattern. To do this, it is essential to discover the injunctions that were transmitted to you within the context of your daily family interactions. When you do this, you discover the beliefs and expectations that are the individual threads of the tapestry. *Then* you have the ability to choose which to keep, which to eliminate, and what new ones you'd like to add.

As post-hypnotic suggestions, family injunctions are followed by most of us unconsciously.[3] Often, we only become aware of these injunctions when our steps forward, into experiences or contexts different from our family's, cause discomfort or fear. In this chapter, we'll focus on injunctions and myths, looking both at their obvious content *and* at the powerful unspoken beliefs, values and norms that underlie them.

THE VARIETIES OF FAMILY INJUNCTIONS

There are as many variations in family injunctions as there are people in families. Certain themes show up, though, in a large sample of injunctions. Over the years, I have had the opportunity to gather together hundreds of examples of these family messages in my *Recreating the Self* workshops. In the workshops, participants are asked to list, on large sheets of newsprint, family injunctions that have given them the most trouble or have been the most influential. At the end of the exercise, the sheets of paper are taped on the walls, creating a gallery of family injunctions. It's always noteworthy to see how similar the themes are that appear on those sheets of paper, how familiar the sayings. There is a moment in nearly every workshop when you can hear a pin drop, the time when everyone is reading the injunctions. Someone always makes at least one comment about what a miracle it is that we make it as well as we do in spite of them!

For the exercises you'll be doing in this chapter, family myths and injunctions fall into several categories. You'll explore both positive and negative injunctions, as well as look at family myths that encourage denial and discourage development and change. In the next chapter, you'll have an opportunity to choose whether you want to continue to carry the beliefs, myths and injunctions your family passed along to you. You'll have an opportunity to "give back" any you decide you don't want.

While you'll define both positive and negative family myths

and injunctions in this chapter, emphasis will be placed on those that have held you back in life.[4]

FAMILY MYTHS ABOUT THE WORLD

In most families, there are myths and injunctions about the nature of the world outside. For some lucky people, family beliefs describe a benevolent world where each person has a right and ability to achieve whatever she wants. For others, family beliefs convey messages about the inherent dangers in the world, about how you can't trust people who aren't family. These kinds of beliefs are bolstered by myths that are told repeatedly.

A personal experience that occurred a few years ago convinced me of the post-hypnotic power of family injunctions. Growing up, I recall hearing the phrase, "Life begins at 40." I heard it as a positive statement, although I never thought much about it on a conscious level. When I awakened on the morning of my 40th birthday, I sensed an excitement I couldn't define. I just knew that, beginning that day, my life would be better than ever before. This was such a powerful post-hypnotic suggestion for me that my unconscious acted on the belief that my life would begin in earnest with this birthday. It was as though I could finally give myself permission to move ahead, professionally and personally, which I did with a new kind of enthusiasm and confidence. Giving yourself permission to succeed is an important subject, and we'll return to it in a later chapter.

An important distinction when considering family myths lies with the differences between functional and dysfunctional families. In functional, adaptive families, beliefs about individuals and the world tend to promote individual autonomy, healthy intimacy, and a sense of power in the world. In dysfunctional families, beliefs often shore up a denial system that says the Emperor *does* have clothes, while the child who dares to speak the truth about the Emperor's nakedness is punished or ostracized.

The injunctions found in functional families tend to have a more positive impact on development than those in dysfunctional families. Functional families tend to have flexible rules and roles. They are apt to respond to developmental challenges creatively. For example, as a child grows older, bedtime is moved to a later hour. As the child matures, more autonomy is granted. Because there tends to be a high tolerance for difference, opinions and wishes are valued even when there may be disagreement. The modeling and messages received by a child in a functional family tend to promote open communication, a search for solutions to problems, and a willingness to bring outsiders into the system.

In dysfunctional families, myths often are told that promote beliefs in the importance of strong family "loyalty." Children might be told, for instance, that "blood is thicker than water," so you can only trust family. When "family" is experienced in an abusive environment, the child has to wrestle with the fact that the only people he can trust are those same people who hurt him.[5] Loyalty often means that no outsiders are welcome in the family. Without the influence of outside sources, family myths and beliefs continue to run their course unchallenged. The isolation so typical of many dysfunctional families offers no respite for the child who has no point of reference other than the family myths he experiences on a daily basis.

It's not unusual for dysfunctional family myths to revolve around issues of loyalty, closeness and "specialness," with rules and beliefs that support the family's system of denial.[6] One client, Alex, initially presented his family as "the best." He described a dynamic, beautiful mother and a father who was the most competent, successful agent in his insurance company. Alex's relationship with his brother was friendly but distant.

Over the course of therapy, Alex's family began to look different from the ideal image he first presented. It took time to see through the family's strong myth of excellence and pervasive denial. As Alex listened to the child's truth, he faced the hard fact that his parents were active alcoholics. Even more difficult was the realization that his mother had often fondled him sexually as a young boy.

The range of feelings Alex experienced as he dismantled the family myths were difficult to reconcile. He felt disloyal and guilty whenever he said unflattering things about his parents. He was disappointed and angry as he reclaimed the child's confusion about the sexual abuse he experienced. He discovered numerous injunctions he had been following that kept the family system of denial in place.

For instance, he had been told, "You'll always belong here with us. This is the one place where you're really loved. We know you better than anyone." Because of this injunction, and others that reinforced it, Alex felt guilty whenever he wanted to spend time with other people, or when he brought people home. Alex's mother and father would be friendly to strangers, but Alex could tell they were uncomfortable and displeased. The most difficult part was that the injunction that conveyed to Alex he would always be loved best by his family was accompanied by insults and verbal abuse when his father got drunk and berated him.

It's confusing when the people who love you are also the people who hurt you, and Alex felt this confusion deeply. When he turned to his mother for support before a job interview one time, she said, "What do you mean you feel afraid of that interview? *We're* never afraid of anything!" His first impulse was to be angry with himself for being such a wimp. The confusing thing was that he would then watch his mother run for a drink whenever she was faced with a challenge. This was one more experience to add to his muddled self-image. It was hard for Alex to assess himself with so many double messages running around in his mind.

Adult children of dysfunctional families often experience this kind of confusion. Injunctions and myths conflict with behaviors and statements that convey hidden meanings.[7] If you have had this kind of experience, it's a good idea to be particularly aware of your responses as you get to know the child within. It wouldn't be surprising if you felt some anger towards the child for "lying," for stirring things up, when the child's truth runs counter to family myths and injunctions.

Your family may have had myths that consistently and un-flaggingly portrayed particular family members as wonderful people. Nina comes to mind. In Nina's family, her grandfather was talked about as the rock of gibraltar, a saint who would give anything to anyone. When Nina was a young girl, Gramps died in his sleep at home. Everyone said it was a wonderful thing. He deserved a peaceful death for being such an honest and straight-forward man.

When Nina was in her twenties, she met a cousin she hadn't known before and began to learn more about her grandfather. She discovered, much to her surprise, that Gramps was actually a small-time con man. As a younger man, he would move his fam-ily around in the night to avoid paying rent. Nina learned that Gramps would come home from work and announce that the family was moving once again. Everyone would pack up the truck and off they'd go, to another town or another state, leaving behind unpaid bills and unfinished business.

What surprised Nina most was the response of some of her family members when she shared this new information. They didn't want to hear it. In fact, they got angry at her for spreading "mean untruths" about this good man they all remembered. This was Nina's first *conscious* experience of her family's strong need to keep its myths intact. Eventually, she stopped talking about her grandfather, but things were never quite the same. She no longer felt the comfort and sense of connection she used to have when stories were told about Gramps. She had pierced the family myth.

As an adult, Nina had the option of keeping her mouth shut and simply staying out of the discussions, which she did. If she had learned this new information about Gramps as a child, though, there would have been few options for dealing with it. She would have had to do whatever was necessary to go along with the family. She might have had to bury the new informa-tion and forget it. She might have blamed herself for being so unloving or she might have gotten angry at the person who told her such lies. However she handled it, her immediate need would have been to comply with the way the family viewed Gramps if she hoped to be accepted.

COVERT MEANINGS OF FAMILY INJUNCTIONS

In many dysfunctional families, there is more than one level of meaning in favorite family sayings that are repeated often enough to become powerful, unconscious injunctions. Just about any injunction can have a double meaning, depending on the tone of voice with which it is delivered. Facial expression and body language often convey subtle levels of meaning that may be different from the words used. If one "family favorite" says, "Don't make waves," the underlying message might be, "If you do, you'll upset me and I can't handle that." Another underlying message might be, "So, forget getting anywhere in life. It's not worth the struggle and you can't win anyway."

As you do the exercises that follow, you might ask yourself what the covert meaning is in any of the injunctions you discover. The overt meaning of an injunction or family myth is powerful enough. When it is combined with a covert message, the post-hypnotic effects of the message are even more powerful.[8]

Remember that injunctions usually reflect the values and expectations inherent in family myths. A common example of this is the injunction from the family that says, "We want you to succeed." That's the overt message. Underlying it, though, may be a covert message that says, "But, you'd better not *exceed* us." The second layer of an injunction is often delivered via stories that convey the family myth.

One example comes to mind from a person who described her family as financially stable and comfortable. Cherie was always expected to go to college and succeed. The problem is, she succeeded beyond even her wildest expectations. In response, her father now often talks about how his parents "really knew how to handle money." He tells stories about how they had more money than anyone in the entire extended family network. He emphasizes the fact that his parents never flaunted their wealth. They were frugal people who saved more than they spent. They could fit in anywhere, even with people of much less means. While presenting an overt message of his regard for his parents, her father's voice tone and inflection conveyed to Cherie, without any doubt, that she had better not get too big for her britches. Her income had outstripped everyone else's in the family and her father's discomfort was palpable.

Can you think of yourself or someone else who has gone out into the world and achieved things beyond the norms of the family of origin? How about the first person in a family to go to college? How about the family member who becomes a well-known public figure? Have you noticed that, while family members may say they are proud, sometimes there may be an undercurrent of discomfort around these accomplishments? In some families, certain careers may be considered acceptable for one child, while another child may be expected to get a job that isn't as distracting as a career. She may have the role in the family of being "on call" to meet whatever needs or emergencies may arise, never really released to her own life.

Favorite family stories, fables, and tales often indirectly convey what behaviors and responses will and will not be tolerated. In Cherie's family, stories of her father's parents provided one means of letting family members know that having and spending too much money were not acceptable.

Another person comes to mind. In Eleanor's family, it was her mother who was the primary storyteller. The problem was that Eleanor's mother told stories to keep the kids in line. She had lots of scary tales of bogeymen who could hide under the bed if a child were bad and come out at night and steal the child away. For another person, Fran, there were stories from an aunt who lived in the extended-family home. These stories were of naughty children who were taken off to a certain shopping center and left there for someone else to find.

INJUNCTIONS AS STATEMENTS ABOUT THE SELF

Injunctions given to children don't always deal with norms and values held by the family. All too often, they focus on characteristics of the child *as a person*. The most damaging thing about these kinds of injunctions is that they convey a judgment about the child personally, rather than commenting solely on the child's behavior. It's important to remember that we can always change our behavior, if we choose. When we are told that we are ugly, or uncoordinated, or an "egghead," though, we are faced with something about the very fabric of our being that is difficult, if not impossible, to change.

Injunctions that are directed at the child personally become extraordinarily powerful post-hypnotic suggestions.[9] These suggestions can operate unconsciously throughout childhood and into adulthood, and have the power to create self-fulfilling prophecies, feelings of guilt, shame, self-hate, and essential "badness." They may even prevent you from giving yourself permission to have good things in your life.

Throughout his childhood, Elliott was told, over and over again, that he was stupid. Whenever he would make a mistake, his father would say, "That was a dumb thing to do. Why are you so stupid all the time, stupid?" Elliott's unconscious took in the label and identified it as a strong characteristic in his personality. He had always dreamed of being a trial lawyer. When he entered college, though, Elliott found the anxiety of performing in class and on exams too much to bear. He dropped out and became a highly respected executive in business. Even with his success in business, the legacy of being labeled stupid followed him wherever he went and prevented him from pursuing his love of the law.

Sissy was a woman who had trouble keeping long-term relationships going. As a young girl, whenever Sissy and her mother would have a fight, her mother would say, "You're such a miserable human being. I don't know how anyone will ever want to live with you." Being a miserable human being became an injunction about Sissy as a person, a post-hypnotic suggestion from her mother. As an adult, whenever she had a live-in relationship with a man, she would constantly look for evidence that he didn't want to be with her. She would behave in ways she described as "being miserable to live with," carrying out, unconsciously, the suggestion planted so many years before.

As adults, both Elliott and Sissy experienced the ongoing effects of early injunctions, even when they consciously wished to do otherwise. Early on, certain threads were woven into the tapestry of their perceptual filters that revealed to each of them the many ways in which they would never measure up. Because expectations and reflections of who we are get communicated on a daily, moment-to-moment basis, and from so many quarters, they become as taken for granted as the air we breathe. With repeated reinforcement, both Elliott and Sissy had difficulty perceiving themselves as different from the labels they received as children.

It's important to remember that the injunctions conveyed to you about yourself and the world are powerful messages that have a strong impact on your perception. The threads in the tapestry of your perceptual filter originated in these messages. For example, if you grew up in an abusive home, danger may have been an ever-present reality. You may have learned to anticipate it and to recognize signals that warn of possible danger. This early learning created a lens that may keep you particularly attuned to the potential for danger in your environment and lead you to interpret ambiguous or unclear interactions as potentially dangerous, even if they aren't.

If there were also stories in your family of other abusive people, or of family members who lived dangerous lives, you may tend to focus your lens on the actual danger that does exist in the world. You may discover that you have a tendency to overlook the safety that also exists within your grasp.

SELF-TALK

Accompanying the bias that your perception takes when you look at the world through the tapestry of your particular lens is a phenomenon called, in cognitive psychology, *self-talk*. You may not be aware of your self-talk, but it is there. It is the dialogue you have with yourself about who you are, what you are doing, how well you're doing, whether you're good enough, what people think of you, and so on. It reflects the injunctions you took in as a child, particularly those that were reinforced time and again. Self-talk has to do with the world at large, and may also focus on things about you.

In cognitive therapy, positive change is brought about by identifying negative self-talk and then challenging it.[10] Rather than allowing negative self-talk to be taken at face value, you learn to question the assumptions underlying statements such as, "Joe stood me up for a date last night. I guess I'll never be attractive enough to get the man I want." After challenging your negative self-talk, you are encouraged to respond with a positive statement, such as, "Yes, Joe did stand me up. I guess that's reason enough to realize that Joe isn't the kind of guy I want to have around."

Daniel Araoz, a family therapist who is also a hypnotherapist, has coined the phrase "negative self-hypnosis" for this kind of self-talk.[11] The post-hypnotic impact of family myths and injunctions often is translated into ongoing negative self-hypnotic suggestions that you repeat to yourself all the time. These suggestions are extremely powerful. They can invalidate your best efforts. They have the capacity to immobilize you in situations perceived as terrifying. They can reflect your deepest vulnerabilities or foibles and remind you of humiliating thoughts and experiences from the past.

Even though this chapter focuses primarily on the negative injunctions you received as a child, it's important to remember that there is also positive self-talk, which becomes positive self-hypnosis. As you work with the negative self-hypnosis arising from injunctions you've taken in, you may want to remember that you can also focus on any good expectations you received. In fact, in the second exercise of the two that follow, you can listen for positive injunctions received from your family or other sources.

Take a moment, now, to identify that voice in your head, the one that makes comments about what's going on in your life or about you. It may be vague at first, seeming to be way in the back of your mind. Whether it's a clear voice, or one that's barely noticeable, your *unconscious* listens to and hears it all the time.

ABOUT THE EXERCISE

In the following exercise, you'll be looking for those family stories and anecdotes that let you know which values and norms were acceptable. Remember Nina and the stories about Gramps, and how Cherie's father talked about his parents and their way of handling money? Be sure to consider the fables and tales the family told, the ones that seemed to be important in the family repertoire.

For this exercise, you'll need a pencil and paper. While this exercise involves opening your eyes and writing down the messages you get in touch with, you may want to tape record it anyway. Doing so will help the self-hypnotic component make your experience more powerful. Remember to record only the italicized sentences and to leave yourself some quiet time when you see the word [pause]. As with all the other exercises, feel free to turn off the tape recorder between steps, if you need extra time.

Exercise #10   Discovering Favorite Family Stories

Begin by finding a place where you can be alone for 15 minutes or so. Be sure you have paper and pencil with you, as this is a written exercise.

Take a nice deep breath, now, and allow your eyes to close for a moment. Become aware of the surface that is supporting you. Notice how your body seems to know just how to use that support in ways that are just right for you. [pause]

Take another deep breath, now, and suggest to yourself that you are drifting into a light, comfortable trance state. Notice how your body can settle a bit more, now, as you continue to allow the surface under you to continue giving its reliable, steady support. [pause]

Let your mind begin to drift back to your childhood. You are seeking memories of family stories you heard as you were growing up. They may have been stories about relatives. They may have been fables or tales about other people, stories that were intended to teach you something, to convey a moral to the story.

They may be stories that contain negative messages, or they may contain injunctions that have had a positive impact in your life. As with all of your inner work, accept whatever comes. [pause]

As memories come to mind, write down whatever stories or anecdotes you remember. You'll find that you can open and close your eyes and still remain in your light trance, attuned to the inner awareness that has developed as you've focused on remembering family messages. [pause here for as much time as you need to write down what comes to mind]

Take some time, now, to allow to come to mind whatever hidden messages may have been conveyed in these stories . . . whatever unspoken injunctions were being communicated. [pause]

For a few moments, imagine how these messages—spoken and unspoken—have affected your life. To do this, allow your unconscious to show you some images or memories of choices you have made based on the injunctions conveyed by these stories. [long pause]

As you keep in mind what you've remembered, are you aware, in some new way, of the power of family myths and injunctions in shaping your expectations and responses? [pause] *Can you imagine the child-within taking in these injunctions? Children are like sponges. The whole world is a school and everything in it becomes a teacher. What have you just discovered about yourself, or the world, that you hadn't realized before in quite the same way?* [pause] *How have these old learnings affected your life?* [pause] *Would you like to change the quality of the perceptual filter that arose from these learnings?* [pause]

When you feel you have done all you can for now, allow yourself to reorient to a fully-alert state. Wiggle your fingers and toes to bring yourself all the way back.

Remember that you can return many times and recall other stories and anecdotes from the treasure chest of family favorites that exists within your unconscious memory. In fact, you may find that memories of stories just drop into your mind at times when you least expect them. An anecdote may come to mind as you're walking across a room, or as you're going through a doorway, or as you're engaged in an interaction with someone.

SPECIFIC INJUNCTIONS ABOUT YOU

Now that you've looked at some of the more general messages you received from hearing favorite family stories, it's time to look at specific injunctions communicated to you about yourself or about the world in general. Remember that these injunctions have become post-hypnotic suggestions that operate in your unconscious to create self-fulfilling prophecies. Many of the expectations you carry about what you deserve and can achieve find their origins in messages conveyed to you, sometimes in an offhand way, on a daily basis when you were growing up.

As a trigger for your own exploration, I'd like to list some of the injunctions that show up time after time in workshops. They are the "standards" that seem to emerge in families from all walks of life. As you read through this list of injunctions, perhaps you'll recognize some from your own family. For some injunctions, I've added possible hidden messages in brackets:

- *What will the neighbors think?* [An implication here is that you are less important than the neighbors.]
- *Why can't you be like . . . You're just like . . .* [Whichever way you look at it, you're not enough as you are.]
- *If you can't do it right, don't do it at all.* [The implication here is that it's not safe to take risks because you might make mistakes. The problem is that learning occurs through trial and error. It's appropriate not to do it right at first.]
- *You shouldn't feel that way.* [I need you to feel the way I need you to feel. Forget what your gut is really telling you.]
- *Don't rock the boat. Don't make waves.* [Implies that if you do make waves, something awful will happen. The "something awful" may never be defined. You may just be left with a feeling of anxiety whenever you feel an urge to express yourself honestly.]
- *It's lonely at the top.* [So you might as well settle for somewhere in the middle.]
- *If it feels good, it must be wrong. No pain, no gain.* [Did you have a variation of this one in your family?]
- *Pride goeth before a fall.* [There have been many variations of this one. It gives a strong message that you'd better not feel too good about yourself or your accomplishments.]
- *What do you know . . . you're only a kid.* [Implies that you can't know your own feelings, that you can't see what's happening. Sends a message that you'd better support the denial system . . . you'd better not see that the emperor is naked.]
- *No one will ever be able to stand you.* [A variation on Sissy's theme. This one shows up a lot.]

Positive injunctions have also been listed in workshops with some regularity, as well. Some of these are:

- *Be the best you can be.*
- *That's the way the cookie crumbles.* [Can be positive if it teaches you to tolerate adversity that you can't change. Can be negative if it's an offhand comment when you're really distressed and in need of support.]

• *Nothing ventured, nothing gained.*
• *No matter where you begin, you can pull yourself up by your*
bootstraps.

ABOUT THE EXERCISE

The above is but a small sample of the kinds of injunctions you'll look for in the next exercise. As you work with the exercise, you may find that there are many more injunctions affecting your life than you have realized. When injunctions come to mind, allow yourself to write them down as you recall them. They may not make sense at first, or you may think you're making them up. That's fine. Whatever comes to mind will have meaning for you in some way that will be helpful to know about. Remember, if it's in there as a thought you can have, then it's in there as a possible post-hypnotic suggestion you use on yourself.

As you did in the last exercise have pencil and paper handy. It will help you to focus if you tape record this exercise as well. The myths and injunctions you are noting in these exercises will be useful in the explorations you'll encounter in the next chapter. Give yourself about 15 minutes for this exercise. You'll probably want to come back to this exercise from time to time, as it's impossible to uncover all the important family injunctions in any one sitting.

Exercise #11   Defining Specific Family Injunctions

Begin by allowing your body to settle into whatever is supporting you right now. Make sure you have your pencil and paper nearby, within easy reach.

Take a deep breath and allow your eyes to close naturally. Discover how good it can feel to rest for a little while behind closed lids. You have all the privacy you need . . . all the time you could possibly want to take an inner journey into old learnings. [pause]

As you take another deep breath, now, give yourself permission to drift into a light trance. It's a state in which you can write easily, opening and closing your eyes, even as you maintain a comfortable trance. [pause]

One more nice, deep breath, will allow you to shift into a state of mind that makes communicating with your unconscious even easier, now. [pause]

If it's all right with you, now, ask your unconscious to review messages that were given you by the family . . . messages about yourself as a person, or about the world in general. [pause]

You may find that you recall a particular event at home, or somewhere else, where an adult is saying something about you. What is being said may be positive and may make you feel very good about yourself. Or, what you become aware of may be something that was hurtful to hear . . . and that made you feel bad about yourself. As always, accept whatever comes to mind now. [long pause]

You may remember times when someone was complaining about work, or telling you something about the way things are in the world. Notice how you feel inside when you hear the predictions, fears, prejudices and other beliefs that may have been told to you by this person. [pause]

You may bring to mind something you've thought of many times. It may be that your unconscious presents you with something you haven't recalled in a long time. Or, you may notice that you're suddenly hearing something you've heard a million times before, but this time in a new way. [pause]

Whatever comes to mind, write it down. Remember, you may be surprised to discover that you can remain in a light trance, even as you open your eyes and note what is coming to mind. [pause]

As you write, you might wonder how the messages you are recalling could affect a child hearing them. Would a child feel elated? Confused? Humiliated? Angry? Hurt?

Take a moment to close your eyes and allow your unconscious

to show you how this message about you or the world has af-
fected the choices you've made in your life . . . how this message
is reflected in the quality of life you live now. [long pause]

When you've finished with that message, allow your uncon-
scious to give you whatever other injunctions are available this
time. Go through the same process as you just did with the first
injunction. [long pause]

Repeat the process as many times as you feel you'd like to for
this trance experience. There will always be more to discover
another time.

When you feel ready to come back, take a moment to give
your unconscious permission to continue to give you a conscious
awareness of injunctions that have had an impact on your life.
[pause]

In fact, you might also give yourself the suggestion, now, that
in time you'll discover that themes may emerge. You might tell
yourself that you can discover how family injunctions may have
become themes that run through your life, touching you person-
ally and professionally in ways it's helpful to know about. [pause]

When you feel you've finished, bring yourself back and sit
with your experience for a moment, feeling the tone of what
you've touched as you might the lingering tone of a bell just
rung.

Let yourself know that your awareness will develop, that you
will realize which injunctions you want to eliminate from your
internal self-talk . . . and, most importantly, you'll know just
which positive injunctions you want to put in their place to
counteract the effects of old, negative ones you used to have in
your life.

Be sure to give yourself permission to uncover the positive, as
well as the negative, messages about you and about the world in
which you live. For most adult children of dysfunctional families, there is likely to be a greater proportion of negative messages than positive ones. To overlook the positive, though, would
be to remain unconscious of empowering post-hypnotic suggestions that you may choose to reinforce in your current life.

Keep the written notes from both parts of this exercise. You may find them useful as starting points in the exercise you'll find in the next chapter.

ORAL HISTORIES

There are other ways to uncover important myths, beliefs and injunctions that have come to you from your family. One way is to obtain oral histories from family members who were adults when you were young.[12] If your parents are living, and you see them, you might ask them what their life was like before you were born. You might also want to ask your mother about her pregnancy with you, and your birth. If your grandparents are living, if you have contact with great aunts, other elderly relatives, or friends of your parents, it can be extremely useful to engage in a process of exploring their viewpoints, experiences and memories.

Questioning parents and other relatives about holidays, birthdays, special memories, and important people opens up family worlds that you may have never before discovered. Asking about experiences that shaped their lives and things that are most important to them will give you a more intimate understanding of people who may have had some influence in shaping your life. In the responses to questions, and between the lines, the content of an oral history will reveal hidden expectations, values and norms that may have been passed along for generations . . . all the way to you.

It's also helpful to talk to your own brothers or sisters as you begin to explore family injunctions. It's important to keep in mind that, in a very real sense, each child grows up in a different family. Your siblings' experiences will be different from yours. If you cannot find validation for your perspective on the family, let that be all right. Keep in mind that the addition of each new child changes the family system, and what feels harmful to one child may be completely overlooked by others.

A note of caution: In your search for family myths and beliefs, be sure to include only those family members with whom you have a positive relationship. Nothing is gained from reinvolving yourself with someone who was abusive or bad for you in any way. Also, if members of your family are uncomfortable or angry with your questions, it may be that there is a denial system still intact that won't budge. If this is the case, leave it alone. Trying to push beyond the family's denial is likely to win you disapproval, a label of "troublemaker," or some other label that is even less benign.

GENOGRAMS

Another way to explore expectations and beliefs that have been modeled for you in the family is to construct a *genogram*. In the Notes section, at the back of the book, you'll find listed two excellent references that can guide you through the process of constructing your own genogram.[13]

Essentially, genograms are like a family tree, made into a diagram with symbols that represent members of your family. Genograms provide a visual map of family relationships and patterns across several generations and allow you to see where patterns of closeness and distance, substance abuse, success and failure and others run through your family. They also give you yet another way to look at what issues, problems and beliefs may have been passed down to you through two or three generations in the families of both your parents. For example, in constructing a genogram, you may discover that a pattern of alcoholism or other substance abuse shows up in three generations, even though no one ever talked about it as a family problem.

You may uncover family secrets, which are powerful realities in the family unconscious.[14] Family secrets contain and convey expectations and beliefs that influence you and operate in your life, even if they have never been discussed openly. There may be previously hidden suicide attempts or hospitalizations for psychological problems that emerge as you gather information for the genogram. These kinds of secrets tend to operate under the surface in the family. Unconscious expectations, fears or beliefs related to the secrets may result in heightened sensitivity to certain kinds of events and behaviors.

For example, you may discover that Uncle Harold didn't really move to Florida because of arthritis, as you'd been told all your life. Instead, you find out that he was sent to jail when you were just a baby and it was too embarrassing for the family to admit. If it turns out that you look like Uncle Harold, you may have received subtle, negative messages that never were discussed openly. For instance, your parents may have worried, without realizing it consciously, that you would grow up to be like Harold. As a result of their fears, they may have been overly concerned about your grades or your behavior at school. They may have been harder on you than on the other kids, demanding better grades and more help around the house from you.

Because none of this was ever talked about openly, you may have grown up feeling as though nothing you did was good enough, that your parents seemed to worry even when things were going well. It wouldn't be too surprising if you actually had gotten into trouble at school from time to time. It may have been the only way you could express your internal distress at the level of expectation placed on you. Incidents at school may have caused your parents to crack down even more, and so a cycle of recreating Harold might have continued, fueled by the hidden family secret.

As you gather information in oral histories, or construct genograms, be alert for subjects and events that you haven't heard about before. These, too, may have become powerful hypnotic suggestions within your unconscious.

In the next chapter, you will find it useful to have available some sense of the family myths and the injunctions that have influenced your life so far because you will learn a way to give back suggestions that you no longer wish to follow.

Chapter 9

GIVING BACK HAND-ME-DOWNS

A common complaint of adult children of dysfunctional families is that they aren't living up to their potential. Another is that relationships just don't seem to work over the long run. Are either of these themes familiar to you? If you look over the family myths and injunctions you identified in the last chapter, can you find some of the post-hypnotic suggestions that may have contributed to your experiences in these areas?

Once you've identified one or two injunctions that have affected you negatively, take a moment and think of the person who gave you the suggestions conveyed in the injunctions. If possible, imagine that person's face and hear that person's voice. What additional suggestions are communicated to you by that facial expression? What do you hear in that tone of voice that says as much as, or more than, the actual words used? What happens if you imagine the posture of the person involved? If the posture were threatening or intimidating in any way, the suggestion you received would have even more impact.

NONVERBAL ELEMENTS OF FAMILY INJUNCTIONS

Much of the power in the injunctions that still fuel your behavior and beliefs came from the nonverbal elements present when the injunctions were delivered. As you explore the exercises contained in this chapter, it's helpful to realize that there will be parts of you responding to the "nonverbals" contained in suggestions you choose to eliminate. Whenever you connect with any part of yourself, accept whatever fear, guilt, apprehension, or other discomfort may arise. All responses will have meaning you can welcome because, until you experience your deeper responses to the suggestion, they continue to have power. Remember, if there is an unconscious belief that differs from one you hold consciously, the unconscious one will prevail in influencing your behavior.

When you think of the nonverbal elements in the post-hypnotic suggestions you received, do you feel any fear, anger or guilt? It's not unusual for the nonverbal parts of a suggestion to carry a strong emotional charge. The child within responded to the emotional quality of the suggestion when it was given. Your spontaneous responses to these suggestions will tell you a lot about how you felt when you first experienced them.

The primary focus in this chapter will be to identify the people who conveyed the post-hypnotic suggestions you want to eliminate from the beliefs, assumptions and expectations that comprise your perceptual filter. Then, you'll have an opportunity to give these suggestions back to their "rightful owner." The injunctions you receive growing up are a lot like hand-me-downs. Did you ever receive hand-me-down clothes or toys? If you did, you know that hand-me-downs may be perfect for the person who first chooses them, but they often aren't quite right for someone else. In fact, sometimes they don't fit at all. Instead, they may pinch, and squeeze, or rub you the wrong way.

Of course, some hand-me-downs are real treasures, to be kept as precious heirlooms. If there are any that have become empowering, positive post-hypnotic suggestions, give yourself permission to bring them even more consciously into your internal self-talk. Maybe you'd even like to thank the person who gave them to you. The nice thing to know, and perhaps the hardest, is that it's up to *you* whether or not you keep messages you received as a child.

You may know already that someone in your family criticized you, teased you mercilessly, or abused you psychologically in some other way. You may even remember exactly what that person said. What may puzzle you is that your conscious awareness of these suggestions hasn't taken away their power to influence you. Because of the emotional charge created at the time you received them in childhood, they continue to play an important role in the quality of what you perceive about yourself and the world.

Remember that your self-hypnosis is made more powerful when you add an emotional component, such as a desire for something you seek to achieve. When you consider that family injunctions are usually delivered with some kind of feeling and that they usually elicit a feeling response from a child, it's not surprising to know that they carry tremendous power. Making conscious the emotional charge that you took in when you received negative suggestions begins the process of taking away that power.

One of the benefits of exploring family injunctions in trance is that you can become aware of the underlying, nonverbal and emotionally charged elements of the suggestions you received. Using your hypnotic eyes, ears and feelings, you can look more deeply, under the surface of the words used. When you do, you can get in touch with powerful, unconscious suggestions taken in by the child within.

For example, Justin consistently found that he couldn't make enough money to be really comfortable in his life. Even as his salary increased with each promotion, he always seemed to have "the wolf at the door," as he described it. Justin was aware that his family had negative, judgmental feelings about people who have lots of money. He was also aware that these judgments affected his own ability to feel good about having sufficient income to more than meet his needs.

During a trance, Justin found himself face to face with several important members of his family: his stepfather, his mother and his grandfather. He asked his unconscious for an impression of the boy in him who was most affected by messages about money. He immediately became aware of a boy about 14 years old. This was a child within he hadn't met before, and he was intrigued. As he listened with his hypnotic ears, Justin could hear his step-father talking about "those rich people who don't care about anyone but themselves." The tone of voice his stepfather used was angry. Justin's grandfather also talked of "those people" who took advantage of others just so they could have money. He also heard his mother talking about the "spoiled rich kids" at his school, and how they got everything they wanted, even though they didn't do any work for it.

As he turned his attention to the boy, Justin became aware of a deep conflict, a feeling of anxiety and shame. The boy couldn't reconcile his wish to succeed and have a good life with the values expressed in his family. He felt ashamed at his ambition to become a successful businessman, because he didn't know how to do that without incurring his family's disapproval. It wasn't that his stepfather wasn't successful enough in his chosen field. It was just that Justin's stepfather and his grandfather were men who hadn't aspired to positions of authority, who had never wished to climb the corporate ladder.

As an adult, Justin had a strong desire to go as far as he could in business. With determination, he had done pretty well. Now, he wanted to be free to do even better. When he asked his unconscious for an symbol to represent all the negative messages from his family about money and success, he became aware of the lid to a garbage can. Then he noticed that there was a gar-bage can there, too. Inside it was a beautiful golden serpent trying to get out. Justin removed the lid and allowed the serpent to emerge. When asked to become the serpent, Justin reported an expansive feeling inside, "like being bathed in liquid sun-shine." He realized, anew, how much he wanted to find his own place in the world, in his own way.

Still in trance, Justin imagined himself giving the lid and the garbage can back to the family, telling them that he could no longer put a lid on his ambitions. He experienced their disapproval, but he continued in spite of it. Then, Justin realized that the boy in him needed some reassurance. The boy was feeling anxious and afraid that he would be rejected. As he reassured the boy, Justin noticed that there was another feeling there, too. The boy had a glimmer in his eye, a small smile forming on his lips. He was excited at the prospect of having permission to follow his own talents and wishes. Justin could feel anticipation stirring in the boy, and he encouraged it. In fact, he said he was the boy's future self and looked forward to expressing, fully, the boy's ambition and talents in the adult world.

For Justin, this was a beginning. It was the first time he had *felt* the power of the suggestions his family had given him about money and success. It was the first time he really *experienced* how strong a role their disapproval played in his fear of really going forward in his own way. There was still a lot of exploration left to do. He wanted to remember more of the specific injunctions and their accompanying post-hypnotic suggestions so he could give them back, consciously.

What was important, though, was that he had the garbage can and lid as symbols of a strong family injunction that was holding him back. Whenever he found himself uncomfortable about going for a promotion or some other achievement, he would remember the garbage can and take a moment to give it back to its rightful owners. He also continued to develop a relationship with the 14-year-old boy, a relationship that turned out to be fulfilling for both of them.

HAND-ME-DOWNS AS SYMBOLS

As you work with the hand-me-downs you received, it's helpful to keep in mind that, most often, you'll be working with *symbols*, the language of the unconscious.[1] Hand-me-downs can be represented by any symbol you bring to your experience. Often, your work will be more powerful when you are able to allow your unconscious to communicate in its own language, as Justin's did with the lid and garbage can. With practice, you'll find that you can allow symbolic representations of hand-me-downs to drop, easily, into the front of your mind.

GUILT AND FEAR

Often, as was true for Justin, the most difficult part of the trance work of giving back hand-me-downs is imagining confronting, directly, the person who gave them to you in the first place. People have a whole range of responses to this idea. When they first begin to work with this exercise, guilt and fear are commonly reported feelings. Some people also surprise themselves with the anger they feel. Even though it can be confusing to experience powerful anger at someone you love, it is an important step in discovering that you have the ability to refuse to accept any message that isn't good for you.

Since guilt is the most common response to the idea of giving back hand-me-downs, let's look at it first. Remember, children do whatever is necessary to keep their environment safe. They do this even when it means giving up their own truth, their inner experience of what's happening, in order to meet the demands and needs of caretakers. This is an essential self-protective response. Without it, the child would be at risk for abandonment in the form of rejection, disapproval, emotional withdrawal by, or actual loss of, the parent or caretaker.

Guilt is a protective response. Let's look at a couple of ways it works to protect the child. First, it keeps the child from saying that the Emperor has no clothes. It prevents the child from openly confronting family dynamics which, if described directly, would be too upsetting to handle. A second important function of guilt is to keep the child from acknowledging her inner truth. If the guilt were to shift and become anger, for instance, the child might either really see what's going on or confront it—and then be in danger of abandonment or injury. Either way, a threat would be present.

Also, it's helpful to remember that, within family systems, children play a complex role in the marital relationship of parents.[2] When the family is dysfunctional in its patterns of intimacy and interaction, the child may find himself caught up in the conflicts and unmet needs of the adults. The child may also know, unconsciously, that if he were to refuse his role, the marriage might flounder. Again, the threat of abandonment could arise.

As you explore giving back hand-me-downs, be particularly attuned to the possibility that guilt may be present. It won't always be, but if it's there you need to deal with it first. As with any other response that comes up in trance, accept it. It's an important message that tells you the child within needs comfort. In fact, whenever there's guilt about giving back hand-me-downs, it's extremely helpful to reinforce the fact that *you* are now the most important adult in the child's life. Remember that the child in you has protected your parents, or other people who gave you negative messages, from his or her true feelings about things in order to be safe. It's frightening to the child within to give up this protective relationship. To overwhelm a parent with the truth might mean another form of abandonment.

When Harriet first began to work with giving back hand-me-downs, she experienced a good bit of guilt and anxiety. Her history was that of a childhood spent in a nuclear family, with her mother and father, a younger brother and sister. Harriet was one of those people who had played a crucial role in holding her parents' marriage together, at great cost to herself. She had difficulty, as an adult, feeling secure and confident in her own opinions and decisions. She would become extremely agitated when things weren't going well and had trouble soothing herself internally.

As a child, Harriet was verbally abused by both her parents, but particularly by her mother. When she started school, things got worse. For reasons she couldn't fathom, her mother would rail at her when she got home from school. Harriet couldn't remember doing anything wrong, but her mother would have a long list of things to complain about. Harriet's main response was to escape to her room, where she would sit by the window for hours, just staring. She wouldn't go out and play, waited to do her homework until the last possible minute, and had to be scolded to come down to dinner. She was deeply depressed and withdrawn. As she thought about it in trance, Harriet was struck by the fact that no one ever came to her room to ask what was wrong, to see if they could be of help. In fact, no one ever mentioned that she might be having problems. Instead, they told her she was "ungrateful" and "sullen."

It's probably not surprising that Harriet blamed herself for her depressed feelings. She would berate herself just as her mother had, calling herself the same names in the same ways. She thought of her parents with great admiration, even though their behavior confused her at times. She had never acknowledged any disappointment or anger with them. To her, they were good people and she automatically blamed her own "quirks" for not being able to be a happier child.

What Harriet didn't know consciously was that, in order for her parents to be sensitive to her depressed state, they would have had to admit that something was wrong in the family. The idea that something in the family might be anything but fine wasn't allowed. To acknowledge problems would have begun to break down the family's denial system, and there simply was no room to allow that to happen.

In her trance work, Harriet discovered that there was a strong family myth that she was the problem and that everything else in the family was just fine. As she began to give back the hand-me-down suggestions that said she was ungrateful and sullen, Harriet realized that her parents were unhappy and vulnerable. In fact, things began to look different as she recalled the family's daily routines and how she fit into the overall dynamic. She decided that her mother was probably an alcoholic and that all the after-school verbal abuse was because her mother had been drinking.

There was no room in the marriage, or in the family, to talk about drinking. It was much easier to focus on Harriet as the problem than to mention the fact that her father would retire to the study every evening, right after dinner, and leave her mother alone. He wouldn't come out until after everyone had gone to bed. Essentially, Harriet's parents no longer had a satisfying relationship, and no one dared acknowledge that fact.

Harriet experienced extreme discomfort and guilt when she began handing back the suggestions she had received from her mother. The family myth was being dismantled and she felt terribly disloyal. She felt guilty for labeling her mother an alcoholic and was convinced that, if her mother ever actually knew, she would be infuriated and hurt. Fortunately, Harriet realized that the power of giving back hand-me-downs was that she was interacting with *internalized representations* of her parents. She was freeing herself from the parents she carried inside, who contributed to her ongoing, negative self-talk.

Harriet's parents were still living and she saw them from time to time. These visits were increasingly comfortable, as Harriet freed herself from the family myth. As giving back hand-me-downs became easier and less guilt-ridden, Harriet realized, more and more, that she didn't have to make herself miserable to protect her parents. Instead, she could be aware, consciously, of the quality of their relationship. Because the adult in her no longer feared abandonment, Harriet could allow her parents to be responsible for themselves. If any feelings of discomfort arose, she could reassure the child within that all would be well and that the child would never be abandoned for standing up for herself.

Acknowledging Your Anger

Part of what helped Harriet shift from her guilt and role as the family problem was the anger she mobilized as she began to give back hand-me-downs. As she freed herself from the family's image of her, she recognized her parents as people with their own difficulties. She also connected with the weight of the burden the child within had carried because of problems her parents refused to acknowledge. She became angry at the denial that allowed her to be labeled in ways that were so destructive to her. In fact, as she increasingly realized that she had done nothing to warrant the kinds of verbal abuse she experienced, her anger allowed her to validate the child as a worthwhile person. She was able to turn around the abusive messages and show the child that they reflected everything about her parents and very, very little about herself.

As with Harriet, your anger will often open the door to a new perspective of yourself and significant caretakers. It's helpful to use your anger to fuel the process of giving back hand-me-downs. It will help you to stand up for the child within, and can foster the adult's ability to be assertive in current relationships. You can also use your anger to fuel a process of achieving things *you* want in life. It is liberating and empowering when acknowledging your anger allows it to shift from a child's helpless rage to an emotion that supports developing self-esteem.

YOUR PARENTS AS PEOPLE

As you consider the injunctions that came from the family, the ones that uphold the family myth at your expense, take a moment to think of your parents as *people,* rather than as Mom and Dad.[3] What are the first names of your mother and father and of other important caretakers in your life? What about teachers and others who gave you negative suggestions you now want to give back? Even if these important figures are no longer living, please know that they are quite alive inside you as internalized parts of your psychological experience. They continue to be mirrors that convey messages to you about yourself and contribute their part to your negative self-talk.

As you think of the first names of your parents and others, also recall what each looks like. Call to mind an image, or an impression, of your mother, for instance. Even if it is vague, allow yourself to accept whatever impression emerges. Now, think of your mother's first name. Then, realize that you are holding an awareness of a *person*, an adult woman with her own internal wishes, fears, memories and dreams. Think of her for a moment, and let yourself wonder *what kind of person* she is, or was. What might you think of her if someone introduced you to her as a stranger?

Do the same for your father, now. How does he look when you call his face to mind? When you put his face and his name together, and consider him as if he were a man you'd never met before, what do you think of him? Can you wonder what his secret ambitions were, before he grew up and took on the responsibilities of raising a family? What do you know of his history before you were born?

If either of your parents were unknown to you, allow yourself to become aware of the fantasies you may have created about this person. Do you imagine he or she was a good person? A magical person? A failure, or negative in some other way? What might this person have looked like? Explore the impressions that come to you from, and about, this internalized fantasy figure.

If you didn't grow up with your parents, do this part of the exercise with whomever the important caretakers and authority figures were in your life. It's a good idea to include grandparents and others whom you had contact with or heard about often.

For some people, this part of the process of giving back hand-me-downs is easy. They already have a good sense of their parents as people, with an awareness of their parents' particular vulnerabilities and imperfections. For others, though, this is a tough assignment. They've never thought of their parents as just people, as adults preoccupied with their own lives. Sometimes, it's surprising to think of being curious about them at all, other than as "mother" and "father."

If, as a child, you were taught to call your parents by their first names, try the process in reverse. Give yourself a chance to think of them as "Mom" and "Dad" and see what new feelings about them emerge in your awareness.

As soon as you put first names to people, rather than labels such as "Mommy" or "Daddy," you begin to experience them differently in a way that automatically starts the process of shifting the family myth. It's hard to stay locked into old ways of seeing people once you begin to consider how they handle life, and themselves, as independent adults out in the world. Once you begin to wonder how they relate to people outside the family, how they cope with stress, and how other people respond to them, you can't continue to overlook the wider range of their strengths and weaknesses. As you do so, you create an opportunity to compare the adult you are exploring with the parent who lived in the family. Does this adult fit with the family myth? Are there any differences between the way you experience the adult now and the way you always thought of his person before?

Sometimes, parents are competitive with their children and seem like children themselves. Whenever the child accomplishes something, the parent either takes credit or tells of a time when he or she did it better. The implicit message is that the child will never do as well as, and had better not try to surpass, the parent. As you explore your parents as people, do you find any memories that would indicate competitive messages like these? Or, have you ever felt that someone close to you didn't like you for reasons you can't figure out? It's not unusual for parents in dysfunctional families to see in their children traits they can't accept in themselves. When this happens, the child is often picked on, or blamed, for the very things the parent does or feels but cannot acknowledge. The injunctions arising from this dynamic are powerful indeed, and are well worth discovering consciously.

FAMILY ROLES

Recalling the power of roles in the family system, you might take a moment to consider how the roles in your family played out.

Remember that, as with Harriet, children often function to divert attention from a troubled marriage. Sometimes, parents who cannot share intimately with one another, or who can't communicate their wishes and fears, need a child through whom they can express these kinds of feelings. They may need a child who can be creative, sensitive, strong or boisterous—a child who will perform to meet unmet and unexpressed needs in the parent.

For example, were you the good child around whom your parents could come together with pleasure? Were you the bad child, over whom your parents could have arguments and heated fights that they couldn't have over the real issues of conflict in their marriage? Were you the sickly child who allowed your parents to share something by being concerned about you? Were you the strong child who would step in and take over if things seemed to be too much for your parents to handle? If you had brothers or sisters, which one of you got into trouble the most? The child who acts up most in a family often serves to protect the other children from being the focus of parents' unresolved conflicts, from the parents' need to have something to argue about other than their relationship. Also, the "problem child" in a family provides a focus around which family members can be brought together in mutual communication and activity.

Let yourself wonder about the suggestions that were an inherent part of your role in the family. These injunctions are implicit, powerful, and usually, unconscious. Even if you're unaware of them, they are there, and it's helpful to make them conscious so you can decide if you want to keep them. You can ask your unconscious to begin to give you a more conscious awareness of what you learned about yourself through playing out your prescribed role. For example, do you experience yourself as a "goof-off"? Do you feel as though you'll always have problems, that things just don't work out well for you? Do you consider yourself always second best, or is there an unquestioned assumption that you'll make it no matter what you do? These kinds of assumptions often find their beginnings in the messages conveyed to you as you fulfilled your family role.

As you think about your family, its myths and roles, become aware of any discomfort that may arise, or any objections you may have about exploring your family in this way. Chances are good that, consciously or unconsciously, you protect at least one family myth, because everyone has been a child in an environment that was, in some way, less than perfect. Every child has a need to keep the environment safe, so it's helpful to accept any mixed feelings you may have towards the process of confronting and dismantling family myths. In fact, as you look at the implications inherent in the role you played in the family, you might jot down any ideas or insights that come to mind. They may be valuable to come back to later, when you've gone further down the road to reclaiming yourself . . . to see just what distortions you learned, and accepted, about yourself as a child.

ARE THE MEMORIES OF THE CHILD WITHIN REAL?

As you work with the material in this book, give back hand-me-downs and change relationships with family members, you may find yourself confronted with the question: Are the memories of the child within real?

For many of us, listening to the story of the true self may elicit doubt about the actuality of what we remember. Partly this is because, as we delve into past events, we may challenge and sometimes dismantle family myths. This brings its own kind of discomfort. Also, it can be uncomfortable to uncover memories that may be impossible to validate.

If you find yourself wondering about the validity of the memories you experience as you give back hand-me-downs, it's helpful to realize that you are dealing with an internalized reality that has special meaning for *you*. When memories revolve around your family, it's helpful to know that each child grows up in what is experienced as a *different* family. This difference in perspective arises because of birth order, your role in the family, stage of development of the parents' marriage when you grew up, changes in socioeconomic status, and other factors.

The important thing to know is that each person has a unique perspective on events that may have been shared by other members of the family. You may all partake of certain common myths aned family stories, but your interpretation of these, as well as your memories related to them, will have the stamp of your own developing beliefs and expectations.

Throughout the process of reclaiming the child and recreating the self, then, it's helpful to keep in mind that you can accept whatever comes, even when it can't be validated by others. All that's really important to validate for yourself is that *something happened to the child or you wouldn't have the wounded places you experience inside.* Whether or not anyone agrees with you, remember that children aren't born shamed, or self-conscious, or terrified, or self-hating. These things children learn through interactions with other people.

In fact, recent studies in split-brain research have demonstrated that it is a normal human capacity, an *inevitability*, to fill in gaps or confusing elements in experience so that they make sense.[4] Because of this natural tendency, it's impossible to avoid unconsciously tailoring your memories to fit your beliefs and internal expectations about reality. It's not something you can keep yourself from doing, and it doesn't make your memories any less significant or meaningful to you. All it means is that you can't expect to have others *necessarily* agree with your version of events.

The broad strokes of your memories will certainly reflect accurately portions of what you experienced as a child. Specifics are less apt to be completely accurate, and you might want to give yourself permission to let this be okay with you. As you work with giving back hand-me-downs and validating the child's truth, what really matters in the long run is that what the child *thought* was going on is resolved and no longer the source of shame, terror, or other psychological discomfort.

EXAMPLES OF HAND-ME-DOWNS

Before you actually do the hand-me-down exercise that follows, I'd like to share several specific examples of what the hand-me-downs of some other people were like. Remember that any message you received growing up may be represented as a symbol, which may be an object, a person, an animal, a creature, some other being, or an abstract form. You may also represent a hand-me-down as a formless feeling or thought that you can give back in whatever way feels right for you. As with all your self-hypnotic work, let your unconscious guide the process, as you allow your creativity to express itself spontaneously, free from the censor of the conscious mind.

Marge was a young woman who had always felt she was basically bad. As a child, she had lived in an extended-family home. There were lots of adults around, but the person who affected her most was a prescription drug addict, a cousin many years her senior. This cousin, a woman, harassed Marge mercilessly. She would tell Marge what an awful person she was. She would blame Marge for "ruining her evening" or "making her crazy." It seemed to Marge as though this person were always there, making comments, yelling at her and generally making her life miserable.

Because of the dynamics in Marge's family, there were no safe adults to protect her. In any interaction with her cousin, Marge was painfully on her own. Because no one would come to her rescue, her cousin's messages had even more power. Marge constantly told herself that if she were lovable, *someone* would have intervened on her behalf. She had no way of knowing, as a child, that the family system operated within a powerful context of denial. To have rescued her, the other adults would have had to acknowledge that there were dysfunctional elements in the family. Instead of facing this, Marge was sacrificed, in a sense, to the larger need to keep a lid on things.

As a result, Marge was convinced no one could love her once they got to know what she was really like inside. Even though she was popular and attractive, she believed she fooled people, that she was a fraud. Given her set of perceptual filters, she couldn't see things any other way. She created self-fulfilling prophecies that brought her a great deal of familiar pain, as lovers verbally abused her before leaving her after several years.

When Marge used the hand-me-down exercise to give back messages from her cousin, she discovered a central theme: her cousin seemed to feel competitive and to have difficulty expressing any regard or admiration for her. In trance, Marge became aware of many small mirrors that represented the negative suggestions her cousin had given her over the years. Among them were phrases such as, "You're such a nasty person." "Couldn't you smile more?" "I don't know how you keep any friends, you're so awful to be around."

As Marge began to place the mirrors at her cousin's feet, in trance, her cousin became more and more agitated. She even began to snarl. It was during this experience that Marge realized her cousin saw all her own self-hate and self-blame in Marge. It was an important revelation. She discovered that her cousin's ambivalence and lack of basic warmth reflected a lot about her, but very little about Marge.

During this experience, Marge's child within was unnerved by her cousin's snarling and hid behind Marge. She was frightened and didn't like the experience at all. She was terrified she'd be in trouble and that her cousin would rage at her. As Marge's insights dawned, she was able to reach out to the little girl and give her a depth of reassurance she hadn't felt before. She connected with a love for the child within that was accompanied by a certain sorrow at the ways the child had been burdened by the projected, disowned parts of her cousin.

As Marge piled up mirror after mirror, almost burying her cousin in them, she realized, perhaps for the first time emotionally, that there was nothing bad about the child. It was both moving and liberating to discover, even in her secret hiding place inside herself, that her cousin *needed* her to be bad. Otherwise, her cousin would have had to deal with her own conflicts about *herself.* Marge understood that she no longer had to sacrifice her own sense of being okay as a person or feel helpless because of the ranting of her cousin.

Marge also included the other adults in her family, as she gave back hand-me-downs received growing up. She acknowledged her feelings of anger at parents who wouldn't protect her. She felt the pain of being abandoned and left at the mercy of someone who seemed only to want to crush her spirit. She also recognized that her family was disengaged.[5] Everyone was busy surviving in his or her own way and had no ability to reach out and connect with someone else who needed help. No one had the capacity to go against the family norms of disengagement, which left Marge very much on her own. Accepting her grief, pain, anger, as well as a determination to give back the humiliating, terrifying and belittling suggestions she received, allowed Marge to begin to change her perceptual filter. As she did so, her self-talk also became more positive and comforting.

After this experience, whenever Marge had to spend time with her cousin, she was able to focus on her as a person, rather than the role she played. As she did, she found that she could relate without having to fend off her cousin's competitive statements. Instead of being indictments confirming the badness in her, Marge now experienced them as comments about her cousin's insecurity and lack of self-esteem. The shift in Marge's perceptions of herself allowed her to be more at ease with her cousin. She felt much better about herself. In fact, rather than perceiving her cousin as powerful, she experienced her as pathetic. Marge was also better able to assert herself with her cousin. She now knew that she could say "no" to verbal abuse. She had the right to leave.

ANOTHER STORY

For Zack, the world often seemed a bit overwhelming and unmanageable. During a trance experience, he found himself standing in front of his father. He had always had what he considered to be a good relationship with his dad, even though he felt somewhat frustrated when his father came home, night after night, and complained about work. It seemed that his father would talk about all the things that were wrong, but then wouldn't do anything to change them. Zack's mother would listen and sympathize, but she couldn't seem to change anything, either.

As a grown man, Zack was not only basically dissatisfied with his work life, but also intimidated by the thought of pursuing a promotion. He didn't like the way things were, but the thought of putting himself out where he might be shot down didn't feel good either. Plus, he could recall all the times his father blamed others for being jealous of him at work. Zack didn't relish the idea of having to deal with other people's competitiveness and disapproval.

As he thought about all the suggestions he had received from his father about how the world was sometimes just too big a place to manage, Zack became aware of an image of a long-sleeved shirt. The shirt was a symbol for an important hand-me-down he wanted to give back to his father. It represented the quality of his father as a male role model, particularly having to do with work and to attitudes about being in the professional world.

What was immediately apparent to Zack was that the sleeves of the shirt were too short for him, and yet they fit his father perfectly. He could see, without any doubt, that the attitudes conveyed to him by his father were part of his father's perceptual filter but didn't need to be part of his. In the symbol of the shirt sleeves, his unconscious had given him a strong message that he needed to find attitudes about work that were right for *him*, that fit *him*.

As he gave the shirt back to his father, he noticed the child within. The boy was about 12 years old and was hanging back, expressing some real discomfort about what was happening. The boy needed reassurance, and a strong pep talk, to get him to feel comfortable with Zack's determination to develop his own attitudes about work. The child within had always taken it for granted that he would have made his father uncomfortable, and would have felt his father's displeasure, if he were to succeed beyond the family's expectations. Never before had Zack realized that he didn't want to recognize his ability to exceed his father. Now that he had developed a relationship with the child within, the prospect of having a father who wasn't all-powerful wasn't so frightening.

LISA'S STORY

Lisa had a different experience of giving back hand-me-downs. She had been working on giving back hand-me-downs to her father, who had been a tyrant in her home. He never allowed her to go out after school, and she wasn't allowed to have friends come home. Father made the rules and the rules were strict. In fact, Lisa had often felt that she could barely wait until she was old enough to move away from home.

During one trance, Lisa found herself on a beautiful farm, inside a large barn. The barn was filled with big baskets of horse manure. Lisa was uncomfortable because the barn was so full of manure. It left little room to move around. She commented on what a lovely barn it was and how nice it would be if it were cleared out. As she explored her experience, she suddenly realized that the manure represented all the "shit" that her father had heaped on her growing up: the rules, the anger, the punishments and the many degrading comments he made about her whenever she wanted to do something different from what he demanded.

Lisa decided to take all the baskets of manure out of the barn and place them in front of her father's house. The child within was about ten years old and was *delighted* with this decision. In fact, she helped haul the large baskets and took great pleasure in leaving them on her father's doorstep. There was no fear in this child. She liked Lisa and trusted her, and was thrilled to have an opportunity to be free of her father's tyranny. Both Lisa and the child within enjoyed the barn as it became emptier and roomier. They were reclaiming it as their own, refusing to continue to store Lisa's father's many negative post-hypnotic suggestions.

MORE ABOUT HAND-ME-DOWNS

Not every hand-me-down emerges as an image or a symbol. Some are simply feelings, sensations, or certain thoughts that you'd like to give back. That's fine, too. There's no need to have a *thing* to give back. You can give back feelings and thoughts by simply saying to the person, "Here, this is yours. I don't want it anymore." You can imagine that the feeling or thought drifts from you, through the air, and into the other person.

Whenever you give back hand-me-downs, it's better to do so *as the adult,* with the child within nearby, watching. As a rule, it asks too much of a child to stand up to someone who was disapproving, or who is an authority figure. *Only* if the child actively wants to give back the hand-me-down, and you are right nearby for protection, might you want to let that happen. If you find that you want the child to give it back, and the child is frightened, allow yourself to explore your demand. It may be that, when you were a child, adults expected you to take care of them, just as you now want the child to take care of you. The expectation that you would take care of the adults is also a hand-me-down, and it may be one you'd like to give back soon.

Some people find that they aren't ready to give back the hand-me-downs they discover. It may be that their guilt is too strong, that they don't want to hurt the other person, or that they just aren't yet ready to be free of an old, familiar suggestion. Allow yourself to accept these feelings if they arise. A solution for some people has been to leave the hand-me-down somewhere *near* the person, rather than demanding of themselves that they actually give it back at that precise moment. In your own best time, you'll be ready to free yourself from whatever negative suggestions you choose to give back. It's fine to take whatever time you need and to remember that you can be gentle and understanding with the parts of you that are too afraid to do the whole job all at once.

You may also find that the other person refuses to take back the hand-me-down, or gets angry, or wants to retaliate in some way. In these cases, remind yourself that this is *your* experience, taking place in *your* hypnotic world, and that *you* are in control. You can't force the other person to like what you're doing, but you can know that you are perfectly safe. The originator of the suggestion you are giving back has no power to hurt you in your inner world. Remember that you, as the adult, have all the resources you need to give back *any* hand-me-down. As is true with all your trance experiences, you can call on your future self to assist you if you feel at all intimidated by the other person's response. If you are faced with this kind of situation, it's all right to put the hand-me-down somewhere near the other person and walk away. Be sure to take the child with you, offering whatever reassurance and comfort the child may need.

ABOUT THE EXERCISE

Before beginning the following exercise, bring to mind an injunction, some quality of your family role, or some other suggestion that you find limits you or makes you feel bad about yourself. Let it be something you'd like to eliminate from your internal self-talk, something you'd feel good about releasing. Have it in mind as you go into trance.

The suggestion you choose to work with need not be dramatic. It might be one of those thoughts that nibbles at the back of your mind and makes you feel insecure. It might be the kind of thought that says, "What if I ——— ?" or, "What if ——— happens?" Of course, it may be dramatic. It may be something that says, "I'm such a terrible person. I'll never get anywhere in life." Because you can do this exercise many times, it's helpful to allow whatever thought pushes to the front of your mind to be the one you choose this time. You'll have many opportunities to go back and work with others.

As with all the exercises in the book, I recommend that you tape record this one. Remember to speak slowly and softly and record the italicized words only. It can be useful to read over the exercise first, before you record it, to familiarize yourself with what it contains. Also, it's helpful to have a paper and pencil nearby, so you can write down your experience when you've finished the exercise. You might also want to write down any new messages that come to mind as you give back hand-me-downs.

Exercise #13 Giving Back Hand-Me-Downs

[Find a place where you will be undisturbed for about 20 minutes. Put yourself into a comfortable trance, and take yourself to a safe, private place in your internal, hypnotic world.]

Once you're settled in your safe place, and seated comfortably with plenty of support, close your eyes. Allow your mind to drift to the injunction or message you decided to focus on this time. [pause]

Become aware of the feelings you have as you recall this message. What does it touch in you? How do you feel right now? [pause]

As you get more in touch with the impact of this message on you, allow yourself to notice whose voice is saying these words to you, whose face is conveying the message. [pause]

As you become aware of the voice and face, ask yourself the following questions:

- *What kind of person would say this kind of thing to a child?*
- *What is a person like who uses this tone of voice?*
- *What kind of person wears his or her face this way?*

[long pause]

Let yourself wonder about this person. Remember, the way a person speaks . . . what a person says . . . the way a person says it conveys a lot about that person. In fact, it says more about that person than it could ever say about you. [long pause]

Allow an awareness of the child within, who received this message, to come into the front of your mind, now. [pause] *What age is the child? Notice what the child feels in response to that message. What is your response to the child?* [pause] *The child may need comfort or reassurance right now, because sometimes it's scary to look so closely at someone who may have been all-powerful in that child's experience.* [pause]

Remember, you're the best person in the world to know what the child really feels, deep down inside. Just let your hypnotic eyes, ears and feelings be sensitive to what's going on in the child, now, and respond to meet whatever need is there. [long pause]

How could any child deserve what the message conveyed? It might be helpful to recall that children are busy being children, discovering the world and who they are in it. Nothing a child does is ever worthy of abuse from someone else. The child is an explorer in a new world and deserves to be welcomed and helped rather than injured or belittled. [pause]

Remember that the messages received by this child are like hand-me-downs. They were made for and by someone else and they don't fit the child within you. In fact, they have never been right for you, because they are all about someone else's beliefs, responses, and ideas. The nice thing to know about hand-me-downs is that you can choose to hand them back. [pause]

If you find yourself feeling any discomfort, or telling yourself that the message wasn't really that bad, remember that some parts of you may be frightened as you give back hand-me-downs that others gave you. Accept the reluctance frightened parts of you may have during this process. In fact, accept whatever comes. Everything is important information and tells you something of how dangerous it would have been, then, to reveal your true feelings. [pause]

Now, perhaps you could allow your unconscious to give you, in the front of your mind, an image of an object or symbol that represents the hand-me-down you'd like to give back. It can be anything at all, even a feeling or a thought with no form. [long pause]

If what comes to you doesn't seem to make sense, that's fine too. Accept it anyway. It has meaning in the unconscious, and it's helpful to go with whatever pushes to the front of your mind and stays there, even if you wish it were something different. [pause]

As you accept impressions from your unconscious, you are developing a relationship of trust that is most helpful to have whenever you go inside to work with parts of yourself.

Take a moment, now, to become the object or symbol and discover its meaning for you. You may know immediately what it conveys, or you may not, and that's fine, too. Give yourself whatever time you need to get in touch with what meaning the symbol holds for you. [pause]

If feelings begin to surface as you explore the symbol of the hand-me-down you want to give back, allow yourself to become fully aware of them. [pause]

Do the feelings imply that you may have been too frightened to disagree at the time the message was given to you? Did you have a need to protect a caretaker by agreeing? Would a family myth have been shattered if you had questioned the message conveyed to you? Give yourself a moment to consider whatever comes to mind, now. [pause]

Allow yourself, as the adult, to give back the message to the person who originally created it. This is the person to whom it really belongs. [pause]

If you can't bring yourself to give it back all the way, set it down somewhere near the other person, in a place where you can leave it behind. If you need help with this, call on your future self. [pause]

What does the other person do as you give back the hand-me-down? Let yourself be aware of that person's response . . . and how you feel about it. [long pause] *Remember that you are an adult now and can handle whatever emerges. Also, you have your future self available for support, should you need it.*

As you become aware of the other person's response to your giving back the hand-me-down, you might also notice the child's response. [pause]

Does the child need reassurance? The important thing to know is that you are there to protect the child and to defend your own right to refuse to accept hand-me-downs that really belong to someone else. [pause]

You might even become aware of a sense of power that develops as you give back the hand-me-down. The child may also shift from, perhaps, initial fear to a feeling of surprise and delight that there is unexpected support available. [pause]

If you find that you just can't give back the hand-me-down, now, and that you can't leave it behind, either, that's okay. You are discovering just how powerful the family myths have been in your life. You are learning how, as a child, you probably felt unsafe and had to protect the family myth in order to stay away from those uncomfortable feelings. [pause]

Remember, your future self is always present and will help you to create an internal healing process that will allow you to give back whatever hand-me-downs you want to eliminate from your perceptual filter. There's no right or wrong time to do this . . . there's only the time that is best for you. Be gentle with yourself, and know that you will get there when you're ready. [pause]

Once you feel finished for now, allow yourself to become aware of the fact that you are still in your safe place. You've been there all along, and the child is there with you. This safe place exists in your present-day adult world in which the child lives with you, now. Be sure to leave a part of you there with the child, and ask your unconscious to develop new, positive and healthy awarenesses to replace the hand-me-down you've just given back. [pause]

And, even as you go on to other things that may invite your attention once you're out of trance, know that in the timeless unconscious, the process of reclaiming the self of the child-within continues. There's no need to be aware of the entire process. It goes on in the safety of the back of your mind in all the ways that are best for you. In fact, when you return to your *safe place the next time you go into trance to give back another hand-me-down, you may become aware of what has evolved since you were here last.*

And so, bring yourself all the way back, now, and take a moment to sit with the experience you've just had as you would the lingering tone of a bell just rung. [pause]

Take a moment or two to write down any impressions you'd like to keep and then wiggle your fingers and toes to bring yourself all the way back.

The process of giving back hand-me-downs continues over time. As you give back certain suggestions, others that are related but hadn't been conscious tend to emerge. You may discover, as you make conscious more of the suggestions you received from people who may have been important to you as you grew up, that your relationships with these people begin to shift. You may discover that you feel more like an adult with them, instead of always feeling as though you become a child again in their presence. You may discover that you no longer feel a need to disagree with them over values or opinions. Instead, they become just other adults with other opinions instead of the mirrors they were before. As they cease to be mirrors to the child in you, their comments and values no longer hold the power to make you feel bad or diminished.

In time, you may discover that you can give back hand-me-downs on the spot in situations where you find yourself feeling vulnerable or caught up in an interaction that triggers your negative self-talk. You can learn to recognize these hand-me-downs right when they are delivered and choose to give them back, mentally, at that moment.

During a self-hypnosis course that lasted several weeks, a participant, Scott, found that whenever he went into trance, his older brother's voice would be there, telling him he wasn't doing it right. The voice told him he was dumb even to try to learn self-hypnosis. Throughout the course, Scott was coached on how to tell his brother to get out of his head, that he wasn't interested in those kinds of opinions. In time, Scott got so good at telling his brother to get out of his head and let him do his trance that he was able to clear away other kinds of self-abusing thoughts almost as soon as they arose. Before, he would hear negative self-talk and begin to feel defeated or angry with himself. Now, he developed an ongoing process of giving back burdensome and destructive suggestions whenever they came into conscious awareness.

One strategy that you might find empowering is to have a "secret alliance" with the child within whenever you visit people with whom you feel at risk of receiving negative hand-me-downs. You can take the child within along with you, without anyone knowing the child is there. During conversations or interactions with others, it's possible to have a running commentary going on with the child, inside your own head. You can give supportive responses to the child within, which counter whatever is said or done by others that, in the past, would have made you feel small, vulnerable or bad about yourself in some way.

One woman, Carrie, took the child within to a large sales meeting, where she would be one of only a few women. She hadn't had much experience with sales and felt nervous about interacting with so many men around a subject that was new to her. She reported, after she returned from the meeting, that all went well. At one point, she was responding to a comment made by one of her colleagues and she noticed the little girl next to her, looking up at her. For Carrie, the sudden awareness that the little girl was admiring her was enough to let her know that she was on top of things and handling them effectively. Throughout the meeting, Carrie held two tracks of awareness. On one track, she actively listened and responded to her colleagues. On the other, she would check in with the little girl and share private comments, in her own mind, about how glad she was that the child was there to share the moment with her.

Another client, Howard, brought the child within along on a visit to his parents' home. He had always felt like a little boy when he was with them, and he hoped that, by bringing along the child, he would be able to maintain his awareness as an adult. The strategy worked. Whenever he began to feel intimidated by either of his parents, he would comment to the little boy that it must have been really tough when he was young and all alone. He would say that he was glad to be able to be with the little boy this time, to help him see that what his parents were saying had lots to do with them and their values, but little to do with young Howard.

Both Howard and Carrie learned how to deal with negative self-talk and hand-me-downs passed along in current interactions before these suggestions became entrenched. They were able to clear their thinking on the spot and put in positive comments and reassurances where before there had been diminishing messages. Through a process of becoming comfortable dealing with authority figures in their trance experiences, Howard and Carrie developed an ability to do so, tactfully, in their ongoing adult interactions with other people. By including the child within in their awareness, they maintained their adult stance, regardless of what was happening in their interactions with others. Whenever they forgot to include the child within, they reported that it was all too easy to experience themselves as if they *were* the child and to lose their adult perspective.

More and more, as you identify and give back suggestions that have caused you to support family myths and deny your true self, you'll discover the child within coming to life. The child becomes lighter in spirit—more spontaneous, creative, joyous— as you unburden yourself from the terrible weight of negative hand-me-downs. You are healing the child, even as you empower yourself. As you clear away the internalized suggestions that have limited your self-expression, you may discover doors opening that enable you to become more than you ever imagined you could be.

Chapter 10

山

MANIFESTING A NEW YOU

While much of the work you've done in this book has focused on healing the past, the most important time in which you live is the present. Healing the past, reclaiming the child within, and recreating yourself only have meaning if the quality of your current life is improved. Remember, *you* are the point of power in the present. What counts is what you do today.

In this final chapter, we'll explore some ways you can put together the self-hypnotic techniques you've learned to create a more satisfying and personally rewarding present. A major focus will be on giving yourself permission to have a better life. I know of no other issue that is more central, ultimately, to becoming the person you want to be.

As adult children of dysfunctional families, many of us have a hard time realizing that we have a right to express ourselves in ways that are meaningful to us. We've been so accustomed to responding to the demands and needs of others, or so attuned to the possibilities of abandonment, that we haven't learned to listen to ourselves.

Remember that the false self is created in order to cope with confusing, chaotic and often frightening patterns of interaction that exist in dysfunctional families. Once the false self is established, we lose touch with the deep place inside that nurtures our unique talents. Instead, we learn to be in touch with the need to adapt and comply or to struggle against our circumstances in order to get what we want.

Another thing that's lost when we have to be a false self in order to survive is a sense of our own purpose, the meaning we attach to being alive. It's not unusual to hear adult children say that they can't figure out what they really want to be, professionally. Many adult children feel alone and disconnected in a very large world or are too frightened to take the risks necessary to move beyond the safety of old, familiar patterns.

An important part of recreating your self is to reconnect with a sense of purpose, with the things in life that carry meaning. As you reclaim the true self, you discover a deeper part of you that feels an urge to express itself in some meaningful way. This part is much more willing than the false self could ever be to take whatever constructive risks are necessary to get you where you need to be.

To reclaim your true self, then, means to get back in touch with a fundamental experience of your right to be in the world and to act in your own behalf to create a life you enjoy—and a life that is rewarding as well. As you work with the material in this chapter, keep in mind that there is no question about your having a right to have a life that works for you. The only question is how to let yourself know it—and then, live it.

CREATING A DAILY ATTUNEMENT PROCESS

In Chapter 3 I suggested "attuning" to the child within and the future self everyday is a powerful way to give yourself permission to create the life you want to have. This needn't take a lot of time. Most people put aside 20 minutes, more or less, for this process. The key element in recreating yourself is regularity and a *desire* to help things move along more quickly. Remember that desire, the emotional component of your inner work, gives a boost to anything you seek to achieve. The more you *want* to get somewhere, the faster you'll get there. A few minutes spent really *wanting* to achieve what you imagine will be more powerful than a half-hour spent wishing you were finished.[1]

As with all other inner work, when you put together your daily attunement, be creative and flexible. There is no "right" way to do this. There is only your way, and it will continue to evolve and change over time.

I usually recommend doing this particular process in the morning or whenever your day begins. Spending focused, quiet time with important parts of yourself sets the tone for the rest of the day. Giving yourself positive and accepting messages creates an internal environment of support and self-acceptance. Can you imagine what your day might be like if you went out into the world feeling this way?

For this reason, you may want to keep the morning attunement focused on several primary processes. First, it's always helpful, during this inner time with yourself, to make contact with the child within, if only for a moment. Because you're such an important mirror for this child, a daily reaffirmation of your love and regard will promote your healing process. This is also a good time to connect with the future self, to imagine your optimal life path, and to give yourself permission to have a better life.

You may find that the more intense work with corrective regression, giving back hand-me-downs, or other interventions on behalf of the wounded child are more effective at other times in the day. Sometimes, doing the child-within work can stir up feelings that may leave you in a vulnerable state. It's helpful to be able to allow these feelings, to be conscious of them, and to have the luxury of staying with them when they come into your awareness. If you're on your way to work, this might be more difficult to do than if you're home for the day and have time to let yourself feel connected with the child's experience.

The key thing to keep in mind is that the first attunement of the day is meant to empower you, to provide a strong foundation of internal equilibrium and well-being. In this way, you give yourself an opportunity to engage your daily activities from a state of mind that says, "I can."

A description of some of the elements that are helpful to include in the attunement process follows. If you're already familiar with these elements, such as affirmation or visualization, you might ask your unconscious to give you some new ideas for how to use them in your inner work. If there's anything here you haven't done before, your unconscious will automatically knit whatever will be useful for you into your current understanding.

Remember that this is a broad outline that includes the general elements of the attunement. *Your* inner process will reflect your own needs, preferences and style of using self-hypnosis. You may also find that adding or subtracting certain elements works better for you. The order in which the suggested steps are presented provides a progression from a breathing exercise that centers and settles you to more active visualization and mental rehearsal exercises that program your unconscious for what you want to achieve. Feel free to change the order so that it fits your own internal style and comfort.

SUGGESTED OUTLINE FOR MORNING ATTUNEMENT

- Color breathing
- Safe place/optimal life path
- Connect with child within and future self
    Request child within to give you his/her talent
    Tell future self how much you want to go forward; imagine being pulled forward
- Continue with other inner work
- Post-hypnotic suggestions
- Come back

Below are descriptions of these different elements, with suggestions of how you might use them.

COLOR BREATHING

I use color breathing as the first part of a morning attunement because of its centering quality. Many meditative traditions use breathing to focus and settle the mind. Color breathing, which I use as the first part of a morning attunement, combines breathing, visualization, and affirmation in a process that can help you focus your mind and center your body. This approach makes available the power of your unconscious to help you bring into your life whatever you seek to achieve.[2]

In general, color breathing involves imagining a color that represents a particular outcome you wish to achieve. Together with the imagined color, you combine a natural process of inhalation and exhalation, along with visualization and affirmation, to create an intense focus on your intended goal.

First, let's look at how you might choose colors. One way is to allow the unconscious to give you a spontaneous awareness of a particular color that is related to a particular idea. You might imagine that you want to increase your physical or psychological health. If you do, ask your unconscious to give you a color that represents the kind of health you seek and then allow yourself to accept whatever comes. You may find that over time the color changes or is replaced by another one. That's fine, too.

For some people, vigorous colors such as red, green or bright yellow convey a sense of well-being and health. Psychological health sometimes represents itself as soothing blues, purples or pastels, or as vivid, intense colors that carry lots of energy. There are no "right" colors. In fact, the colors that come to mind from the unconscious have such personal meaning that it can limit you to base your colors on what other people have experienced. The important thing to know is that *any* color may represent any goal you seek to achieve. As with all your inner work, accept what your unconscious gives you and allow it to develop in its own way over time.

You may discover that, instead of just a color, you become

aware of a particular object of a particular color. One woman in a workshop became aware of black and white triangles. Another suddenly felt surrounded by red roses. Accept whatever your unconscious chooses to represent the color you will breathe.

Perhaps you've gotten to a point where you want to bring more loving, reliable people into your life, but you're not sure how to accomplish this goal. A good place to begin is with the color breathing. You can ask your unconscious for a color that represents people who are supportive and positive. As you do the color breathing, you also convey to your unconscious that you're ready to look at, and deal with, any limiting beliefs you may have about the kinds of people you think you deserve in your life. Whatever affirmations you choose to use with the color that represents more positive relationships in your life also act as powerful suggestions to the unconscious to create new beliefs about people. Each time you breathe the color, you encourage yourself to learn that you have a right to have people around who are good for you. Remember to connect with your *desire* to have things change for the better.

If, as is true with many adult children, you need to increase your financial security, you might want to color breathe on the subject of money. When you ask your unconscious for a color to represent financial security, the color gold, or a combination of gold and silver, may come to mind. I have heard people report an entire range of colors, from dark to light and pale to vivid, to represent financial security. Again, let your own creativity and personal world of meaning draw on the color that is best for you.

Parenthetically, adult children of dysfunctional families often have difficulties with money and the concept of abundance. Because of the chaos, unpredictability and unreliability often experienced growing up in a dysfunctional home, financial security can become a conflicted, elusive reality. Part of giving yourself permission to have a better life includes having the right to meet your needs comfortably, whatever that may mean to you personally.

As you develop the colors to use in the exercise, you may be surprised to discover that your unconscious often gives you combined colors. In the unconscious, there are no limits when working with imagery. Colors become multidimensional. They combine and shimmer in an infinite number of possible combinations. If your unconscious gives you a color that is really made up of many colors intertwined, creating something you've never seen before, allow it. It will convey a combination of elements that speak to you in new, important ways.

You can focus on almost anything as part of the color-breathing exercise. In addition to the unlimited colors you have available, you can also create as many affirmations as you want to further support what you seek.[3] These affirmations become powerful post-hypnotic suggestions. It's helpful to remind yourself of your affirmations at times throughout the day. To do so reinforces the impact of these post-hypnotic suggestions on your unconscious processes.

Some sample affirmations follow, to show you ways in which you might construct your own. In general, though not always, it's best to make up your own affirmations, rather than to use someone else's. There will be ways to word your affirmations that make them personal and most powerful for you. Keep in mind that it's best to avoid words like "try" and "not." You may need to look back at the Chapter 3 on self-hypnosis, in the section on language (pp. 76–77). The same rules apply to affirmations.

Remember that the unconscious acts on what you affirm. Keep your affirmations in the present tense, which implies to the unconscious that what you seek exists already. It will then work to conform to that reality.

If you were to color breathe for health, you might say to yourself:

My body is healthy, vibrant, vital and resilient.
I have more energy than I ever imagined possible.
As the day goes on, I am surprised to discover that I am even more energized and creative than when I started.

For financial security, you might use affirmations like the following:

I am magnetic to money. I attract to myself, and have, all that I could possibly need.
I am financially independent, and I allow it to be easy.

For friends, an affirmation might be similar to the one for money:

I am magnetic to loving and supportive people.
I draw to myself people who are good for me and for whom I can be a good friend.

When you've finished breathing the color and saying the affirmations to yourself, it's time to take a few moments to focus on an image that represents the outcome you seek.[4] You may choose simply to focus on an image of an object or symbol, or you might want to use mental rehearsal to imagine yourself as you want to be.[5]

If no visual image comes to mind, spend a few moments imagining how you will *feel*—in your body, emotions and mind—when you *have* achieved what you seek. Remember to include as many of your senses as possible. For example, hear the sounds associated with your achievement. Smell the smells. Imagine the surroundings. Taste the flavors.

When you come to the imagery portion of the color-breathing exercise, it's okay to spend only a minute or two imagining the outcome you seek. Most important is to allow yourself to have whatever *experiential* sense of achievement feels most powerful. At times, this part of the exercise will be more vivid than at other times. That's fine. Remember that the intensity and focus of your self-hypnotic trances will shift, on given days, from being more focused to, perhaps, feeling loose and drifting.

An example of an image for visualizing health might be to see your body as it would look if it were perfectly healthy. For friends, you might imagine that you are standing within a group of people who are all smiling at you. You might hear their voices talking to you with interest and feel a sense of camaraderie with them. Use as many of your senses as you can whenever you visualize the outcomes you seek. The more senses you use, the more powerfully your unconscious will respond to what you imagine.

For physical health, you might imagine yourself doing exercises you really enjoy. You could imagine, also, that you've just finished exercising and that you have that good feeling of satisfaction and well-being that comes when the body has exerted itself in a healthy way. You might imagine that you are looking in a mirror and that you like what you see—someone who is radiant and vital. You might imagine how your body feels when it's at its peak of health, even if you haven't yet achieved that goal. It might be that a powerful image for you is to see yourself eating fresh, healthful foods. It helps to draw on all your senses, noticing the flavors, colors, and textures of the foods your body prefers when it is at its peak of well-being.

When color breathing for financial security, you might visualize an image of your checkbook with a balance that is always sufficient. You might prefer a money tree, imagining that you are going to the tree and gathering as much money as you'd like to have. You might finish by imagining that you go to the bank and deposit the money in your checking or savings account. You might also find it powerful to imagine how it feels to be able to earn your own way in the world, to be a capable, creative and successful person, *in whatever ways that has meaning for you.*

When preparing your color-breathing exercise, as you think about the kinds of things you want to achieve in your life, consider, also, what you would most like to contribute. Whenever anyone does color breathing in order to have something come to them, such as increased responsibility, psychological ease or comfort, or money, I recommend that they link the idea of receiving with the concept of giving, of creating an inherent reciprocity.

For example, if you are looking for a job, you might tell yourself that there are people who need what you have to offer and that you just haven't met them yet. When you do meet them, you'll find your job. This kind of suggestion reaffirms that you have a unique talent that is valuable to others. It buoys your self-confidence and encourages you to take the risks that job hunting and career development often require.

If you seek increased psychological ease, a healing from the chaos of the dysfunctional family, perhaps you could imagine that your increased ease makes it more possible to express yourself. By expressing yourself more actively and creatively, you automatically contribute something to the world.

If you want to increase your income, you might envision success as an automatic response to your contributing something to others. You have something to offer to people that they need, and they have money with which to pay for what you offer. It becomes a give-and-take proposition, whereby you can constantly affirm to yourself that you are worthwhile, that you have something to offer, and that others will benefit from what you have to give.

Be sure to interpret these suggestions in whatever ways make sense to you. Sometimes adult children of dysfunctional families get fed up with having to think about how they affect the world at large. That's how they spent their entire childhood, and possibly much of their adulthood, as well. If the above suggestions feed into that place in you, then ignore the linkages between giving and receiving for now. It's better to affirm *your* needs— something most adult children have to learn to do—than to get involved in worrying about reciprocity. There may come a time when it will be comfortable to include this concept, emphasizing how it affirms that you have something to offer, but it's not at all necessary. Whatever leaves you feeling most empowered is the best approach to follow.

Sometimes, you may discover that your imagery or affirmations reflect limitations you are in the process of overcoming. If you think this may be happening, or if the color breathing seems not to be creating any change in your life, take some time to look for beliefs or family injunctions that may be getting in your way. Later, when you have time, giving back a few hand-me-downs or doing a corrective regression might help to get things moving again.

It's a good idea to give yourself permission to experiment with how many different subjects you want to deal with on any given day. I usually color breathe on two or three different things. I usually teach people to "breathe" each color three times, which means dealing with combinations of three. If you choose one subject, you can do one round of three breaths, or several rounds of three breaths each. You may find that more than three rounds of three breaths (nine breaths, altogether) takes more time than you want to give to this one portion of your morning attunement. Or, you may find that, at times, the color breathing is all you really want to do and you may feel quite comfortable doing many rounds of three breaths. Also, as is true with everything else here, if rounds of three breaths don't feel right to you, do whatever combination seems best. Some people may prefer to do seven breaths, or four, or just one. Accept the most natural and focused rhythm for you.

The color you choose to breathe is imagined out in front of you as a mist, a cloud, a light, or any substance that comes to you naturally. As you inhale, imagine that the light enters your lungs and fills your entire chest. Hold your breath as you mentally repeat your affirmation. Then, as you exhale, imagine that the color moves out through your whole body and into the surrounding environment. Along with the color, send the *intention* embodied in the affirmation, imagining that it, too, goes out into the environment.

With *each* breath, imagine the color entering you. Hold the breath while you repeat the affirmation, and then exhale both the color and the intent of the affirmation at the same time. Imagine that they flow throughout your body and out into the world. Remember that, with each breath and each repetition of the affirmation, you are giving your unconscious a powerful message that mobilizes it to respond. You are creating self-fulfilling prophecies that are positive and that will give you an opportunity to overcome the limiting beliefs and patterns of interaction you learned when you were young.

If you find that you have difficulty holding your breath as you repeat your entire affirmation in your mind, allow yourself to exhale a little bit and take in some more air and color. Breathing from your diaphragm, along with practice, can increase your ability to hold your breath longer. Also, there may be times when you won't be able to hold your breath at all, as when you have a cold. During these times, simply imagine the color filling you, repeat the affirmation to yourself, and then imagine the color and the intent of the affirmation flowing out of you together, unrelated to your breathing.

If you don't have time in the morning, color breathing can be done anytime, anywhere. At bedtime, color breathing is a way to give yourself powerful suggestions your unconscious can work on while you sleep. You might also find you like to color breathe when you first awaken in the morning, in those moments before you actually get up. If you have a long train ride, it's possible to do your color breathing while you travel. There's really no limit to the potential places and times you can attune to your inner process. As with all the techniques presented in the book, let your own needs and creativity be your guide.

Also, the affirmations used with color breathing may be repeated mentally throughout the day, to reinforce the outcomes you seek. Even if you aren't in a place where you feel comfortable visualizing the color and doing the breathing, there's nothing to prevent you from repeating your affirmations to yourself.

There's no need to tape record the color-breathing exercise or sample attunement. It's a good idea to learn to do this inner work as you would a meditation. Let it be a process that finds its own way as you go along. To tape record it would set it too firmly in place. Just let yourself read over the steps in Exercise 15 (p. 268) several times. You might find it helpful to put them on an index card or a sheet of paper to have in front of you as you attune. You can then refer to the steps if you need to, as you go along. It's also helpful, at first, to write down any affirmations you choose to use during your morning attunement, until you have them memorized. Remember that affirmations said in trance become powerful post-hypnotic suggestions. As with all the other exercises in the book, you'll find the short forms of both the color breathing and the morning attunement formats at the back of the book.

Another important thing to know about working with color breathing and affirmations is that there will come a time when the affirmations become rote and less engaging than they once were. This is a signal that you've built in the post-hypnotic suggestions implied by the affirmations and that it's time to move on to something else. It may be that you need to create an updated affirmation about the same issue, or it may be time to begin color breathing about another issue. You can let your own internal sense of connection with the affirmation be your guide. The more energized you feel when you repeat an affirmation, and the more focus and interest you find arising in you, the more effective things will be. If you have no emotional connection with the affirmation, change it.

The same principle applies to the imagery portion of color breathing. If you find that the image changes spontaneously, and you're comfortable with that change, go with it. If you discover that you're bored with visualizing a particular image, and that you have trouble concentrating on it after having used it for a while, it's probably time to let it go. If you choose to continue using the same affirmation, you may want to update the old image or let it go and create a new one. Whenever you change to a new affirmation, allow your unconscious to give you a new image to accompany it.

Usually, the need to change an affirmation or image won't arise for several months, perhaps even more. There are some images and affirmations I've used for a year or longer that still carry energy. Some have become less entrancing in a month. There's no set rule. Use your internal sensory awareness as your best guide. The important thing to know is that it's perfectly all right to have a given affirmation or image around for a long time. It doesn't mean that you're not getting anywhere. It simply means that it continues to be a powerful message in the process of recreating yourself.

SAFE PLACE/OPTIMAL LIFE PATH

The next part of your morning attunement might be to go to your safe place or to find yourself walking along your optimal life path. Remember that you can imagine an optimal path related to anything at all. Perhaps, from time to time, you will want to find yourself walking along one that pertains to the color breathing you have just done.

There's no need always to find yourself on a path. You can connect with your future self and the child within, as well as other parts, just as well in any safe place that may come to mind during a given attunement. In fact, it's helpful to switch from always walking on your path to finding yourself in a variety of safe, sacred, or special private places from time to time. It's important for the attunement process to remain vital, and changing locations can help to enliven your experience and keep your curiosity engaged.

Remember to use all your senses to explore the place you have entered when you go inside during this phase of your attunement. Notice, first, whether you are indoors or outdoors. There can be safe, private places wherever you choose to find them. You may discover that some have elements of both indoor environments and the outdoors. Create and allow whatever you need at any given time.

Sometimes, you might connect with a particular place and tend to go there time and again. It becomes the place of choice. That's fine, too. You may find that it helps you to have the regularity of a special environment that is consistently available to you. Go with that, if it emerges. Also, go along with any changes that occur, should they emerge over time. In one way or another, your process is furthered as your inner experience develops and evolves.

As you will do with the color-breathing images, draw on all your senses. If you're outdoors, smell whatever natural fragrances are present. Listen for natural sounds. Become aware of colors, shapes and textures that capture your attention. *Feel* your feet on the ground, if you're walking; imagine your body supported, if you're sitting down. Be in your body, experiencing the temperature of the air on your skin. Notice whether there's a breeze, or if the air is still.

If you're indoors, notice what patterns of light and shadow

may be present. Discover the nature and texture of any walls that may be there. If there are windows, take a look at what you see, if you can see through them. Also notice the scents that may be present or the sounds that are particularly reassuring. Feel the support that is available if you choose to sit down.

If you're walking along a path, what's underfoot? Notice how it feels to be there. Again, bring in all of your senses. Become aware of the surrounding environment, as well. If you come to this path often, you might take a look around and see if you've progressed, or if you are exploring a certain portion of the path in some detail. Sometimes, the path has something to teach you and you wouldn't want to move along until you've discovered the awarenesses that are available at that particular place.

CONNECTING WITH THE CHILD WITHIN

Once you've become aware of the place you've chosen to be, take a moment to recall the child within. Allow the child to join you. You might ask your unconscious to present you with the facet of the child that holds your talent. We *all* have a talent of some kind. It may not be an "artistic" talent or something that the world would flock to your door to see, but *each and every person has something to express in this world*—and so do you.

As important as anything else you've done in reclaiming the child and recreating the self is to develop a strong desire to express yourself. This doesn't mean that you have to "go out and *be* somebody." It just means that you have the right to be *you,* whomever that may be. To do so you need to have available the talents and skills held within the true self of the child. Remember, the child is like the seed of a tree. All of the potential to be the best adult you can be is held within the true self of the child. As you create a supportive internal environment, you give the child permission to release that potential into your adult life.

Giving the child permission to release your talents and potential isn't always simple. You may find that certain objections arise, either in you or in the child. These suggest the presence of beliefs that block you from becoming all you can be. It's helpful to remember that blocks are gifts from the unconscious. They tell you where you still have work to do in giving back hand-me-downs and changing your expectations and beliefs. They reflect what the protective voices are saying to you and show you ways in which parts of you fear going forward.

Next, it's essential to convey your love to the child, a love you feel deeply and actively. You might imagine that the child sits in your lap, or you might kneel down in front of the child. Experiment, for a moment, by pretending that you are actually with that child right now. Look at the child and say, "I love you so very much. I'm so glad you're in my life."

How did that feel? Are you comfortable telling the child about the love you experience? Do you feel receptive to the child? Are you glad that the child is in your life? These are important questions. If you find you're uncomfortable, that's good to know. It's more information about old feelings you didn't realize were still hanging on. Any discomfort you feel can point the way to old images of yourself, old post-hypnotic suggestions that you still carry around, that tell you that you're not okay.

Whenever you discover discomfort around giving yourself loving and supportive messages, it's helpful to pay particular attention to any shame the child within may be experiencing. The wounded child in you feels so basically unworthy that, as you love and reassure him or her, the entire process of becoming more of what you can be is enhanced.

As you interact with the child, remember to reaffirm that you are willing to hear the child's story, to listen to the child's truth, and to know, consciously, where and how the child became so wounded. This child is the seed of your potential and deserves your respect and attention.

When you're talking with the child in you, do so in whatever ways are comfortable, using whatever phrases are natural for you. The important thing is that you convey your love and your gratitude that the child exists.

It's also helpful to be willing to play. The child within may want to explore your safe place or run along your optimal path. You may discover that there is a strong curiosity in the child. Give yourself permission to respond to that by participating in the wonder and playfulness of creating an adventure together.

You may be surprised to discover how quickly the child within responds to the positive mirroring you offer when you request the talent the child has kept safe all these years. As the child experiences your desire to utilize your inherent abilities, there is usually a rapid response. Children are resilient, and the child in you is no exception. The child within understands respect and will respond eagerly and with enthusiasm *in his or her own best time.*

Be sure to avoid rushing or making demands on the child. Think of a young animal that's been mistreated. When you reach out to feed it, sometimes it pulls away. It has learned not to trust the human hand. If you remain present, without chasing after it, you'll find that the animal will usually approach, in time. Do the same for the child in you. Give that child a chance to realize that you truly mean it, that the love you offer is real and reliable.

And, as always, be gentle with yourself. Give yourself the same understanding and love you seek to give to the child. If you have mixed feelings, or just can't seem to find the kind of love I'm describing here, accept that. In your own good time, you'll discover how to love the child in positive and personally meaningful ways. The more you can give yourself permission to find your own way, the more quickly and easily you'll surprise yourself with new and positive feelings about the child . . . and yourself.

Contact with the child needn't be lengthy. It can take place in just a minute or two. The important thing is to make a connection and to reaffirm your love for the child and your wish to express yourself fully. There may be days when you want to sit with this experience for as long as you can. At other times, you may have decided to focus on other things and this contact will take but a moment of your attention. It's regularity that counts, more than the amount of time spent. Your goal is to reinforce the connection made and then to nourish it.

CONNECTING WITH THE FUTURE SELF

Next, it's helpful to take a few moments, or many minutes, to reconnect with the future self. You can imagine that the future

self is there with you, already nearby. Remember that to experience what it's like to *be* your future self creates a magnetic,
unconscious pull that draws you towards becoming that more
evolved, more mature you. It's enough to have a vague impression of the future self, or you may find that you experience this
part of you vividly. The clarity of your impression will probably
differ from time to time. Be sure to accept whatever you experience, realizing that each day presents a new opportunity to practice self-acceptance.

There are many ways to connect with the future self. You
might imagine what it would be like to hold the hand of your
future self, or to feel a supportive, reassuring hand resting on
your shoulder. These are images and sensations you can draw on
to increase feeling supported and reassured in any situation later
in the day. It may be that, at a given time, it's more powerful for
you to "see" the future self and imagine what it feels like to be
that person. The important thing is to reinforce the connection
with, and to rekindle your desire to become, your future self.

It's also helpful to take a moment to recall the thread that
connects your heart to the heart of the future self, as well as the
thread that connects you and the child within. Remember that
these threads are magnetic and that the one you share with the
future self guides, *draws* you, into your optimal future. Give
yourself permission to experience what that pull feels like, to
imagine that you can feel yourself being drawn forward.

There are many ways to interact with your future self during
this portion of your inner work, other than those mentioned
above. You might want to engage in a dialogue, and ask the
future self some questions. You might have a problem or a challenge that would benefit from some input. At times like these,
you might allow yourself to *become* the future self and see the
problem from the perspective of this wiser you. You can then
allow the back of the mind of the future self to fill the back of
your present-day mind with "memories" of how you got from
where you are today to where you need to be. To do this, just
give yourself a few minutes where your conscious mind just drifts
or focuses on the scenery around you, as your unconscious takes

in whatever the future self has to offer. Remember that the memories of the future self become the new ideas, responses, and moments of inspiration that lead you forward, today, step by step.

Also, remember to say to the future self, "I want to be you," "I am becoming you," or "I am you." You can discover other phrases that suit your experience at any given time, things to say that reaffirm your desire to become your future self.

CONTINUING OTHER INNER WORK
At this point in your attunement, you might want to do some additional inner work. As time permits, *any* self-hypnotic work can be done now. You may find that you'd like to spend a few minutes doing some mental rehearsal of an upcoming event, experiencing yourself handling it effectively and constructively.[5] It might be helpful to spend some time asking your unconscious to work on a specific problem for you, while your conscious mind drifts and enjoys the comfort of your trance time.

Whenever you ask your unconscious for this kind of help, you can also suggest to yourself that the answer will come at a moment when you need it most, even if it's when you expect it least. Also, there's no need to feel that you must do anything at all. It's up to you, your time schedule and whatever needs may make themselves known to you.

POST-HYPNOTIC SUGGESTIONS
Before you finish your attunement, you might want to take a moment or two to give yourself some post-hypnotic suggestions. One that I use every day suggests that, as the day progresses, I will feel even more energized and creative than I did in the morning. I also tell myself that I'll be fully alert all day and will be open to creative inspiration from my unconscious, as needed. One colleague tells himself that he'll automatically go in and out of trance throughout the day, whenever that would be helpful to him and his work.

Other possibilities might involve telling yourself that you'll be surprised to discover how comfortable you are in a certain situation that may be coming up. It may be helpful to give yourself suggestions that provide specific cues linked with certain states of mind. For example, you might tell yourself that when you reach for the telephone you'll discover that, at some point in the beginning of your call, you have a wonderful feeling of confidence in your stomach and you didn't even realize you could have it so easily.

It may be that it would be helpful simply to tell yourself a word that creates an inner state you'd like to have. You might give yourself the suggestion that whenever you say the word "settle" you will automatically become calmer and more focused.

Your post-hypnotic suggestions may be long or short, one word or many. They may also deal with short-term or long-term results. Use your creativity to guide you in choosing what would be the most helpful to give yourself at any particular time.

COMING BACK

After you've finished all the different activities you want to include in your attunement, it's time to come back. There are several ways to reorient quickly to full alertness. First, you can simply tell yourself that it's time to come back and then begin to wiggle your fingers and toes. You may choose, instead, to sit with your experience for a moment, exploring the state of your body and mind, savoring whatever lingering sensations you may have before opening your eyes and coming all the way back. You can also count, mentally, from three to one, suggesting to yourself that when you say the number one your eyes will open spontaneously and automatically and you'll be all the way back. Use whatever form of returning from trance that works best for you on any given day.

If you have the time, and you keep a journal of your daily attunements, you might want to take a moment at the end to write down any thoughts or experiences you'd like to remember. Keeping a journal is a good idea in general, and you may discover that you'd like to have several, each devoted to a different aspect of your inner work. One journal might focus on your morning attunements. Another might focus on your self-hypnotic work with the child within. As with everything that relates to your inner process, it's all up to you. Give yourself permission to have things be just the way you'd like them to be to meet your needs in the best ways possible.

Also, throughout the day, if you notice negative self-talk running through your mind, replace it with positive affirmations. You might choose the ones you used during color breathing. You might have others that you say to yourself on a random basis. Whatever affirmations you use, it's helpful to remember that they are constructive and empowering self-hypnotic suggestions.

Whenever you notice that your self-talk is of the negative variety, be gentle with yourself. Use every opportunity to affirm your worth as a person, your humanness and fallibility, and your strengths. It's healing to be able to laugh at yourself, rather than to become mired in self-criticism and self-blame. Every moment of every day provides unlimited opportunities to choose to be a loving, validating and respectful mirror for yourself and to forgive yourself when you fall back into old patterns you learned as a child.

My wish for you is that, if you haven't already, you'll develop a habit of going inside every day to do some kind of attunement that allows you to reconnect with important parts of yourself. When you do, your unconscious understands that you are eager to remember, to learn and to go forward into your optimal future. And, it *will* respond.

You can give yourself an opportunity—and permission—to discover the new behaviors, ideas, and responses that will enter your life unexpectedly, as your unconscious creates an internal readiness for the outcomes you seek. Let yourself be delightfully surprised by the unending magic of your unconscious, and by its ability to create in your life the self-affirming and positive things you deserve.

Exercises: Short Forms

Exercise #1   Self-Hypnotic Induction

• Settle yourself in a place where you can be alone, undisturbed, for the next 15 minutes or so.

• Allow yourself to sit with enough support for your back to allow you to surrender to that support and find comfort in it.

• Take a deep breath as you roll your opened eyes toward the ceiling.

• As you exhale, allow your eyelids to close naturally, while your eyes find their proper resting place behind those lids.

• Take two more deep breaths, holding your breath for a few moments before you exhale. Notice that with each breath your body settles just a bit more.

• If there is any tension present, bring it along. It will ease as you become more absorbed in your inner experience.

• Allow any distractions to become leaves on a stream, floating into, and then out of, your awareness.

• Discover yourself in a safe place that may be indoors or outdoors. The important thing about it is that it is *your* place. It is a private place and, in it, you are perfectly safe.

• Notice the colors, shapes and textures in your safe place . . . and any other qualities of the environment that come into your awareness. Become aware of how it feels to touch things there, of what natural smells and sounds are there.

• You may discover, as your trance develops, that there is a certain feeling of safety or comfort somewhere in your awareness . . . maybe as a sensation in your body. Let it develop, now.

• If your mind is blank and no impressions come, remember the creative void. Your unconscious is still searching for just the right impression to give you.

• What would those impressions be, if you *were* able to be aware of them?

• If you haven't already, allow your eyes to close, there in that safe place, as you deepen your awareness of any comforting sounds or smells that may be there.

• At this point, give yourself some quiet time just drifting in trance, or do whatever inner work you have planned for this time. Give yourself as much time as you'd like.

• Once you've completed your inner journey, take a few moments, now, to give yourself some positive post-hypnotic suggestions.

• To bring yourself back, now, simply count from three to one, mentally, with the suggestion that when you say the number "one" to yourself, your eyes will pop open automatically and spontaneously and you'll be all the way back.

• Take a moment to sit with the tone of your experience as you would the tone of a bell just rung.

• When you're ready to be all the way back, simply wiggle your fingers and toes and go on to your next activity.

Exercise #2   Identifying Protective Parts

• Put yourself into trance and think about a way you limit yourself.

• Let an impression of a person, animal, other kind of being, or an object that represents this part of you come from the back of your mind to the front of your mind.

• Notice what qualities the part expresses and your responses to them.

• Become the part and experience what it's like to be that part.

• Ask yourself, as the part, "What is my function? What do I do to protect [your name]?"

• Discover a screen on which is projected a memory or image that conveys to you the time in childhood when this part was created.

• Once you've understood the protective origins of this part, give it your appreciation for working so hard to keep you safe.

• Ask it if it will consider updating the *kind* of protection it can provide you, now that you're an adult.

• Allow an impression to pop into your mind that represents the part in its updated form. Become this part and *feel* the changes that have been made.

• When you've had a few minutes to sit with your experience, bring yourself back to an alert state, wiggle your fingers and toes, and jot down some notes about your experience.

Exercise #3   Identifying Resource Parts

• Put yourself into trance and think about a specific quality of skill you would like to develop.

• Allow an impression of that quality or skill to emerge as an object, person, animal, being, color, sensation or state of mind.

• Become aware of the qualities that part conveys to you and of your responses to those qualities.

• Explore what it's like to *be* that object, person, animal, being, color, sensation or state of mind.

• Let your unconscious create an image of a situation in which you are expressing this skill or quality successfully. Explore the sensations of the skill or quality somewhere in your body or feelings.

• Enjoy your experience of this resource state. Affirm your pleasure at having it in your life.

• Give your body and mind time to learn how it feels, on deeply-unconscious and nonverbal levels, when you have developed this skill or quality fully.

• Come back, now, all the way into full alertness, bringing along any sensations or images you would like to keep.

• Take a moment to jot down your experience and remember that your unconscious continues to develop the theme of your experience even as your conscious mind goes on to other things.

Exercise #4: Discovering Your Future Self

• Begin your trance in whatever way works best for you. Allow yourself to begin in a safe place where you can sit down and drift into a reverie.

• Imagine yourself walking on a path. It is your optimal life path.

• Simply notice all the qualities around you—the color and texture of the path; the natural sounds and smells drifting on the air; the quality of the surrounding environment.

• Because this is an optimal path, it is a place where you are absolutely safe, a place where you connect with everything you need to complete the journey you have begun.

• Allow the child within to be there with you. The child can be whatever age is most appropriate to the issue you are addressing now.

• Notice how it feels to have the child there with you, and notice the child's state of mind. Whatever it is, simply accept it.

• Any mixed feelings you may become aware of might indicate that your intent to go forward on this path has triggered a protective part or a limiting belief it would be worthwhile to note and explore later.

• Take a moment to look back and see how far you've come. What is it like back there?

• Look forward again and notice someone approaching. It is your future self, a more evolved, wiser part of you that has already made the journey you are beginning.

• Allow impressions of the future self to simply drop into the front of your mind from the back of your mind. Accept whatever comes.

• If you will, take a moment now to *become* the future self . . . to experience the perspective, internal feelings and state of mind of this future you.

• Take a moment to look at the present-day you through the eyes of the future self. Give yourself an opportunity to experience the love and acceptance you can feel toward yourself.

• Notice how the future self feels toward the child within and how the child within responds to the future self.

• Perhaps for a moment, now, you might allow the future self to convey to the back of your mind the important steps you took to get from your present-day self to the future self. Allow this process to be *unconscious*. Whatever you need to know will come to you at exactly the right time and in all the right ways.

• As your present-day self, perhaps you could ask your future self to be your guide.

• Take a moment to say to the future self, "I want to be you." Notice how it feels to say this.

• Notice that you, the future self, and the child within can begin moving further along your optimal life path. Each step conveys to your unconscious your willingness to make whatever changes are necessary to achieve what you seek on this path.

• When you're ready, leave a part of you on the path, continuing to go forward, as the rest of you comes back to the present.

• Wiggle your fingers and toes to bring yourself all the way back.

Exercise #5:   Your Thread of Connection

• Put yourself into trance and find yourself in a safe, private place, a place where you can communicate clearly with parts of you that live in the unconscious.

• Notice that the child within is present. Allow that child to be whatever age spontaneously springs to mind.

• Allow your future self to be there as well.

• Coming from the chest area of the future self and connecting with your chest, in the area of your heart, there is a thread of some color. It may be gold, or silver, or some other color that has meaning for you.

• The thread represents a living, vital connection between you and the future self. It is magnetic and pulls you automatically into your optimal future. It draws you, automatically and inevitably, towards that future self.

• Notice, now, that a similar thread comes from your chest area and connects with the area of the child's heart. This thread represents your connection with the child within. It is also magnetic and draws the child toward you, toward becoming who you are today.

• Remember, just as the future self is the promise that you make it, you are the promise that the child makes it.

• Take a moment or two, now, just to feel the power of these connections, to imagine the magnetic quality at work. Imagine that the thread magnetically draws you toward your goals in all the ways that are best for you.

• Notice that the child is drawn along, automatically, as well.

• For just a moment, say "yes" to the future self and sense how your commitment to become your future self intensifies the color of the thread. The magnetic quality of the thread is also intensified when you do this.

• To come all the way back, simply wiggle your fingers and toes and hold onto any lingering feelings of connection you may want to keep.

Exercise #6   Discovering the Child in You

• Put yourself in trance in whatever way works best for you.

• Take yourself to a safe place and settle in.

• Allow an impression to come from the back of your mind to the front of your mind that represents the child-within at a particular age. Let yourself be surprised by the child that comes to mind. You may be aware of a photograph or an image of the child.

• Ask yourself, now, the following questions:

> What do I think of this child?
> What kind of child is this?
> Is the child happy? Sad? Angry? Withdrawn?
> What is my response to this child?
> Am I happy to see the child? Irritated? Indifferent?

• Allow the child to come to life, as though the child were actually there with you right now.

• Reach out to the child, make contact in some way that feels right to you and that is okay with the child.

• Remember to allow the child whatever response arises naturally. Explore your feelings about the child's response.

• If the child is willing, perhaps you can hold him or her for a moment and discover how that feels to each of you.

• When you're ready to come back, remind yourself that a part of you stays with the child, continuing to develop the relationship. Then, bring yourself all the way back to an alert state of mind and wiggle your fingers and toes, and spend a few minutes writing down your experience.

Exercise #7: Corrective Regression

• Allow yourself to go into trance, now, and take yourself to a safe place inside.

• Notice that nearby is an old scrapbook. It holds important memories from childhood. You may find photographs, words, images, vague impressions or blank spaces that seem to speak to you in a way you don't understand consciously.

• Turn the pages and discover that you seem to stop at a particular page. Notice what it contains.

• Allow your mind to go back, now, across time and space, to the time and place related to whatever you've discovered in the scrapbook. Remember to go back *as the adult,* as an observer.

• Notice where you find the child. Become aware of what is happening there.

• Let yourself run through the entire scene once or twice, observing whatever you need to become aware of.

• Step in, now, and help the child in whatever way the memory requires. Be sure to take along your future self if you need help.

• Become particularly aware of how the child is feeling in response to the help you're giving. Accept the child's feelings, whatever they may be.

• Now, bring the child with you back to your present, to your safe place or to your current home, if that's a safe place.

• Become aware of a bodily sensation you can use as a signal that the child is in need.

• Be sure to leave a part of you there with the child, allowing the relationship to continue to develop, allowing yourself to continue to listen to the child's story.

• When you're ready to reorient, bring yourself all the way back, wiggle your fingers and toes, and spend a few minutes writing down your experience.

Exercise #8   Bonding With the Infant

• Put yourself into trance in whatever way is best for you right now. Find yourself in a safe place.

• Allow your mind to drift back, all the way back, to the time right after you were born.

• Become the infant. How do you feel? Where are you? Take a moment to discover what the environment is like . . . whether it's bright or dim . . . quiet or noisy . . . warm or cold. Allow any sensation or awareness that your unconscious wants you to have to come into your experience now.

• Now, become the adult you are today, looking at the infant. What are your responses to the infant? Remember to accept everything that comes to mind.

• Is the infant agitated or sleeping?

• If it's all right with you, reach out and pick up the infant.

How does it feel to hold that tiny, new life? Give yourself a minute to explore your responses.

• If the infant is stressed, you might want to gently massage the infant's arms and legs with your fingers. You have the capacity to help that child relax and find comfort.

• If you don't know what to do, allow your future self to help you.

• Notice that there will come a moment when the infant looks at you. Stay with that eye contact. Remember that you are an important mirror for the infant. Allow yourself, if you will, to reflect love, acceptance . . . perhaps even your pleasure at the fact that this unique person is alive.

• When you're ready, bring the infant back to your safe place. In every real sense, the infant lives with you now. You are the most important source of soothing and comfort in that infant's world.

• Be sure to leave a part of you there with the infant and come back when you're ready. Wiggle your fingers and toes to bring yourself all the way back.

Exercise #9   Healing the Shamed Child in You

• Put yourself into trance in whatever way is most comfortable for you this time. Find yourself in a particularly private, safe place.

• Allow an impression of the shamed child to come to mind. The impression may be of a child-within, or it may be a symbolic representation of some kind. Accept whatever comes now.

• What does the shamed part of you look like? What qualities does it convey? What responses arise in you now?

• Take a moment and *become* the shamed part of you. Experience what it's like on the inside.

• Become your present-day self again and, if it's all right with you, reach out to that shamed child. What does it feel like to make contact with this part of you? Allow any mixed feelings you may have to be present. Simply accept and validate them. They have something important to tell you.

• Give yourself permission, now, to open your heart to the shamed child. This part of you has a story to tell . . . a story of how the shame came to be. What feelings arise in you, as you open up to this child?

• Take whatever amount of time you'd like, now, to spend getting to know the shamed child. If you need help, call on your future self. Remember, the shamed child and the future self have already developed their healing relationship.

• Allow yourself to remember that whenever you reach inside and spend time with the shamed child, you give your unconscious the message that you are willing to remember. You are willing to hear and accept the child's story. You are ready to heal the old wounds that created the shame.

• Ask your unconscious to guide the process of remembering and healing. It will happen in your own best time, in your own best way.

• Come back now, leaving a part of you there with the child to continue developing a relationship of openness and acceptance.

Exercise #10 Discovering Favorite Family Stories

• Find a place where you can be alone for at least 15 minutes. Be sure to have paper and pencil with you.

• Put yourself into a light trance and let your mind drift back to your childhood.

• Focus your attention on family stories you heard growing up. They may have been stories about relatives or other people. They may have been fairy tales that were family favorites, passed down from generation to generation.

• Pay particular attention to the morals of the stories, and to the feeling quality they convey.

• Look for both positive and negative messages and injunctions conveyed by the stories.

• As memories come to mind, write down whatever stories or anecdotes you remember, as well as the beliefs and expectations they convey to you.

• Give yourself a moment to find whatever hidden messages or injunctions may be held in the stories.

• Take a moment, now, to imagine the child within taking in these messages.

• Imagine how both the overt and covert messages in the stories have affected your life from childhood to the present.

• Ask yourself if you would like to change the quality of the perceptual filter that is related to these injunctions.

• When you feel you've remembered all you can for this time, bring yourself back with the thought in mind that your unconscious can continue to bring injunctions to mind from time to time, even when you're engaged in other activities.

Exercise # 11   Defining Specific Family Injunctions

• Find a place where you can sit undisturbed for 15 minutes or so. Be sure to have a pencil and paper handy.

• Put yourself into a light trance and ask your unconscious to review messages given you by the family, messages about yourself as a person, or about the world in general.

• Allow your unconscious to bring to mind a memory in which someone is saying something about you. It may be a positive statement that makes you feel very good about yourself, or it may be a negative statement that leaves you feeling bad.

• Or, you may find that you are being told something about the world. Someone may be complaining about work, or expressing fears, prejudices or other beliefs. Become aware of how you feel as you experience these.

• Whatever comes, write it down, even if you've thought of it many times before. Write it down, even if it's vague and you're not sure what it means.

• As you write, you might wonder how the messages you recall could affect a child hearing them. Would a child feel elated? Confused? Humiliated? Angry? Afraid?

• Take a moment to close your eyes and allow your unconscious to show you how this message has affected the choices you've

made in your life . . . how the message is reflected in the quality
of life you live now.

• Repeat the process with as many injunctions as you'd like,
realizing that you can return to this process as often as you'd like.

• When you're ready, bring yourself back with the suggestion
that your unconscious can continue to bring internal messages to
mind, even when you're not in trance.

Exercise # 12   Discovering Your Parents as People

The following questions may be asked about any important caretaker or adult figure from your childhood. If the person you are
considering is no longer living, change the questions to the past
tense.

• Bring to mind an image of this person's face . . . voice . . .
body.

• Recall this person's first name.

• What kind of person wears a face like this . . . uses a voice like
this . . . uses gestures like this?

• What interests does this person have?

• Does this person have close friends? What are they like?

• Does this person get along well in the world, personally and
professionally? Would you consider this person to be confident
and compentent?

• What kinds of vulnerabilities, unresolved issues or conflicts
do you recognize in this person, now that you are an adult and
can see things in a new light?

• Is this the kind of person you like to be around?

• Would you choose this person as a friend, now that you are an
adult?

• What feelings do you have when you think of this person?
How about the feelings of the child within?

• Take a few minutes simply to note your responses. You might
want to write them down for use in the next exercise.

Exercise #13   Giving Back Hand-Me-Downs

• Put yourself into trance and go to your safe place.
• Bring to mind a hand-me-down, a negative message delivered to you by someone when you were a child, that you'd like to give back.
• Whose voice is telling you these things?
• Whose face is conveying this message?
• Ask yourself:

   What kind of person would say this to a child?
   What kind of person uses this tone of voice?
   What kind of person wears his or her face this way?

• How does the message impact the child?
• Bring to mind an object or symbol that represents the message.
• How does it feel to think about giving this hand-me-down back to its rightful owner?
• As the adult, give the message back to the person who gave it to you.
• How does the person respond?
• How does the child respond?
• Be back in your safe place, now, with the child. Take a few moments to be connected there, with the safety of that place, and with your increasing acceptance of, and love for, the child-within.
• Reorient to a fully-alert state when you're ready and take a moment to write down anything you'd like to remember.

Exercise #14   Morning Attunement Outline

• Color breathing: Choose any area(s) you want to develop, any achievement(s) you want. Breathe each color three times.
• Take yourself to a safe place, or find yourself on your optimal life path.
• Connect with both the child within and the future self:

Mirror your love and approval to the child;
Ask the child to "give you" his/her talent;
Tell the future self how much you want to go forward;
Imagine being drawn/pulled forward by the future self;

• Continue with other self-hypnotic work, if you choose.
• Give yourself post-hypnotic suggestions.
• Reorient and take a moment to sit with whatever good feelings you have tapped during your time in trance. Experience how your body feels when it is centered and settled. Tell yourself you can carry this feeling with you throughout the day.

Exercise # 15   Color Breathing

• Choose something you want to achieve/develop/heal.
• Allow your unconscious to present you with a color that represents what you seek.
• Imagine the color in front of you as a light, a mist, a cloud, or in whatever way is natural for you.
• Take a deep breath and, as you do, imagine that you are filling up with this color.
• Hold your breath and repeat, mentally, your affirmation(s).
• As you exhale, imagine the color flowing throughout your body and out into the world, along with the intent of the affirmation.
• Recall the concept of reciprocity. Giving and receiving are two sides of one coin.
• Take two more breaths, filling yourself again with the color and, again, repeating the affirmation(s) mentally to yourself before you exhale.
• Then, allow an image to come to mind that represents the attainment of what you seek. Spend a moment or two visualizing/sensing/experiencing the image.
• If you want to reorient yourself at this point, simply sit for a moment experiencing whatever focus, clarity or internal equilibrium you may be feeling. Then, bring yourself back.
• If you choose to continue with your inner work, do so now and then come back.

NOTES

CHAPTER 1. CAN THE SELF BE RECREATED?

1. Information about the brain is constantly being updated as new discoveries are made. *The Social Brain: Discovering the Networks of the Mind,* by Michael S. Gazzaniga, offers an overview of split-brain studies and how the brain organizes perception. See p. 47 for a discussion of the right brain/left brain concept.

2. For therapists who are interested in learning more about Ericksonian hypnosis, there are training groups around the country. Contact the Milton H. Erickson Foundation, 3606 North 24th Street, Phoenix, Arizona 85016, 602-956-6196, for information on training available in your area.

3. I first heard this story at a workshop conducted by David Calof in New York City.

4. Erickson describes these states in transcripts of actual sessions found in *Hypnotherapy: An Exploratory Casebook,* by Milton H. Erickson, Ernest L. Rossi, and Sheila I. Rossi, p. 367.
   Also see Ernest L. Rossi's book, *The Psychobiology of Mind-Body Healing,* especially pp. 136–137 on the natural trance state that occurs every 90 minutes throughout the day.

5. See Emily Marlin's book, *Hope: New Choices and Recovery Strategies for Adult Children of Alcoholics,* Chapter 1, which describes functional and dysfunctional patterns in families.

Also, *Facing Shame: Families in Recovery,* by Merle A. Fossum and Marilyn J. Mason, provides an in-depth look at how patterns operate in "respectful" and "shame-bound" families, pp. 19–36.

Chapter 2. Early Learnings: Laying the Foundation

1. For therapists interested in an in-depth study of the developing sense of self, see the following books by Heinz Kohut: *The Analysis of the Self, The Restoration of the Self* and *How Does Analysis Cure?*

   Also see *The Theory and Practice of Self Psychology,* by Marjorie Taggart White and Marcella Bakur Weiner, which provides an easily-understood overview of self psychology.

2. Empathy is a major factor in the theory and practice of self psychology. Alice Miller, in *For Your Own Good: Hidden Cruelty in Child-Rearing and the Roots of Violence,* describes how a lack of empathy creates deep wounds in a person's sense of self. For therapists, her *Thou Shalt Not Be Aware: Society's Betrayal of the Child* addresses issues of self and empathy in the therapy setting.

3. See *Resilience,* by Frederic Flach, for a thoughtful exploration of the benefits of developing a resilient attitude towards life events.

4. To read further about the power of unconscious beliefs, see *Severe and Mild Depression: The Therapeutic Approach,* by Silvano Arieti and Jules Bemporad, especially pp. 419–429.

5. See *Oneness and Separateness: From Infant to Individual,* by Louise J. Kaplan.

6. For more information on the developmental phases of separation-individuation, see M. S. Mahler, F. Pine, and A. Bergman, *The Psychological Birth of the Human Infant.*

7. See John Bradshaw's book, *Healing the Shame That Binds You,* for a discussion of the many ways children can experience abandonment in dysfunctional families.

8. Self psychology addresses the need for mirroring throughout life via relationships we all have with "selfobjects." See *The Theory and Practice of Self Psychology* for examples of mirroring in the therapy process. Also, *Self Psychology in Clinical Social Work* by Miriam Elson explores the function of mirroring, p. 107.

9. See *The Drama of the Gifted Child* by Alice Miller, pp. 9–14.

10. Also, for a description of how we split off and project parts of the self that have been abused and suppressed, see Miller's *For Your Own Good,* pp. 79–91.

CHAPTER 3. SELF HYPNOSIS: A TECHNOLOGY FOR CHANGE

1. The Ericksonian principle of open-ended suggestions is helpful for giving plenty of room for the individual's creativity to have free rein. See *Hypnotic Realities*, by Milton H. Erickson, Ernest L. Rossi, and Sheila I. Rossi, p. 27.

2. For therapists interested in utilizing naturally occurring trance states in therapy, see "Interspersal of Hypnotic Phenomena within Ongoing Treatment," by R. Reid Wilson, in *Ericksonian Psychotherapy, Vol II: Clinical Applications*, edited by Jeffrey K. Zeig, pp. 165–178, and *Erickson Monographs, No. 5, Ericksonian Hypnosis: Application, Preparation and Research*, edited by Stephen R. Lankton, pp. 1–6.

3. See "Depth of Trance and Susceptibility to Suggestion," by Seymour Holzman, in *Hypnosis Questions and Answers*, edited by B. Zilbergeld, M. G. Edelstien, and D. L. Araoz, pp. 126–128.

4. In more directive forms of hypnosis, depth of trance is measured in a number of ways. The following books list some of these:
   You Can Do It With Self-Hypnosis, by Charles E. Henderson, pp. 59–66;
   Self-Hypnotism, by Leslie M. LeCron, pp. 51–52;
   Hypnosis With Friends and Lovers, by Freda Morris, pp. 51–53;
   Self-Hypnosis, by Marshall B. Stearn, pp. 26–28.

5. For more on pain control, see the following:
   "Hypnosis and Pain Management," by Dabney M. Ewin, in *Hypnosis Questions and Answers*, pp. 282–288;
   "Hypnotherapy with Chronic Pain: An Ecosystemic Approach," in *Ericksonian Monographs, No. 2, Central Themes and Principles of Ericksonian Therapy*, edited by Stephen R. Lankton, pp. 69–82;
   Ericksonian Psychotherapy, Vol II: Clinical Applications, Section IX on Pain Control, pp. 437–472;
   "Pain and Pleasure: Awareness and Trust," by N. M. Poncelet, in *Ericksonian Monographs, No. 3, Treatment of Special Populations With Ericksonian Approaches*, edited by Stephen R. Lankton and Jeffrey K. Zeig, pp. 25–43;
   "The Use of Posthypnotic Suggestions in the Hypnotherapy of Pain." In *Ericksonian Monographs, No. 5, Ericksonian Hypnosis: Application, Preparation and Research*, pp. 85–104.

6. There are many good books on meditation. An overview of meditative approaches may be found in Daniel Goleman's *The Meditative Mind*. Also see *The Miracle of Mindfulness*, by Thich Nhat Hanh, and *Freedom in Meditation*, by Patricia Carrington.

7. Thanks to Robert Gerard, Ph.D., for sharing this concept with me early in my explorations of consciousness. It has saved me from stresses that otherwise would have occurred, had I worried about "being blank."

8. This represents an open-ended suggestion. For a discussion of this kind of suggestion, see pp. 76–79 in *Hypnotic Realities*. Sidney Rosen gives an example of the open-ended approach in his article, "Hypnosis as an Adjunct to Chemotherapy," in *Ericksonian Psychotherapy, Vol II: Clinical Applications*, p. 388.

9. The beginning of this induction is based on the eyeroll technique developed by Herbert Spiegel. For more information on Dr. Spiegel's approach, see *The Inner Source: Exploring Hypnosis With Dr. Herbert Spiegel*, by Donald J. Connery. Also see *Trance and Treatment*, by Herbert Spiegel and David Spiegel.

CHAPTER 4. THE SELF: PARTS OR WHOLES?

1. There are many recent books and articles on dissociation and its role in protecting abuse survivors from overwhelming memories. Most focus on the relatively extreme cases that result in multiple personality and atypical dissociative disorders. See *Childhood Antecedents of Multiple Personality Disorder*, edited by Richard P. Kluft.

   For most adult children, the protective parts that evolve during childhood create ego states or personality fragments that resemble the "subpersonalities" found in Psychosynthesis, rather than well-defined personality alters. See *What We May Be*, by Piero Ferrucci, pp. 47–58.

2. See *Healing the Child Within*, by Charles L. Whitfield, for a description of common responses in children of dysfunctional families. Also see Melody Beattie's *Codependent No More*.

3. See *Through Divided Minds*, by Robert S. Mayer. It recounts Dr. Mayer's own story of how he was introduced to the phenomenon of multiple personality disorder.

4. The discussion of ego states and protective parts in this chapter is necessarily simplified. There is a burgeoning specialization of therapists who work with dissociative disorders and multiple personality disorder. Research in the field is creating a growing and increasingly sophisticated database that describes the richness and complexity of dissociative phenomena. If you are interested in the subject, I recommend *Dissociation*, the journal of the International Society for the Study of Multiple Personality and Dissociation. Information about *Dissociation* may be obtained from the Ridgeview Center, 3995 South Cobb Drive, Smyrna, GA 30080. For information on the Society, contact 2506 Gross Point Road, Evanston, Illinois 60201, 312-475-7532.

5. For further information on this aspect of dissociation, see Bennett G. Braun's articles: "The BASK Model of Dissociation" and "The BASK Model of Dissociation, Part II—Treatment."

6. See *Unity and Multiplicity,* by John O. Beahrs, "Ego States and Hidden Observers," by J. G. Watkins and H. H. Watkins, "The Theory and Practice of Ego State Therapy," also by Watkins and Watkins.

7. John Beahrs uses this analogy in *Unity and Multiplicity,* p. 69.

8. See the reading list for additional references related to multiple personality and dissociation.

9. See *Unity and Multiplicity* for a discussion of the need to engage parts in learning new, constructive functions, pp. 111–140.

CHAPTER 5. THE FUTURE SELF

1. For Erickson's approach to "pseudo-orientation in time," see Milton H. Erickson, *Life Reframing in Hypnosis,* edited by Ernest L. Rossi and Margaret O. Ryan, pp. 195–200.

2. Jean Houston talks about engaging the child in a forward-moving process guided by the "extended self," the "entelechy" of you, "who you would be and could be if your potentials and capacities were fully realized." See *The Possible Human,* p. 93.

CHAPTER 6. THE CHILD WITHIN: RECLAIMING THE SELF

1. See Alice Miller's *Thou Shalt Not Be Aware,* pp. 192–195.

2. For incest survivors, *The Courage to Heal,* by Ellen Bass and Laura Davis, describes ways of tapping into forgotten memories and feelings. See, especially, pp. 70–85.

3. See Alice Miller's *For Your Own Good,* p. xi and Chapter 1, "Poisonous Pedagogy," pp. 58–65.

4. In the dissociative disorders, the dissociation is involuntary and unconscious. When working with the child within, the dissociation is conscious and intentional, and promotes the development of an adult observer who can soothe distressing feelings.

5. A review of the February Man technique may be found in the article, "The February Man: Facilitating New Identity in Hypnotherapy," by Milton H. Erickson and Ernest L. Rossi. Also see, *The February Man: Evolving Consciousness and Identity in Hypnotherapy,* by Milton H. Erickson and Ernest L. Rossi.

6. See the article by Rothlyn Zahourek, "Imagery."

7. See Gershen Kaufman's *Shame: The Power of Caring,* pp. 3–32; and, John Bradshaw's *Healing the Shame That Binds You,* pp. 25–70 for further descrip-

tions of how caretakers and other important adults pass along to children their own unacknowledged, internalized shame messages.

8. I've heard numerous stories from clients about how they never really liked children prior to connecting with the child within. After developing a positive, empathic relationship with this part of themselves, some people report a shift that surprises them. They begin to enjoy interacting with, and getting to know, children in a new way.

9. I was introduced to the concept of corrective regression by Sidney Rosen, M.D., during an advanced training course in Ericksonian hypnosis.

10. See *The Courage to Heal*, pp. 118–121, for a discussion of grieving. Jane Middleton-Moz and Lorie Dwinell also discuss the grieving process in *After the Tears: Reclaiming the Personal Losses of Childhood*, pp 81–109 and pp. 111–122. Charles Whitfield talks about grieving and recovery in *Healing the Child Within*, pp. 85–105.

CHAPTER 7. HEALING THE INFANT AND THE SHAMED CHILD

1. In *Oneness and Separateness: From Infancy to Individual*, Louise Kaplan explores how the child's early interactions with parents create a sense of "constancy." See pp. 25–58.

2. John Bradshaw refers to the effects of "toxic shame" in *Healing the Shame That Binds You*. See, especially, pp. 71–112.

3. See *Shame: The Power of Caring*, pp. 9–11, where Gershen Kaufman describes an early experience of being shamed in school.

CHAPTER 8. THE POWER OF FAMILY MYTHS

1. See *Genograms: The New Tool for Exploring the Personality, Career, and Love Patterns You Inherit*, by Emily Marlin, pp. 83–108, *Facing Shame: Families in Recovery*, pp. 46–47, and *Black Sheep and Kissing Cousins*, by Elizabeth Stone, for examples of family myths and stories, and their effect on family members. Also see *Personal, Marital and Family Myths*, by Dennis Bagarozzi and Stephen Anderson.

2. In *Listening: The Forgotten Skill*, Madelyn Burley-Allen describes perceptual filters and their relationship to beliefs. See, especially, p. 31.
   Louis Foresdale's *Perspectives on Communication* describes how "you don't perceive what you don't believe," and illustrates the power of preconceptions on how we experience and interpret our reality. See p. 117.
   Also see *The New Hypnosis in Family Therapy*, by Daniel Araoz and Esther Negley-Parker, on "mind-sets," pp. 8–12.

3. An example of the power of family messages taken in and responded to unconsciously can be found in *Using Hypnosis in Family Therapy*, by Michele Ritterman, pp 128–142.

4. Daniel Araoz, in *The New Hypnosis in Family Therapy*, emphasizes the importance of shifting negative self-talk, pp. 10–12, 16.

5. See *Healing the Incest Wound*, by Christine A. Courtois, pp. 42–46.

6. *Facing Shame: Families in Recovery* offers a review of rules in "shame-bound" families that operate to keep old behaviors in place, pp. 86–104. See, especially, pp. 96–98 on denial and pp. 102–103 on "no-talk" rules.

7. Michele Ritterman provides numerous examples of these kinds of "embedded messages" in *Using Hypnosis in Family Therapy*. For an illustration of the subtlety and power these messages convey, see pp. 115–117.

8. In her "Case Study of a Suicidal Woman," Ritterman describes the impact of covert messages. See, particularly, pp. 213–219, *Using Hypnosis in Family Therapy*.

9. Remember that injunctions that come from people who are important to us are part of the mirroring process that shapes our sense of self.

10. See, for example, *Feeling Good*, by David D. Burns, which describes a cognitive therapy approach to challenging negative self-talk.

11. In *The New Hypnosis*, by Daniel Araoz.

12. See *Family Reconstruction: Long Day's Journey Into Light*, by William F. Nerin, p. 58.

13. See Emily Marlin's *Genograms: The New Tool for Exploring the Personality, Career, and Love Patterns You Inherit* and *Genograms in Family Assessment*, by Monica McGoldrick and Randy Gerson.

14. Emily Marlin talks about family secrets on pp. 99–102 in *Genograms*.

CHAPTER 9. GIVING BACK HAND-ME-DOWNS

1. In *Psychosynthesis*, Roberto Assagioli says that, "one should attempt to use the mode in which the unconscious normally operates, which is by way of symbols," when an attempt is made to "address the unconscious," p. 180.

   In *What We May Be*, Piero Ferrucci talks about Carl Jung's theory that symbols have a "transformative impact on the psyche," p. 118.

2. For a discussion of the inevitability and power of triangular relationships in families, see *Family Evaluation*, by Michael Kerr and Murray Bowen, pp. 134–162.

3. Exercise #12 at the back of the book outlines this process.

4. See *The Social Brain* by Michael Gazzaniga, pp. 3–8.

5. See *Families and Family Therapy,* by Salvador Minuchin, pp. 54–56, for a discussion of disengaged families.

CHAPTER 10. MANIFESTING A NEW YOU

1. See "The Neuropsychology of Achievement" audiotape series (San Leandro, CA: Sybervision Systems, 1982. In particular, Tape 1, "Your Holographic Brain: The Power of Three-Dimensional Visualization," says, "The more sensory-detailed and emotionally-charged the image, the greater impact it will have . . ."

2. For a color-breathing approach that focuses primarily on physical health and healing, see Linda Clark and Yvonne Martine's *Health, Youth and Beauty Through Color Breathing.*

3. To learn more about affirmations, see *You Can Heal Your Life,* by Louise Hay.

4. Visualization is a powerful component of any inner work. The following books offer guidelines for using visualization: *Visualization: Directing the Movies of Your Mind,* by Adelaide Bry; *Creative Visualization,* by Shakti Gawain.

5. For more information on mental rehearsal, see *In the Mind's Eye: The Power of Imagery for Personal Enrichment,* by Arnold Lazarus, and *Mind Power: Getting What You Want Through Mental Training,* by Bernie Zilbergeld and Arnold Lazarus.

REFERENCES

Araoz, D., and Negley-Parker, E. *The New Hypnosis in Family Therapy.* New York: Brunner/Mazel, 1988.

Araoz, D. *The New Hypnosis.* New York: Brunner/Mazel, 1985.

Arieti, S., and Bemporad, J. *Severe and Mild Depression: The Therapeutic Approach.* New York: Basic Books, 1978.

Assagioli, R. *Psychosynthesis.* New York: Viking Press, 1965.

Bagarozzi, D. A., and Anderson, S. A. *Personal, Marital and Family Myths.* New York: W. W. Norton, 1989.

Bass, E., and Davis, L. *The Courage to Heal.* New York: Harper & Row, 1988.

Beahrs, J. O. *Unity and Multiplicity.* New York: Brunner/Mazel, 1982.

Beattie, M. *Codependent No More.* New York: Harper/Hazeldon, 1987.

Bradshaw, J. *Healing the Shame That Binds You.* Deerfield Beach, FL: Health Communications, 1988.

Braun, B. G. The BASK Model of Dissociation. *Dissociation,* 1:1, March 1988.

Braun, B. G. The BASK Model of Dissociation, Part II—Treatment. *Dissociation,* 1:2, June 1988.

Bry, A. *Visualization: Directing the Movies of Your Mind.* New York: Barnes & Noble, 1979.

Burley-Allen, M. *Listening: The Forgotten Skill.* New York: John Wiley & Sons, 1982.

Burns, D. D. *Feeling Good.* New York: Signet, 1981.

Carrington, P. *Freedom in Meditation.* Kendall Park, NJ: Pace Educational Systems, 1977.

Clark, L., and Martine, Y. *Health, Youth and Beauty Through Color Breathing.* Berkeley, CA: Celestial Arts, 1976.

Connery, D. S. *The Inner Source: Exploring Hypnosis With Dr. Herbert Spiegel.* New York: Holt, Rinehart and Winston, 1982.

Courtois, C. A. *Healing the Incest Wound.* New York: W. W. Norton, 1988.

Elson, M. *Self Psychology in Clinical Social Work.* New York: W. W. Norton, 1986.

Erickson, M. H. The February Man: Facilitating New Identify in Hypnotherapy. In: M. H. Erickson, E. L. Rossi, and S. I. Rossi, *Hypnotherapy: An Exploratory Casebook.* New York: Irvington, 1979.

Erickson, M. H. *Life Reframing in Hypnosis.* E. L. Rossi, and M. O. Ryan (Eds.). New York: Irvington, 1985.

Erickson, M. H., and Rossi, E. L. *The February Man: Evolving Consciousness and Identity in Hypnotherapy.* New York: Brunner/Mazel, 1989.

Erickson, M. H., Rossi, E. L., and Rossi, S. I. *Hypnotherapy: An Exploratory Casebook.* New York: Irvington, 1979.

Erickson, M. H., Rossi, E. L., and Rossi, S. I. *Hypnotic Realities.* New York: Irvington, 1976.

Ewin, D. M. Hypnosis and Pain Management. In: B. Zilbergeld, M. G. Edelstien, and D. L. Araoz (Eds.) *Hypnosis Questions and Answers.* New York: W. W. Norton, 1986.

Ferrucci, P. *What We May Be.* Los Angeles: J. P. Tarcher, 1982.

Flach, F. *Resilience.* New York: Fawcett-Columbine, 1988.

Foresdale, L. *Perspectives on Communication.* New York: Random House, 1981.

Fossum, M. A., and Mason, M. J. *Facing Shame: Families in Recovery.* New York: W. W. Norton, 1986.

Gawain, S. *Creative Visualization.* New York: Bantam Books, 1982.

Gazzaniga, M. S. *The Social Brain: Discovering the Networks of the Mind.* New York: Basic Books, 1985.

Goleman, D. *The Meditative Mind.* Los Angeles: J. P. Tarcher, 1988.

Hanh, Thich Nhat. *The Miracle of Mindfulness.* Boston: Beacon Press, 1976.

Hay, L. *You Can Heal Your Life.* Santa Monica, CA: Hay House, 1984.

Henderson, Ch. E. *You Can Do It With Self-Hypnosis.* Englewood Cliffs, NJ: Prentice-Hall, 1983.

Holzman, S. Depth of Trance and Susceptibility to Suggestion. In: B. Zilbergeld, M. G. Edelstien, and D. L. Araoz, (Eds.) *Hypnosis Questions and Answers.* New York: W. W. Norton, 1986.

Houston, J. *The Possible Human.* Los Angeles: J. P. Tarcher, 1982.

Kaplan, L. J. *Oneness and Separateness: From Infant to Individual.* New York: Touchstone, 1978.

Kaufman, G. *Shame: The Power of Caring.* Cambridge, MA: Schenkman Books, 1985.

Kerr, M., and Bowen, M. *Family Evaluation.* New York: W. W. Norton, 1988.

Kluft, R. P. (Ed.) *Childhood Antecedents of Multiple Personality Disorder.* Washington, DC: American Psychiatric Press, 1987.

Kohut, H. *The Analysis of the Self.* New York: International Universities Press, 1971.

Kohut, H. *The Restoration of the Self.* New York: International Universities Press, 1977.

Kohut, H. *How Does Analysis Cure?* Chicago: University of Chicago Press, 1984.

Lankton, S. R. (Ed.) *The Ericksonian Monographs, No. 2, Central Themes and Principles of Ericksonian Therapy.* New York: Brunner/Mazel, 1987.

Lankton, S. R. (Ed.) *The Ericksonian Monographs, No. 5, Ericksonian Hypnosis: Application, Preparation and Research.* New York: Brunner/Mazel, 1989.

Lankton, S. R., and Zeig, J. K. (Eds.) *The Ericksonian Monographs, No. 3, Treatment of Special Populations With Ericksonian Approaches.* New York: Brunner/Mazel, 1988.

Lazarus, A. *In the Mind's Eye: The Power of Imagery for Personal Enrichment.* New York: Guilford Press, 1977.

LeCron, L. M. *Self-Hypnotism.* New York: New American Library, 1970.

Mahler, M. S., Pine, F., and Bergman, A. *The Psychological Birth of the Human Infant.* New York: Basic Books, 1975.

Marlin, E. *Genograms: The New Tool for Exploring the Personality, Career, and Love Patterns You Inherit.* Chicago: Contemporary Books, 1989.

Marlin, E. *Hope: New Choices and Recovery Strategies for Adult Children of Alcoholics.* New York: Harper & Row, 1987.

Matthews, W. J., and Daniel, R. M. Hypnotherapy With Chronic Pain: An Ecosystemic Approach. In: S. R. Lankton (Ed.) *Ericksonian Monographs, No. 2, Central Themes and Principles of Ericksonian Therapy.* New York: Brunner/Mazel, 1987.

Mayer, R. S. *Through Divided Minds.* New York: Doubleday, 1988.

McGoldrick, M., and Gerson, R. *Genograms in Family Assessment.* New York: W. W. Norton, 1985.

Middleton-Moz, J., and Dwinell, L. *After the Tears: Reclaiming the Personal Losses of Childhood.* Deerfield Beach, FL: Health Communications, 1986.

Miller, A. *The Drama of the Gifted Child: How Narcissistic Parents Form and Deform the Emotional Lives of Their Talented Children.* New York: Basic Books, 1981.

Miller, A. *For Your Own Good: Hidden Cruelty in Child-Rearing and the Roots of Violence.* New York: Farrar, Straus, Giroux, 1983.

Miller, A. *Thou Shalt Not Be Aware: Society's Betrayal of the Child.* New York: Farrar, Straus, Giroux, 1984.

Minuchin, S. *Families and Family Therapy.* Cambridge, MA: Harvard University Press, 1974.

Morris, F. *Hypnosis With Friends and Lovers.* New York: Harper & Row, 1979.

Nerin, W. F. *Family Reconstruction: Long Day's Journey Into Light.* New York: W. W. Norton, 1986.

Poncelet, N. M. Pain and Pleasure: Awareness and Trust. In: S. R. Lankton and J. K. Zeig (Eds.) *Ericksonian Monographs, No. 3, Treatment of Special Populations With Ericksonian Approaches.* New York: Brunner/Mazel, 1988.

Ritterman, M. *Using Hypnosis in Family Therapy.* San Francisco: Jossey-Bass, 1983.

Rossi, E. L. *The Psychobiology of Mind-Body Healing.* New York: W. W. Norton, 1986.

Schwarz, R. The Use of Posthypnotic Suggestions in the Hypnotherapy of Pain. In: S. R. Lankton (Ed.) *Ericksonian Monographs, No. 5, Ericksonian Hypnosis: Application, Preparation and Research.* New York: Brunner/Mazel, 1989.

Spiegel, H., and Spiegel, D. *Trance and Treatment.* New York: Basic Books, 1978.

Stearn, B. *Self-Hypnosis.* Sausalito, CA: Park West Publishing, 1982.

Stone, E. *Black Sheep and Kissing Cousins.* New York: Penguin Books, 1988.

Watkins, J. G., and Watkins, H. H. Ego States and Hidden Observers. *Journal of Altered States of Consciousness,* 1979–80.

Watkins, J. G., and Watkins, H. H. The Theory and Practice of Ego State Therapy. In: H. Grayson (Ed.) *Short-Term Approaches to Therapy.* New York: National Institute for the Psychotherapies and Human Sciences Press, 1979.

White, M. T., and Weiner, M. B. *The Theory and Practice of Self Psychology.* New York: Brunner/Mazel, 1986.

Whitfield, C. *Healing the Child Within.* Deerfield Beach, FL: Health Communications, 1987.

Zahourek, R. P. Imagery. In: R. P. Zahourek (Ed.) *Relaxation and Imagery: Tools for Therapeutic Communication and Intervention.* Philadelphia: W. B. Saunders, 1988.

Zeig, J. K. (Ed.) *Ericksonian Psychotherapy, Vol. II: Clinical Applications.* New York: Brunner/Mazel, 1985.

Zilbergeld, B., and Lazarus, A. *Mind Power: Getting What You Want Through Mental Training.* Boston: Little, Brown & Co., 1987.

Zilbergeld, B., Edelstien, M. G., and Araoz, D. (Eds.) *Hypnosis Questions and Answers.* New York: W. W. Norton, 1986.

ADDITIONAL READING

~~~

CHILDHOOD, ABUSE AND FAMILY ISSUES

Forward S., and Buck, C. *Betrayal of Innocence: Incest and Its Devastation.* New York: Penguin Books, 1978.

Lerner, H. *The Dance of Anger.* New York: Harper & Row, 1985.

Mills, J. D., and Crowley, R. J. *Therapeutic Metaphors for Children and the Child Within.* New York: Brunner/Mazel, 1986.

Paul, J., and Paul, M. *Do I Have to Give Up Me to Be Loved By You?* Minneapolis, MN: CompCare Publishing, 1983.

Pearce, J. C., *Magical Child.* New York: Bantam Books, 1977.

Pearce, J. C., *Magical Child Matures.* New York: Bantam Books, 1986.

Poston, C., and Lison, K. *Reclaiming Our Lives: Hope for Adult Survivors of Incest.* Boston: Little, Brown & Co., 1989.

Schaef, A. W. *Co-dependence: Misunderstood and Mistreated.* Minneapolis, MN: Winston Press, 1986.

SELF-HYPNOSIS, VISUALIZATION, MENTAL REHEARSAL

Borysenko, J. *Minding the Body, Mending the Mind.* Reading, MA: Addison-Wesley, 1987.

Bristol, C. M. *The Magic of Believing.* New York: Pocket Books, 1969.

Harman, W., and Rheingold, H. *Higher Creativity: Liberating the Unconscious for Breakthrough Insights.* Los Angeles, J. P. Tarcher, 1984.
Mann, S. *Triggers: A New Approach to Self-Motivation.* Englewood Cliffs, NJ: Prentice-Hall, 1987.
Pearson, C. *The Hero Within.* San Francisco: Harper & Row, 1986.
Petrie, S. *Helping Yourself With Autogenics.* West Nyack, NY: Parker Publishing, 1983.
Straus, R. A. *Strategic Self-Hypnosis.* Englewood Cliffs, NJ: Prentice-Hall, 1982.
Zdenek, M. *Inventing the Future.* New York: McGraw-Hill, 1987.

OF PARTICULAR INTEREST TO THERAPISTS

Bliss, E. L. *Multiple Personality, Allied Disorders and Hypnosis.* New York: Oxford University Press, 1986.
Braun, B. G. (Ed.) *Treatment of Multiple Personality Disorder.* Washington, DC: American Psychiatric Press, 1986.
Dolan, Y. *A Path With a Heart: Ericksonian Utilization With Resistant and Chronic Clients.* New York: Brunner/Mazel, 1985.
Erickson, M. H. *Healing in Hypnosis.* (Vol. I) New York: Irvington Publishers, 1983.
Ochberg, F. *Post-Traumatic Therapy and Victims of Violence.* New York: Brunner/Mazel, 1988.
Putnam, F. W. *Diagnosis and Treatment of Multiple Personality Disorder.* New York: Guilford, 1989.
Ross, Colin A. *Multiple Personality Disorder: Diagnosis, Clinical Features, and Treatment.* New York: Wiley, 1989.
Rossi, E., and Cheek, D. B. *Mind-Body Therapy.* New York: W. W. Norton, 1988.
Wallas, L. *Stories for the Third Ear.* New York: W. W. Norton, 1985.
Zeig, J. *Experiencing Erickson.* New York: Brunner/Mazel, 1985.

INDEX